DIFFERENTIATED LITERACY INSTRUCTION

assessing • grouping • teaching

Julie W. Ankrum

INDIANA UNIVERSITY OF PENNSYLVANIA

Routledge
Taylor & Francis Group

LONDON AND NEW YORK

Library of Congress Cataloging-in-Publication Data
Names: Ankrum, Julie W.
Title: Differentiating literacy instruction : assessing, grouping, teaching/
  Julie W. Ankrum, Indiana University of Pennsylvania.
Description: Scottsdale, Arizona : Holcomb Hathaway, [2017] | Includes
  bibliographical references.
Identifiers: LCCN 2016033125 (print) | ISBN 9781621590569 (print book)
Subjects: LCSH: Individualized reading instruction. | Ability grouping in
  education.
Classification: LCC LB1573.45 .A65 2017 (print) | DDC
  372.41/7-dc23
LC record available at https://lccn.loc.gov/2016033125

Photo credits: *front cover (left to right)*, Wavebreak Media Ltd/123 RF, dolgachov/123RF, Cathy
Yeulet/123RF, *(main)*, tomwang/123 RF; *back cover*, Inspirestock International/123 RF; *page 1*,
Wavebreak Media Ltd/123 RF; *page 17*, stylephotographs; *page 31*, racorn; *page 45*, Wavebreak
Media Ltd/123 RF; *page 83*, Wavebreak Media Ltd/123 RF; *page 99*, Parinya Binsuk; *page 100*,
Edhar Yuralaits; *page 103*, iofoto; *page 121*, Wavebreak Media Ltd/123 RF; *page 141*, racorn; *page
151*, Wavebreak Media Ltd/123 RF; *page 161*, Cathy Yeulet.

Please note: The authors and publisher have made every effort to provide current website
addresses in this book. However, because web addresses change constantly, it is inevitable that
some of the URLs listed here will change following publication of this book.

First published 2017 by Holcomb Hathaway, Publishers, Inc.

Published 2017 by Routledge
2 Park Square, Milton Park, Abingdon, Oxon OX14 4RN
711 Third Avenue, New York, NY 10017, USA
Routledge is an imprint of the Taylor & Francis Group, an informa business

Contents

Differentiated Instruction
BUILDING BACKGROUND   1

Classroom Context I
LITERACY INSTRUCTION IN A PRIMARY-LEVEL EXEMPLARY CLASSROOM   17

Classroom Context II
LITERACY INSTRUCTION IN A MIDDLE-LEVEL EXEMPLARY CLASSROOM 31

Managing Small-Group Reading Instruction
KEEPING ALL STUDENTS ENGAGED IN LITERACY LEARNING 45

5 Starting with Assessment
BEGINNING WITH THE END IN MIND   83

Analyzing the Assessments

USING DATA TO DESIGN DIFFERENTIATED INSTRUCTION   103

Planning the Lesson Focus   121

Selecting Texts 141

Providing Differentiated Support for Students 151

Parting Thoughts 161

Instructional Tools   164

A.1 Peer Conference Form   164

A.2 Self-Editing Checklist   165

A.3 Literacy Center Routine Reminders   166

A.4 Reading Ticket   167

A.5 Using the Dictionary Handout   168

A.6 Fluency Self-Checklist   169

A.7 Building Compound Words Using Ladybug Wings   170

A.8 Scaffolding Handout for Informational Text   171

A.9 Scaffolding Handout for Narrative Text   172

Assessment Tools   173

B.1 Concepts About Print Assessment   173

B.2 Letter/Sound Identification Assessment   174

B.3 Generic Retelling Assessment Template   178

B.4 Written Retelling Rubric for Narrative Text   179

B.5 Written Retelling Rubric for Informational Text   180

B.6 Example Interest Inventory   181

B.7 Blank Running Record Form   182

B.8 Example Qualitative Spelling Inventory   183

Planning and Data Tools   184

C.1 Planning for Assessment   184

C.2 Template for Assessment Data Compilation Form   185

C.3 Literacy Assessment Correlation Chart   186

AUTHOR INDEX   187

SUBJECT INDEX   189

Preface

I clearly remember so much about my first year of teaching: the way I arranged my classroom, my colorful bulletin boards, advice from my mentor teachers, and the excitement of the students. I remember my own excitement, which turned into fear when I came to the quick realization that I didn't *really* know how to teach reading! I have discussed this with colleagues from all over the country, and many of them faced the same dilemma. The truth is that pre-service teachers are required to learn a wide range of topics in their preparation programs; as a result, they are asked to absorb much information in a short period of time, and this approach doesn't always ensure deep learning. Teaching is complex, and preparing novice teachers for the complexities can be very tricky.

Adding to the challenge, today's classrooms are filled with students possessing a range of cognitive abilities and diverse cultural and linguistic backgrounds. Research tells us that the most effective teachers provide differentiated instruction to meet their students' needs, and differentiated instruction most often occurs during small-group lessons. It is only through these small-group lessons that teachers can address the varying needs of all learners, including English learners, gifted students, and those with special needs.

Developing literate students is a primary goal in education, and thus literacy instruction is now a primary focus in most teacher education programs. Although conventional wisdom and research support small-group, differentiated reading instruction, many classroom teachers struggle with the "what" and "how" of teaching each student at the appropriate developmental reading level. To better prepare educators, teacher-preparation programs across the country must help their students learn effective strategies and techniques to teach *all* learners to read and comprehend texts. It is imperative that we provide practical information to help pre-service teachers learn and become comfortable with these instructional techniques.

The goal of this practical book is to help explain the intricacies of differentiated literacy instruction to pre-service teachers. (Novice teachers, and experienced teachers attempting small-group instruction for the first time, will also find it useful as a "how-to" classroom guide.) This book provides a multitude of specific, hands-on descriptions and exhibits to illuminate for teachers the process of differentiated literacy instruction.

The book's first chapters are devoted to describing the "what" and "why" of small-group differentiated reading instruction. Chapter 1 offers background on the history of differentiated reading instruction and discusses current research, policies, and initiatives that support the need for it. Chapters 2 and 3 illustrate effective literacy instruction in exemplary primary- and middle-level classrooms, respectively, and show how small-group reading lessons fit into that instruction.

The remainder of the book is designed to get readers started and then guide them through a plan for flexible differentiation. The chapters are organized in the way I have organized my own thinking and classrooms for small-group teaching. Chapter 4 focuses on preparing the classroom environment to allow for effective management and student engagement. In Chapters 5 and 6, we move into assessing for instruction and interpreting the assessment data. In Chapter 7, we discuss using assessment as a guide to forming small groups and planning and preparing effective lessons. Finally, Chapter 8 discusses selecting texts, and Chapter 9 discusses providing differentiated teacher support for classroom students.

Each chapter provides practical, essential information designed to help teachers formulate and work with small groups and to motivate and teach diverse learners. "Classroom Snapshots" (case studies of real classrooms) demonstrate application of effective instructional techniques. These snapshots offer detailed information about such topics as learning centers, integration of assessment and instruction, and small-group lesson planning. Photographs and charts exhibit actual student work and classroom tools.

Chapters conclude with Practical Application opportunities to ensure that readers can apply what they've read about and learned, and lists of additional resources allow readers to extend their learning beyond the information in the text.

I am confident that this book will provide readers with the necessary background to plan for and achieve effective differentiated literacy instruction. I sincerely hope that readers will revisit the text each year as they teach to continue to refine their instructional techniques and deliver exemplary instruction to all learners.

Acknowledgments

Writing a manuscript, especially for a book, is a humbling experience! Blank pages, ideas, and more blank pages. I am forever grateful to many colleagues, friends, and family for their support during this project. Darla Trent shared her classroom and first graders with me for an entire semester; thank you, Darla, for allowing me to refine my teaching so that I could begin to fill the blank pages. Wendy Jones, Jackie Gillespie, Tricia Parker, Tricia Stuck, and Erin Weber are among the finest teachers I know. Thank you for sharing your classrooms, your insights, and your time with me. I especially appreciate the time you devoted to reading my early drafts and clarifying my thinking. Thank you to the pre-service teachers in my literacy methods courses for raising important questions; because of them I was inspired to write this book.

I never realized how many eyes and ears are required to build the confidence required to complete a book. Thank you to Maria Genest, Beth Belcastro, and Aimee Morewood for listening to my ideas, reviewing my early drafts, and keeping me going with laughter and meals. Jackie Myers, I cannot tell you how much I appreciate your careful review and feedback on every draft that I wrote. Thank you, Andrea Moffatt, for reviewing my drafts, praising me throughout the process, and snapping photos on demand. Thank you so much, Mary Avalos, for sharing your insights about English learners. Susan Sibert, I truly appreciate your help with this as well.

Thank you, Mary Beth McConahey, for commiserating as you wrote your own book, and providing encouragement as I wrote mine. Dalila Berlingo, thank you for sharing your "young learners"—they helped with detail and photos for the book. A huge thank you to Rebecca Sexton for listening to my ideas and cheering me along.

A special thank you to W. Dorsey Hammond, who has served as my unofficial mentor for many years. You talked me through this book before I even knew I was going to write it, and you helped me get unstuck through email conversations along the way.

I would also like to thank the following individuals, who formally reviewed the book at various stages, working with my publisher to refine and improve it: Elsa Anderson, Texas Wesleyan University; Nancy Atkeison-Cherry, Union University; Mary A. Avlaos, University of Miami; Karla Broadus, University of Texas at San Antonio; Linda Champney, Metropolitan State University; Susan Densmore-James, University of West Florida; Genya Devoe, Antioch University Midwest; Lee A. Dubert, Boise State University; Maria Genest, University of Pittsburgh; W. Dorsey Hammond, Professor Emeritus, Oakland University; Barbara P. Laster, Towson University; Mona W. Matthews, Georgia State University; Aimee Morewood, West Virginia University; Nancy Witherell, Bridgewater State

College; Alice F. Snyder, The Ohio State University, Newark; and Jodi G. Welsch, Frostburg State University. I am grateful for their assistance and constructive comments.

And always, to Martin and Hadley: Your humor as I worked through this book lightened the process. Thank you for being proud of me and this project; it means so much!

About the Author

Julie W. Ankrum serves as Assistant Professor at Indiana University of Pennsylvania, where she teaches undergraduate and graduate level literacy courses in the Department of Professional Studies in Education. She earned a Ph.D. in Reading Education from the University of Pittsburgh, an MAT in Reading and Language Arts from Oakland University (Rochester, Michigan), and a BA in Elementary Education from Michigan State University.

Ankrum's classroom teaching experiences provided the foundation for her love of literacy instruction. She taught grades K, 5, and 8 and served as a Reading Recovery teacher in Michigan. Ankrum also co-taught in a first grade classroom during a sabbatical study while teaching at the college level.

Differentiated reading instruction is Ankrum's primary research focus. She also conducts research on effective professional development in literacy. Ankrum has authored and co-authored articles in various journals, and she provides professional development to elementary school teachers.

DIFFERENTIATED LITERACY INSTRUCTION

assessing • grouping • teaching

Differentiated Instruction

BUILDING BACKGROUND

It's mid-September and Mrs. Jones has recently finished collecting her baseline assessments. She has compiled a literacy assessment folder for each of her 22 students, which includes a formal spelling inventory, several writing samples, benchmark running records, and comprehension measures. After analyzing the results, Mrs. Jones noted that two of her second-graders are just beginning to read at the emergent level (see Exhibit 1.2); one of these students is an English learner. Five students are reading just below the beginning second-grade level with strong comprehension, and six students are reading fluently at the beginning second-grade level with weak comprehension. Another six of Mrs. Jones's students are reading fluently and accurately at a mid-second-grade level with strong comprehension, while three of her students are reading and comprehending text at the fourth-grade level or beyond. This is not unusual; in her nine years of teaching second grade, Mrs. Jones has noticed a similar range in her students as each school year begins. Mrs. Jones recognizes that the instruction in her classroom will have to be differentiated to support the strengths and meet the needs of her learners. But what exactly does *differentiate* mean? What components of reading can, and should, Mrs. Jones differentiate? Where does she start with such a complex task?

Mrs. Jones's questions are important. They will be addressed throughout this book, since its specific focus is small-group differentiated reading instruction, an essential component of effective literacy instruction. To differentiate reading instruction in small groups, teachers must possess a deep understanding of differentiated instruction, the reading process, and how to teach it. This book opens with an overview of differentiated instruction (Chapter 1), and then provides examples of effective literacy instruction (Chapters 2 and 3). The remainder of the book is organized in the sequence that a classroom teacher would use to prepare for differentiated instruction. This preparation begins by planning for classroom management and organization, conducting and analyzing student assessments, and grouping of students, and it culminates with daily small-group lessons.

WHAT IS DIFFERENTIATED INSTRUCTION?

Differentiated instruction is what happens when teachers respond to individual differences in students' background knowledge, developmental level, and/or modes of learning. It is student centered, responsive, and informed by assessment. Rather than delivering a one-size-fits-all style of instruction, differentiated instruction is just what the root word *different* implies: teachers provide different types of instruction to meet the varied needs of individual students. Thus, the teaching is student centered. Differentiated instruction is often described as responsive teaching; that is, before introducing new skills or strategies, the teacher considers what the learner already knows (MacGillivray,

Rueda, & Martinez, 2004). To teach responsively, the teacher must assess the students individually to determine how deeply each component of the curriculum must be addressed for each student. In other words, differentiated instruction is informed by classroom-based assessments. Differentiated instruction encompasses "ensuring that what a student learns, how he/she learns it, and how the student demonstrates what he/she has learned is a match for that student's readiness level, interests, and preferred mode of learning" (Tomlinson, 2004, p. 188).

Tomlinson (2000) describes four elements of instruction that may be differentiated to meet the needs of all learners: content, process, product, and learning environment. Exhibit 1.1 provides brief descriptions of these elements, along with a concrete example of each.

WHY DIFFERENTIATE?

Experts agree that differentiating instruction is essential to ensure that all students learn to their potential. According to Vygotsky (1978), learning is enhanced when a student is provided assistance in his or her **zone of proximal development (ZPD)**. Vygotsky defined the ZPD as *"the distance between the actual developmental level as determined by independent problem solving and the level of potential development as determined through problem solving under adult guid-*

Elements of instruction and examples of differentiation.		**EXHIBIT 1.1**
ELEMENT OF INSTRUCTION	**DEFINITION**	**EXAMPLE**
Content	Content is *what* the students need to learn; it may include the method(s) by which students will access the information.	When students demonstrate a need to learn to decode unfamiliar words, the teacher conducts small-group lessons on different developmentally appropriate strategies, such as using the pictures on the page as a clue to decode unknown words for one group and chunking multisyllabic words to decode for another group of students.
Process	Process is *how* the content will be presented and what the students are expected to do in the lesson.	The teacher provides tiered activities; all students work on the same content (such as summarizing a text), but with different levels of support, challenge, or complexity.
Product	Product refers to the assignment that students will complete to practice a skill/strategy or demonstrate their understanding.	A teacher may require all students to research an animal and report on the animal's physical adaptations and habitat. Students are given the option to present their findings in a traditional research paper, a Prezi presentation, a blog, or a mural.
Learning Environment	The learning environment consists of physical spaces in the classroom created to meet students' different modes of learning. In addition, providing spaces that encourage collaborative activities (e.g., designed for language development) based on students' interests and backgrounds creates a sociocultural context for literacy development.	The teacher may create a quiet classroom library where students go to read silently, a listening center where students go to listen to audio books in English or their native language, and a book club area where students gather to read aloud and/or discuss books they are reading.

ance or in collaboration with more capable peers" (Vygotsky, 1978, p. 86, author's italics). Today's classrooms are filled with students who possess a wide range of competencies and experiences; as a result, there are many different optimal learning zones, as well. The variance in student populations continues to increase as schools strive to provide equitable learning opportunities to students with disabilities, students from non-English-speaking backgrounds, and students with diverse cultural experiences (Subban, 2006). The inevitable diversity in classrooms, coupled with our current knowledge of brain development, learning styles, and literacy development, all point to the need to differentiate instruction.

Support from Brain Research

Tomlinson and Kalbfleisch (1998) point to three principles from brain research that dictate the need for differentiated instruction: emotional safety, appropriate challenge, and self-constructed meaning (p. 52). If learners feel emotionally unsafe, for example, as a result of frustration over difficult concepts or pressure to learn at an inappropriate pace, they may shut down altogether, making learning difficult or impossible. Learners who are not appropriately challenged are not able to work within their ZPD (Vygotsky, 1978), making their learning less effective and efficient. Finally, if students are not able to construct their own meaning through associations, the learning cannot reach deep levels. Differentiated instruction aligns with these research principles.

Differences in Student Learning Styles

Even before these brain research findings, effective educators recognized another reason for differentiating instruction when planning lessons: differences in students' learning styles. Dunn and Dunn (1979) explained that individuals respond differently to instruction based on the way in which they focus on, absorb, and retain information. Further, Dunn and Dunn identified 18 dimensions (e.g., emotional, sociological, physiological) that may be used to describe a student's learning style. Considering the number of possible combinations, each classroom is bound to be filled with a variety of preferences for learning new information. One mode of instructional delivery simply cannot meet the needs of all learners.

Students' Stages of Literacy Development

Individuals also differ in their knowledge about literacy, which develops at different rates. Although the rate at which literacy is acquired can vary, many experts agree that children follow a similar sequence of developmental milestones. There seem to be distinct phases of development, each associated with specific reading and writing behaviors. For example, Chall (1983) described six stages of reading development, starting with oral language development and ending with the construction of meaning through analysis and synthesis of information from the text. Pinnell and Fountas (2007) describe a similar phenomenon in reading and writing development; they outline six stages that readers and writers pass through, beginning with the emergent phase and ending as advanced readers and writers. Exhibit 1.2 describes the literacy phases of development that we will reference throughout this book.

Phases of literacy development.   **EXHIBIT   1.2**

EMERGENT PHASE (typical grades: PK–K)

Description: Pre-reading or beginning stage. Students are learning the connection between oral language and print. Students begin to learn that text (often with pictures) tells the story.

Learner Characteristics (reading)

- "Pretend Reading"
  - holds book upright
  - turns pages
  - looks at words and pictures
  - uses pictures to tell story/construct ideas
- Connects stories/books to own experiences
- Talks about favorite stories/books
- Often tells/draws a story in sequence
- Retells stories that have been read aloud, often in sequence
- Reads environmental print
- Develops concepts about print
  - understands concepts of book: right way up, front, back, upside down
  - reads print from top to bottom and left to right
  - begins to recognize most letter sounds
- Begins to develop one-to-one match between the spoken word and the word on the page in reading, as well as concept of word versus letter
- Begins to recognize own name in print
- Begins to recognize meaningful high-frequency words (I, mom, dad, yes, no)
- Begins to demonstrate understanding of sounds in words, syllables, and rhyming words

EARLY PHASE (typical grades: K–1)

Description: Students begin to gain confidence in reading. They understand how print works and begin to cross-check word predictions with visual information (letter–sound correspondence). Beginning readers read for meaning and self-monitor their comprehension of text.

Learner Characteristics (reading)

- Recognizes/describes beginning/middle/end
- Retells story in proper sequence, including key details
- Can recall main idea and details of text
- Begins to identify characters, settings, and major events in stories
- Asks and answers questions before, during, and after reading a text
- Begins to recognize text features in informational text (e.g., table of contents, titles, headings) and understand their purpose
- Makes reasonable predictions before and during reading
- Visualizes events in a story/text
- Can discriminate between fiction and nonfiction text
- Locates known words and uses them to self-monitor reading; possesses a large cadre of sight words
- Is secure with the one-to-one match between the spoken word and the word on the page, as well as the concepts of letter, word, and sentence
- Cross-checks visual information (letter/sound) with meaning (picture clues, context clues) to solve unknown words
- Uses chunks of words to read new words
- Recognizes when reading isn't making sense and can self-correct as necessary
- Begins to integrate all cue sources (meaning/structure/visual; see Exhibit 5.9) during reading
- Reads words in phrases rather than word by word
- Attends to punctuation and pauses appropriately

(continued)

EXHIBIT **1.2**   Continued.

TRANSITIONAL PHASE (typical grades: 1–3)

Description: Readers at this stage are able to use various reading strategies independently. They are able to decode most words automatically and, therefore, can devote more attention to comprehension and fluency.

Learner Characteristics (reading)

- Asks questions before, during, and after reading
- Summarizes accurately with appropriate detail
- Cites evidence from text in summary and retell
- Describes character, setting, problem, and solution
- Determines main idea and important details
- Forms and describes an opinion about a text
- Accurately distinguishes fact from fiction and can identify specific genre (e.g., historical fiction, realistic fiction, procedural nonfiction)
- Connects texts to other texts
- Draws inferences based on prior knowledge and information in text
- Cross-checks and self-corrects automatically
- Begins to solve unknown words by using syllables or meaningful word parts (e.g., root words, prefixes, suffixes)
- Independently looks for known parts of words to read unknown words
- Uses context clues in text to solve the meaning of unfamiliar words
- Applies analogous thinking to read unknown words (e.g., I can read *cheek* and I can read *air;* I can use parts of those words to read *chair*)
- Reads orally with appropriate expression and pauses based on context and punctuation

SELF-EXTENDING PHASE (typical grades: 3+)

Description: Students integrate all cue sources fluently, smoothly, and automatically. They are capable of maintaining comprehension and fluency across complex texts from various genres and with various structures.

Learner Characteristics (reading)

- Intentionally compares what is read to prior knowledge
- Integrates information from the text and prior knowledge to make inferences and draw conclusions
- Applies knowledge of text structures, literary devices, and literary elements to evaluate, interpret, and respond to texts
- Determines a theme of a story or poem
- Interprets and responds to various (i.e., diverse, multicultural, informational, and time period) texts
- Maintains interest, comprehension, and fluency throughout long texts
- Reads independently for a variety of purposes and reads a variety of genres; identifies purpose for reading
- Uses word identification skills automatically
- Recognizes and remembers robust vocabulary words
- Determines meanings of unknown words and phrases through context clues in the text
- Respectfully listens and responds to others' opinions about a text
- Automatically adjusts reading rate to meet the demands of the text

A BRIEF HISTORY OF DIFFERENTIATED READING INSTRUCTION

ifferentiating instruction is not a new construct. In December of 1953, ASCD (formerly the Association for Supervision and Curriculum Development) devoted an entire issue of its journal, *Educational Leadership*, to the topic of differentiation. According to Washburne (1953), teachers voiced the challenges they faced in dealing with individual student differences as early as the late 1800s.

Whole-Class Ability Grouping

One of the first efforts designed to narrow the gap in student achievement was what we now call ability grouping. In the earliest iterations, referred to as **whole-class ability grouping,** students were grouped in classrooms according to their cognitive ability, as determined by the students' mental age (Washburne, 1953). The intent was that teachers could then teach to the whole group, since all students would presumably be learning at the same developmental level. However, as teachers noted, individual differences in ability still existed.

Early attempts to differentiate instruction to meet the needs of individuals in these classrooms included allowing for independent learning through "self-instructive texts," which were quite similar to the workbooks commonly used in classrooms today (Washburne, 1953, p. 140). Through this approach, students were able to read and respond to materials at their own pace and on their own reading level. Another early attempt at differentiating instruction was the **Project Method** (Kilpatrick, 1918), which is akin to the "centers approach" still used in many classrooms. The Project Method allowed students the opportunity to select and complete instructional tasks individually or in collaboration with peers, and members of the group set the pace for learning in this case. Both of these early methods, however, lacked interaction with the teacher; the students guided themselves through learning tasks, and the teacher was primarily responsible for monitoring student behavior.

Within-Class Ability Grouping

While some educators developed ways to scaffold individual learners through ability grouping or individual activities, others found managing individuals or small groups difficult, and some simply could not provide appropriate support for individual students through whole-class lessons. This resulted in less than desired student gains in achievement (Washburne, 1953). Once again, ability grouping took hold in American classrooms. However, rather than homogeneously grouping students into one classroom, it became popular to split students into smaller ability groups within a heterogeneous classroom. This approach, known as **within-class ability grouping,** took a firm hold in the 1950s when published reading programs were designed to support this type of instruction (Barr & Dreeben, 1991). By the 1980s, within-class ability grouping was the predominant form of grouping for reading instruction (Hallinan & Sorensen, 1983; Dreeben & Barr, 1988).

The process of within-class ability grouping seemed to provide the opportunity for differentiating reading instruction. The intent was that teachers would assess students' reading ability and then sort students into smaller homogeneous groups. The next step was for the teacher to design different lessons to meet the needs of the students in each group. In reality, however, structural variables, such as class size, were often the criteria for grouping. It became common practice to divide students into three groups of equal size and deliver the same lesson to all three groups (Dreeben & Barr, 1988; Hallinan & Sorensen, 1983).

Although the smaller subgroups were sometimes more homogeneous than the whole class, there often remained a range of abilities within each group. Since the same lesson was frequently repeated across groups, little differentiation of instruction actually occurred.

Despite the range within the subgroups, a certain amount of tracking existed. That is, students who were identified as struggling readers were often labeled as the "low achieving" group and relegated to membership in this group for a full school year or longer. Barr (1973/1974, 1975) and Allington (1983) characterized this type of instruction as **differential instruction,** as opposed to the differentiated type of teaching that this book advocates. The term *differential instruction* was used because often the instruction for struggling readers was limited to skills-based practice through worksheets, and these readers were exposed to fewer text reading experiences, since story reading for these students occurred at a slower pace than for average or high-achieving peers. At the same time, the advanced readers in the same classroom were provided opportunities to read varied texts at a faster pace and to engage in high-level conversations about the texts (Barr, 1973/1974; Pallas, Entwisle, Alexander, & Stluka, 1994). As a result, the higher-achieving group received more and better instruction (i.e., differential) and in essence learned more than their less able peers (Pallas et al., 1994). Stanovich (1986) described this as the Matthew Effect: the rich get richer and the poor get poorer. This was indeed often the case with ability grouping. Based on his review of research, Allington (1983) argued that "good and poor readers differ in their reading ability as much because of differences in instruction as variations in individual learning styles or aptitudes" (p. 548). As a result, the efficacy of ability grouping came under debate during the 1980s, and whole-group teaching began to take hold again in many classrooms (Moody & Vaughn, 1997).

Whole-Class Grouping

Moody and Vaughn (1997) conducted a study to determine the types of grouping arrangements used in reading instruction. The general education teachers who participated in their study reported that their predominant grouping arrangement was whole group, mainly due to management issues. Teachers found it easier to manage one lesson and one group of students than to plan different activities for multiple groups. However, some general education teachers did utilize small groups in their classrooms for "practice and reinforcement" (p. 6). This study demonstrated that teachers were beginning to use a small amount of differentiated instruction in classrooms, in order to reinforce skills and strategies taught to the whole class. This occurred as ability grouping became an "unpopular" mode of instruction, based on the earlier findings regarding *differential* instruction between groups (Allington, 1983; Barr, 1973/1974; Pallas et al., 1994).

During this time, research demonstrated that teachers did recognize the need to differentiate instruction, even if they did not always do it. For example, Schumm, Moody, and Vaughn (2000) found that although some teachers reported using various grouping arrangements to differentiate reading instruction, most teachers observed in the study delivered instruction to the whole class. Further, even when the observed teachers integrated small-group instruction into their repertoire, none of them differentiated the instruction delivered to the different groups.

During this same period, however, a number of other studies demonstrated that effective literacy teachers used a variety of grouping formats, including whole-group, small-group, and individual lessons (Pressley, Wharton-McDonald, et al., 2001; Taylor, Pearson, Peterson, & Rodriguez, 2003). In addition, the teachers in these classrooms consistently demonstrated the ability to differentiate instruction across flexibly grouped subsets of learners. The term **instructional-level grouping,** in contrast to *ability grouping*, grew in popularity. This was primarily in reaction to the negative connotations regarding differential teaching, which was associated with ability grouping. Ongoing assessment is vital to ensure that students are properly placed with peers at a similar developmental level for reading instruction (instructional level) and moved to a new group as often as needed. This is in contrast to traditional ability groups, where students were typically tracked by ability into one group for the long term.

DIFFERENTIATED READING INSTRUCTION FOR TODAY'S DIVERSE LEARNERS

Current research supports the past findings: differentiating reading instruction does positively impact student achievement (Connor, Morrison, et al., 2011; Shaunessy-Dedrick, Evans, Ferron, & Lindo, 2015; Valiandes, 2015). Although there is no one-size-fits-all model for differentiating instruction, teachers who successfully differentiate do have a common characteristic: a deep knowledge of students' strengths, needs, and interests, as determined by assessment (Ankrum & Bean, 2007; Watts-Taffe, Laster, et al., 2013). Mrs. Jones, the second-grade teacher introduced at the beginning of the chapter, has this deep knowledge about her students. Mrs. Jones's baseline data provides a starting point for this knowledge and for grouping her students, as well as a starting point for beginning instruction. Still, Mrs. Jones will need to continue to monitor student progress in reading development and adjust instruction accordingly throughout the year.

Like Mrs. Jones, most classroom teachers welcome a diverse student population into their classrooms each day. Students come to school equipped with varying background knowledge and exposure to literacy events from home. They also possess varying styles and rates of learning. For some students, this serves as an advantage; if children learn to read early or easily, they may perform at a grade level that is higher than expected for their age. This is true of three of Mrs. Jones's students, who entered her classroom reading above the expected level for second grade. As a result, Mrs. Jones will have to address the needs of these students; this may require her to consider learning styles, modify instructional pacing, or select more challenging texts than the other students require. The instructional foci for her lessons will most likely be aligned with the learner characteristics described for self-extending learners in Exhibit 1.2. For students with limited background knowledge or delayed development due to a slower rate of learning, Mrs. Jones will make different adjustments in her teaching, and focus her teaching points to earlier levels of development described in Exhibit 1.2. The specific adjustments will be determined by the level of literacy development that each student demonstrates.

In addition, students in today's classrooms often represent different cultural foundations, which may affect the understanding they bring to reading and writing. For example, one of Mrs. Jones's students is an English learner and is considered to be reading books (printed in English) at a level that is lower than expected for second grade. This may be attributable to the fact that the student has not developed an understanding of the syntactic structure of English, or perhaps the student has not acquired an adequate English vocabulary to read the words on the page. On the other hand, this student may have experienced delayed language acquisition in his or her first language, which still needs to be addressed. English learners are a diverse group of students, so Mrs. Jones will have to analyze her baseline assessments closely to determine the specific needs of each student. However, she has placed her students in groups with others who have demonstrated a similar level of literacy development, and she will address their specific strengths and weaknesses during small-group instruction. For more information on English learners, refer to the bibliography listed in the Recommended Resources section.

Educational Policy in Support of Differentiation

Small-group differentiated reading instruction is a common feature in effective classrooms (Taylor et al., 2003), and this instructional practice does have a positive effect on student learning (Connor et al., 2011; Shaunessy-Dedrick et al., 2015; Valiandes, 2015). It is only through differentiated instruction that teachers can address the various needs of all learners in today's classrooms, including English learners, gifted students, and those with special needs. This section provides a brief review of the legislation that supports or requires the integration of differentiated instruction in classroom instruction.

National Reading Panel

In 1997, the director of the National Institute of Child Health and Human Development (NICHD) and the Secretary of Education were charged by Congress to assess the efficacy and research base of then-current practices for teaching reading. This resulted in the formation of the National Reading Panel (NRP), a group of 14 individuals, including experts in reading research, teacher educators, reading teachers, school administrators, and parents. The committee conducted a review of research in reading instruction and prepared a final report for Congress in 1999.

The members of the NRP chose to synthesize research detailing effective instructional practices related to the following: alphabetics (phonemic awareness and phonics), fluency, comprehension (vocabulary and reading strategy instruction), teacher education, and computer technology. One of the key themes the panel chose to explore was the "need to develop a clear understanding of how best to integrate different reading approaches to enhance effectiveness for all students" (NICHD, 2000, pp. 1–2). The NRP concluded that because of learner variability, a "one size fits all" approach to reading instruction is not likely to be effective. The panel recommended that teachers base instructional decisions on the needs of their students, not on a fixed sequence of lessons scheduled throughout the school year. This conclusion was drawn by each subcommittee of the panel, which means that experts across all of the focus areas (i.e., alphabetics, fluency, comprehension, teacher education, and computer technology) agreed that differentiated instruction was necessary for student learning.

ESEA/NCLB/ESSA

Congress originally passed the Elementary and Secondary Education Act (ESEA) in 1965. The intent of this legislation was to provide resources to schools to enable equal access to high-quality education for all students. Although the intent of the law was good, little action was taken to improve the equity and quality of education in U.S. schools (Michelman, 2012). Still, the ESEA has been revised and reauthorized eight times in an attempt to improve education, most recently as the Every Student Succeeds Act (ESSA) in 2015.

Prior to the signing of ESSA, Congress passed the No Child Left Behind (NCLB) Act (2001) as a reauthorization of ESEA. One major focus of this legislation was addressing the long-existing achievement gap documented among subgroups of students in U.S. schools. In a policy statement on ESEA, the Department of Education noted, "Achievement gaps have existed for decades between white students and racial minorities, poor students and their more affluent peers, native English speakers and students who are English Learners, and students with disabilities and those without" (U.S. Department of Education, n.d., p. 1). Through NCLB, schools were required to implement plans to reduce the achievement gap among subgroups in their populations. NCLB mandated standardized tests as the primary means for ensuring accountability for raising student achievement for all learners. While it seems natural that educators would differentiate instruction to narrow the achievement gap, the opposite actually occurred. Each state's standardized test became a high-stakes measure for meeting the legislative mandate. Since the achievement measure was a one-size-fits-all task, many teachers took the same approach to teaching (U.S. Department of Education, 2013).

As mentioned above, ESSA was signed into law in 2015. The law includes a provision for tailored interventions in all schools, particularly those where high numbers of children do not succeed (U.S. Department of Education, 2015). The flexibility provided by tailored interventions allows states and local school districts to determine appropriate and differentiated interventions for students. The hope is that when instruction is tailored to the needs of learners, all students will achieve.

What do the Common Core State Standards (CCSS) say about differentiation?

The purpose of the CCSS is to focus on results and not means. The standard's document states, "By emphasizing required achievements the Standards leave room for teachers, curriculum developers, and states to determine how those goals should be reached" (Common Core State Standards Initiative, 2016a). The document further states, "While the standards set grade-specific goals, they do not define how the standards should be taught or which materials should be used to support students. States and districts recognize that there will need to be a range of supports in place to ensure that all students, including those with special needs and English learners, can master the standards. It is up to the states to define the full range of supports appropriate for these students" (Common Core State Standards Initiative, 2016b). Therefore, since the CCSS focus on results, they do not call for, or prohibit, differentiated instruction.

Response to Intervention (RTI)

Differentiated instruction is a major focus in **Response to Intervention (RTI)**. RTI was first introduced in 2004 with the reauthorization of the Individuals with Disabilities Education Act (IDEA). The Act described RTI as an alternative method for identifying students with specific learning disabilities (SLD). The traditional method for identifying a child with an SLD was to measure the child's intelligence quotient (IQ) with a standardized test and then compare the IQ to the child's expected achievement level, as measured through a standardized achievement test. This is referred to as the **IQ–achievement discrepancy model** (Fletcher, 2012), which was the primary method for SLD identification prior to the inception of RTI. Alternatively, the RTI initiative requires early intervention for all struggling learners. Only the students who do not "respond" to the various instructional interventions through improved achievement may then be identified with an SLD.

A standard protocol of implementation for RTI was created, based on the work of Torgesen and his colleagues (Torgesen, Alexander, et al., 2001). This protocol evolved into a popularly implemented model of tiered interventions for students. Tier 1 was described as high-quality, scientifically based, differentiated classroom instruction for all. The intent of this provision was to ensure that classroom teachers employed instructional techniques that have been researched and have demonstrated positive outcomes for students (Hughes & Dexter, 2008). Supplemental instruction was described as Tier 2 intervention: students who did not perform at expected levels on assessments were provided with targeted interventions (Detrich, States, & Keyworth, 2008). This model defined Tier 3 interventions as more intensive individualized interventions designed for students who continued to demonstrate specific needs on assessments (Hughes & Dexter, 2008). Some school districts have moved to a four-tier model, explicitly naming Special Education services as Tier 4, and other districts may have more tiers.

The International Literacy Association (ILA), formerly the International Reading Association (IRA), published a position statement to help educators with their implementation of RTI (IRA, 2010). The document outlined six guiding principles, including (1) core instruction, (2) responsive teaching and differentiation, (3) assessment, (4) collaboration, (5) systemic and comprehensive approaches, and (6) teacher expertise. According to IRA (2010), the first tier of the RTI model is exemplary responsive and differentiated instruction for all students. Further, Tier 2 and Tier 3 interventions require targeted and differentiated instruction based on the needs of the learners as determined through assessment. This type of intervention requires a high level of teacher expertise; teachers must understand the complexities of differentiated instruction to reach all learners effectively and successfully implement RTI.

Support for Differentiation from Professional Organizations

The RTI position statement (IRA, 2010) is only one example of the calls to action for differentiated instruction that have been put forth by professional literacy organizations. In the position statement entitled *Excellent Reading Teachers* (IRA, 2000), the ILA stated that effective teachers "use flexible grouping strategies to tailor instruction to individual students" (p. 1). In other words, the ILA explained that excellent reading teachers differentiate instruction for small groups of students. The National Council of Teachers of English (NCTE) offers a similar endorsement in its *Resolution on Teacher Expertise* (2012). NCTE stated that policymakers and school district decision makers should respect teacher decision-making when they implement differentiated reading instruction to meet the needs of all learners. In addition, ILA and the National Association for the Education of Young Children (NAEYC) published a joint statement, *Where We Stand: On Learning to Read and Write* (NAEYC, 2009), that describes the importance of using differentiated methods for teaching young children as they acquire essential literacy skills.

CONCLUSION

 ifferentiated reading instruction is necessary to meet the diverse needs of students in today's schools. Various educational policies support and endorse the use of differentiation. Effective teachers differentiate lesson focus and text materials, as well as the length and frequency of small-group lessons (Ankrum & Bean, 2007). To accomplish this, teachers like Mrs. Jones must possess a deep knowledge of literacy development and pedagogical practices that enhance that development. Since teaching a small group requires the students who are not part of the group to be actively engaged in meaningful activities, teachers like Mrs. Jones have had to become experts in classroom management. Authentic opportunities for developing literacy are accessible for all students; these opportunities foster self-regulation and a love for learning in students. Because differentiation is complex, it can be a daunting task for teachers. The remainder of this book will provide details for getting started and effectively differentiating reading instruction throughout the school year.

Practical Application

1. Consider Tomlinson's elements of instruction that may be differentiated, as described in Exhibit 1.1. Describe three different products that students may create to demonstrate the ability to describe the elements of a story (e.g., character, setting, and plot) that you read to your class.

2. The following table summarizes the reading development of the students in Mrs. Jones's second-grade class:

GROUP	DESCRIPTOR	NUMBER OF STUDENTS
One	Beginning to read at emergent level	2 (1 English learner)
Two	Reading below second-grade level with strong comprehension	5
Three	Reading fluently at second-grade level with weak comprehension	6
Four	Reading fluently and accurately at second-grade level with strong comprehension	6
Five	Reading and comprehending text at fourth-grade level	3

Use Exhibit 1.2 (literacy phases of development) to answer the following questions:

   a. What competencies are the students in Group One likely to demonstrate?
   b. Which phase of development are the students in Group Two most likely working in?
   c. Students in Group Five can be described as self-extending readers, and these students can comprehend texts that are considered appropriate for fourth grade. Search online for a list of books appropriate for fourth-graders. Select one book that you know from the list and describe why it is appropriate for self-extending learners.

Recommended Resources

The following texts provide in-depth information on teaching English learners.

Avalos, M. A., Pasencia, A., Chavez, C., & Rascon, J. (2007, December). Modified guided reading: Gateway to English as a second language and literacy learning. *Reading Teacher*, 61 (4), 318–329.

Ball, A. (2006). Teaching writing in culturally diverse classrooms. In C.A. MacArthur, S. Graham, & J. Fitzgerald (Eds.), *Handbook of writing research* (pp. 293–310). New York: Guilford Press.

Barrera, R. B., & Jimenez, R. T. (2000). *Literacy practices for Latino students.* Washington, DC: U.S. Department of Education, Office of Grants and Contracts Services. Retrieved from http://www.ncela.gwu.edu/pubs/reports/literacy/index.htm.

de Oliveira, L. C., Klassen, M., & Maune, M. (2015). *The Common Core State Standards in English language arts for English language learners* (pp. 39–52). Alexandria, VA: TESOL Press.

de Oliveira, L. C., & Silva, T. (Eds.) (2013). *L2 writing in secondary classrooms.* New York: Routledge.

Gort, M. (2015, Special Edition Fall). *Understanding and fostering the language and literacy development of young bilinguals.* Columbus, OH: Crane Center for Early Childhood Research Center and Policy, The Ohio State University.

Graves, M., August, D., & Mancilla-Martinez, J. (2012). *Teaching vocabulary to English language learners.* New York: Teachers College Press.

Harman, R. (2013). Intertextuality in genre-based pedagogies: Building lexical cohesion in fifth-grade L2 writing. *Journal of Second Language Writing, 22,* 125–140.

Nation, I. S. P. (2013). *Learning vocabulary in another language.* Cambridge, UK: Cambridge University Press.

Short, D., & Echevarria, J. (2005). Teacher skills to support English language learners. *Educational Leadership, 62* (4), 8–13.

Valdés, G., Menken, K., & Castro, M. (2015). *Common core bilingual and English language learners: A resource for educators.* Philadelphia: Caslon Publishing.

REFERENCES

Allington, R. L. (1983). The reading instruction provided readers of differing abilities. *The Elementary School Journal, 83* (5), 548–559.

Ankrum, J. W., & Bean, R. (2007). Differentiated reading instruction: What and how. *Reading Horizons, 48* (1), 133–146.

Barr, R. (1973/1974). Instructional paces and their effect on reading acquisition. *Reading Research Quarterly, 9* (4), 526–554.

Barr, R. (1975). How children are taught to read: Grouping and pacing. *The School Review, 83* (3), 479–498.

Barr, R., & Dreeben, R. (1991). Grouping students for reading instruction. In R. Barr, M. Kamil, P. Mosenthal, & P. D. Pearson (Eds.), *Handbook of Reading Research Vol. 2* (pp. 885–910). New York: Longman.

Chall, J. S. (1983). *Stages of reading development.* New York: McGraw-Hill.

Common Core State Standards Initiative (2016a). English Language Arts Standards. Retrieved from http://www.corestandards.org/ELA-Literacy/introduction/key-design-consideration/.

Common Core State Standards Initiative (2016b). Read the Standards. Retrieved from http://www.corestandards.org/read-the-standards/.

Connor, C. M., Morrison, F. J., Fishman, B. J., Giuliani, S., Luck, M., Underwood, P., et al. (2011). Testing the impact of child characteristics x instruction interactions on third graders' reading comprehension by differentiating literacy instruction. *Reading Research Quarterly, 46* (3), 189–221.

Detrich, R., States, J., & Keyworth, R. (2008). Response to intervention: What it is and what it is not. *Journal of Evidence-Based Practices for Schools, 9* (2), 60–85. Retrieved from http://search.proquest.com/docview/622048607?accountid=14709.

Dreeben, R., & Barr, R. (1988). The formation and instruction of ability groups. *American Journal of Education, 97,* 34–61.

Dunn, R. S., & Dunn, K. J. (1979). Learning styles/teaching styles: Should they ... can they ... be matched? *Educational Leadership, 36,* 238–244.

Fletcher, J. M. (2012). Classification and identification of learning disabilities. *Learning About Learning Disabilities,* 1–26.

Hallinan, M. T., & Sorensen, A. B. (1983). The formation and stability of instructional groups. *American Sociological Review, 48,* 838–851.

Hughes, C. A., & Dexter, D. D. (2008). Selecting a scientifically based core curriculum for Tier 1. Retrieved from http://www.rtinetwork.org.

International Reading Association (2000). *Excellent reading teachers: A position statement of the International Reading Association*. Newark, DE: IRA.

International Reading Association (2010). *Response to intervention: Guiding principles for educators from the International Reading Association*. (Position statement). Newark, DE: IRA.

Kilpatrick, T. H. (1918, September). The project method. *Teachers College Record, 19*, 319–334.

MacGillivray, L., Rueda, R., & Martinez, A. (2004). Listening to inner city teachers of English language learners: Differentiating literacy instruction. In Fenice Boyd (Ed.)., *Multicultural and multilingual literacy and language practices* (pp. 114–160). New York: Guilford.

Michelman, B. (2012, Spring). The never-ending story of ESEA reauthorization. *ASCD Policy Priorities, 18* (1).

Moody, S. W., & Vaughn, S. (1997). Instructional grouping for reading. *Remedial & Special Education, 18* (6), 347–356.

National Association for the Education of Young Children (2009). *Where we stand: On learning to read and write*. Washington DC: NAEYC.

National Council of Teachers of English (2012). *Resolution on teacher expertise and the Common Core State Standards*. Retrieved from http://www.ncte.org/positions/statements/teacherexpertise.

National Institute of Child Health and Human Development (2000). Report of the National Reading Panel. *Teaching children to read: An evidence-based assessment of the scientific research literature on reading and its implications for reading instruction: Reports of the subgroups (NIH Publication No. 00-4754)*. Washington, DC: U.S. Government Printing Office. Retrieved from http://www.nichd.nih.gov/publications/pubs/nrp/Documents/report.pdf.

Pallas, A. M., Entwisle, D. R., Alexander, K. L., & Stluka, F. (1994). Ability-group effects: Instructional, social, or institutional. *Sociology of Education, 67* (1), 27–46.

Pinnell, G. S., & Fountas, I. C. (2007). *The continuum of literacy learning*. Portsmouth, NH: Heinemann.

Pressley, M., Wharton-McDonald, R., Allington, R., Block, C., Morrow, L., Tracey, D., Baker, K., Brooks, G., Cronin, J., Nelson, E., & Woo, D. (2001). Strategy instruction for elementary students searching informational text. *Scientific Studies of Reading, 5* (1), 35–59.

Schumm, J. S., Moody, S. W., & Vaughn, S. (2000). Grouping for reading instruction: Does one size fit all? *Journal of Learning Disabilities, 33* (5), 477–488.

Shaunessy-Dedrick, E., Evans, L., Ferron, J., & Lindo, M. (2015). Effects of differentiated reading on elementary students' reading comprehension and attitudes toward reading. *Gifted Child Quarterly, 59* (2), 91–107.

Stanovich, K. E. (1986). Matthew effects in reading: Some consequences of individual differences in the acquisition of literacy. *Reading Research Quarterly, 21* (4), 360–407.

Subban, P. (2006). Differentiated instruction: A research basis. *International Education Journal, 7* (7), 935–947.

Taylor, B. M., Pearson, P. D., Peterson, D., & Rodriguez, M. C. (2003). Reading growth in high-poverty classrooms: The influence of teacher practices that encourage cognitive engagement in literacy learning. *Elementary School Journal, 104* (1), 3–28.

Tomlinson, C. A. (2000, August). Differentiation of instruction in the elementary grades. *ERIC Digest*. Champaign, IL: ERIC Clearinghouse on Elementary and Early Childhood Education. (ERIC Document No. ED443572). Retrieved from http://www.education.com/reference/article/Ref_Teacher_s_Guide/.

Tomlinson, C. A. (2004). Sharing responsibility for differentiating instruction. *Roper Review, 26* (4), 188–200.

Tomlinson, C. A., & Kalbfleisch, M. L. (1998, November). Teach me, teach my brain: A call for differentiated classrooms. *Educational Leadership, 56* (3), 52–58.

Torgesen, J., Alexander, A., Wagner, R., Rashotte, C., Voeller, K., & Conway, T. (2001). Intensive remedial instruction for children with severe reading disabilities: Immediate and long-term outcomes from two instructional approaches. *Journal of Learning Disabilities, 34*, 33–58.

U.S. Department of Education (2013). *The opportunity of ESEA flexibility*. Retrieved from http://www2.ed.gov/policy/elsec/guid/esea-flexibility/resources/esea-flex-brochure.pdf.

U.S. Department of Education (2015). *Every Student Succeeds Act: A progress report on elementary and secondary education*. Retrieved from https://www.whitehouse.gov/sites/whitehouse.gov/files/documents/ESSA_Progress_Report.pdf.

U.S. Department of Education (n.d.). *The opportunity of ESEA flexibility*. Retrieved from http://www2.ed.gov/policy/elsec/guid/esea-flexibility/resources/close-achievement-gaps.pdf.

Valiandes, S. (2015). Evaluating the impact of differentiated instruction on literacy and reading in mixed ability classrooms: Quality and equity dimensions of education effectiveness. *Studies in Educational Evaluation, 45*, 17–26.

Vygotsky, L. S. (1978). *Mind in society: The development of higher psychological processes*. Cambridge, MA: Harvard University Press.

Washburne, C. W. (1953, December). Adjusting the program to the child. *Educational Leadership, 11* (3), 138–147.

Watts-Taffe, S., Laster, B. P., Broach, L., Marinak, B., Connor, C. M., & Walker-Dalhouse, D. (2013). Differentiated instruction: Making informed teacher decisions. *The Reading Teacher, 66* (4), 303–314.

Classroom Context I

LITERACY INSTRUCTION IN A PRIMARY-LEVEL EXEMPLARY CLASSROOM

his chapter provides one example of a typical day of literacy instruction in a primary-level classroom, and Chapter 3 provides an example from an intermediate/middle-level classroom. Grades K through 2 are generally considered primary grades in elementary schools, and grades 3 through 6 are considered intermediate or middle-level grades. Although the remainder of this book focuses on small-group reading instruction, this chapter and Chapter 3 provide an overview of effective literacy instruction to show differentiated instruction in the context of a school day.

Welcome to Ms. Palmer's classroom. She has been teaching first grade for nine years, and last spring she was nominated by her district's administrators and literacy specialists as an exemplary teacher of literacy. As you read, consider what exemplary instruction looks like in action. How does Ms. Palmer fit the necessary lessons into each day? How does she know which content to teach in whole-class lessons and how to differentiate her instruction in small-group lessons? How does Ms. Palmer find the time to monitor the progress of individual students?

CHARACTERISTICS OF RESEARCH-BASED EFFECTIVE PRACTICES

his section describes research-based effective practices that award-winning teachers such as Ms. Palmer and Mr. Metzgar (Chapter 3) use in their teaching. As a result of these teaching practices, many students in Ms. Palmer's and Mr. Metzgar's classrooms consistently demonstrate higher than expected achievement in reading and writing. The accompanying box describes the research-based characteristics of exemplary literacy instruction in these classrooms.

Research-based characteristics of exemplary literacy instruction

Teachers who engage in exemplary teaching of literacy:

Use a variety of instructional grouping arrangements throughout the day. The teacher presents information and guides discussion with the whole class, small groups, and individuals at different times throughout the day. Examples include:

- **Whole class:** Interactive read-aloud, shared reading, modeled writing, show and tell (oral language and listening in primary grades)
- **Small group:** Guided reading, guided writing, buzz groups (oral language and listening in primary grades)
- **Individual:** Teacher–student reading/writing conferences

Predominately use small group as the grouping arrangement each day. The teacher devotes more time to teaching students in small groups than teaching with the whole class. This allows the teacher to provide differentiated instruction in the students' zones of proximal development. Examples include:

- **Guided reading:** The teacher conducts differentiated small-group lessons and discussion about carefully selected texts.
- **Guided writing:** The teacher meets with small groups to discuss differentiated writing strategies and skills.

Include differentiated instruction, based on assessment, daily. These teachers use various classroom-based authentic assessments to inform and plan instruction that is tailored to students' needs. This is critical for effective differentiation in small-group and individual lessons. Examples of differentiated instruction are described in detail throughout this book.

Model instruction daily. The teacher provides explicit instruction in literacy skills and strategies by modeling processes for the students. This can occur in any instructional grouping format, but it generally occurs with the whole class on a daily basis. For example,

- **Think-aloud.** The teacher uses this technique to demonstrate the cognitive process during a read-aloud (interactive read-aloud) or a writing demonstration (modeled writing).

Scaffold instruction to meet the needs of individuals. Scaffolding is a term to describe tailored instructional support that is provided to enable students to accomplish more difficult tasks than they could without assistance to aid their learning. The teacher uses various techniques to help students grasp new information. For example,

- Visual prompts (posters, anchor charts, handouts),
- Verbal prompts during guided instruction.

Require and model high-level thinking. The teacher engages students in the application of high-level thinking skills during literacy tasks and discussions. Conversations require students to go beyond basic recall of text materials. Examples include:

- Making connections to the world and other texts.
- Evaluating characters' motives.
- Citing evidence from a text.
- Judging the trustworthiness of a source.

Expect students to be engaged in authentic activities throughout the instructional block. The teacher prepares opportunities for active responses (e.g., reading, writing, manipulating, discussing) to instruction rather than passive responses (e.g., fill-in-the-blank worksheets, listening to lectures, round-robin reading). For example,

- Students spend large chunks of time independently reading and writing full-length authentic texts.
- Students engage in cooperative activities at literacy centers.

Use various genres and text types for instruction and recreational reading. The teacher intentionally selects varying text types (e.g., narrative, expository; traditional, electronic) at varying levels of difficulty for instructional purposes. The classroom library is well stocked with a variety of texts to facilitate independent text selection and exploration. For example,

- The teacher may model strategies for navigating and/or writing informational texts to the whole class and then revisit these strategies during small-group instruction.

Hold high expectations for all learners. All students are considered successful readers and writers and part of a learning community. The teacher tailors instruction to start at a developmentally appropriate level for each child and provides rigorous and scaffolded instruction to help that child develop as much as possible during the school year. For example,

- The teacher uses high-level vocabulary to converse with students about literacy activities. The teacher might describe the "similarities and differences between realistic fiction and fantasy" or ask children to "respond to the text in writing" with children as young as kindergarten. Each child is then expected to respond according to his or her developmental level.

Ensure high levels of student engagement. Most children are on-task and actively engaged in literacy tasks throughout the instructional block. A limited amount of time is spent on transitions or off-task behaviors. For example,

- Multiple activities may occur at one time. While the teacher meets with a small group of students to discuss a text, the other children are working quietly at literacy tasks. Individuals may be reading or writing independently while small groups of children collaborate to create an annotated mural.

Sources: Ankrum, Morewood, Bean & Genest (2008); Block & Mangieri (2003); Lyon & Weiser (2009); Pressley, Allington, Wharton-McDonald, Block, & Morrow (2001); Sailors (2013); Taylor, Pearson, Peterson, & Rodriguez (2003, 2005); Wolfersberger, Reutzel, Sudweeks, & Fawson (2004).

DAILY INSTRUCTIONAL COMPONENTS OF THE LITERACY BLOCK

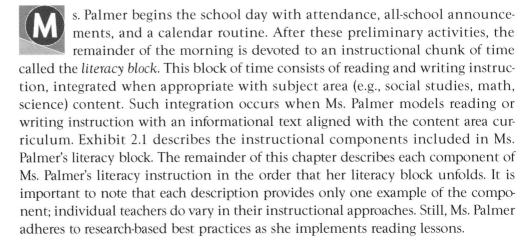 Ms. Palmer begins the school day with attendance, all-school announcements, and a calendar routine. After these preliminary activities, the remainder of the morning is devoted to an instructional chunk of time called the *literacy block*. This block of time consists of reading and writing instruction, integrated when appropriate with subject area (e.g., social studies, math, science) content. Such integration occurs when Ms. Palmer models reading or writing instruction with an informational text aligned with the content area curriculum. Exhibit 2.1 describes the instructional components included in Ms. Palmer's literacy block. The remainder of this chapter describes each component of Ms. Palmer's literacy instruction in the order that her literacy block unfolds. It is important to note that each description provides only one example of the component; individual teachers do vary in their instructional approaches. Still, Ms. Palmer adheres to research-based best practices as she implements reading lessons.

Interactive Read-Aloud

At the beginning of the literacy block, Ms. Palmer invites all of the children to sit on the carpet in the whole-class meeting area. Ms. Palmer has found that the children tend to be more actively engaged in a lesson when they are in close proximity to her; this is especially true when she asks them to participate in

Components of literacy instruction.		**EXHIBIT 2.1**	

COMPONENT	INSTRUCTIONAL FOCUS	GROUPING ARRANGEMENT	APPROXIMATE TIME FRAME
Interactive read-aloud	Comprehension Fluency	Whole class	15 minutes
Differentiated small-group reading: guided reading (combined with literacy centers, discussed in Chapter 4)	(Varies, depending on strengths and needs of learners) Comprehension Vocabulary development Fluency practice Word study	Small groups (1 to 3 groups per day meet with teacher)	45 minutes
Shared reading experience	Comprehension Vocabulary development Fluency practice Word study	Whole class	15 minutes
Independent reading/ individual reading conferences	Assessment Varied instruction, depending on need	Individual (2 to 3 per day)	15 minutes
Writing instruction: writing workshop Mini-lessons	Writing process and strategies Spelling Grammar	Whole class	20 minutes
Independent writing (while the teacher conducts small-group lessons and individual conferences)	Writing process and strategies Spelling Grammar (Varies depending on strengths and needs of learners)	Small group or individual	40 minutes

conversations about texts. Once the students are settled and their attention is focused, Ms. Palmer begins to conduct an Interactive Read-Aloud (IRA). Pinnell and Fountas (2011) describe the IRA as "a teaching context in which students are actively listening and responding to an oral reading of a text" (p. 189). It is through a daily IRA that teachers are able to model proficient, fluent reading, as well as conduct think-alouds to provide insights regarding the cognitive processing involved in reading and responding to a text. Because the IRA is conducted as a whole-class lesson, teaching points are typically aligned with grade-level standards. When a read-aloud is interactive, the students are invited to share their thinking during the lesson; this allows the teacher to assess the students' understanding and plan for subsequent instruction. In this IRA, Ms. Palmer plans to model the strategy of asking questions while reading.

The children are quickly drawn into Ms. Palmer's introduction of *Chester's Way*, by Kevin Henkes (1988). After a brief introduction, Ms. Palmer reads the picture book to the class, stopping periodically to model her thinking. For example, she states, "I wonder why Chester always eats the same thing for breakfast." As she reads the story, Ms. Palmer also asks the students, "What are you wondering as I read this page?" and allows volunteers to share their thinking. She continues alternating reading with stopping to ask various questions. At one point, she states, "I have another question! I wonder why Lily always carries a disguise with her? Why might she need a disguise?" At another point in the book, Ms. Palmer explains that good readers ask questions and then read on to find the answers. Before she can demonstrate this, Finn (a student in the class) exclaims, "That's why Lily always has a disguise, so she can be brave and protect her friends!" Ms. Palmer praises Finn for noticing this and finding the answer to the question she posed. Throughout the reading, Ms. Palmer also pauses to allow the students to make predictions about what may happen next in the story and to elicit questions that students have as she reads. Ms. Palmer uses the IRA and questions and responses such as these to "show" students the thinking that readers do. In addition, the interactive discussion helps to maintain student engagement while Ms. Palmer demonstrates reading strategies.

Ms. Palmer conducts an IRA each day, typically with a new text; however, she may revisit *Chester's Way* if she finds it necessary to teach new strategies or review strategies. She is careful to select texts that represent various genres over the course of the school year to ensure that her students have multiple opportunities to interact with texts of varying types and complexity, as emphasized in the Common Core State Standards. Ms. Palmer is also careful to demonstrate grade-level-appropriate reading strategies, as outlined by her school district's curriculum, which is aligned with the CCSS (since her state has adopted the standards). High-level conversations may center on the use of these strategies, the author's intent or purposes in writing, text features and elements, vocabulary development, or any other topic that will help Ms. Palmer's students navigate new texts in their own reading.

At the end of each IRA, Ms. Palmer reviews the main teaching point(s) she has modeled, in this case the strategy of asking questions. A typical review consists of Ms. Palmer restating the strategy modeled and then requesting that the children try it in their own reading. For example, after closing *Chester's Way*, Ms. Palmer comments on an "interesting part" of the story and then states, "Good readers ask themselves questions while they read. Remember when I did that? I wondered why Chester always had the same thing for breakfast. I also asked myself why Lily would always carry a disguise. These questions made me want to keep reading and gave me a purpose to read. Remember to stop and think about the questions that pop into your head as you read." This instructional charge is considered a *statement of transfer*, or an intentional directive that Ms. Palmer uses to solidify new skills and strategies for her learners. In this case the statement is meant to encourage the children to apply the modeled strategy in their independent work.

Differentiated Small-Group Reading Instruction: Guided Reading

Ms. Palmer also uses the statement of transfer, described above, as a transition cue. After describing what she expects the students to do as they work independently (in this case, as they read), Ms. Palmer issues a few reminders about the tasks the students will complete in their literacy centers. (See Chapter 4 for a complete explanation of literacy centers.) She dismisses the children to their centers and monitors each small group as they begin the authentic tasks in each area. As the focus of this book is to describe differentiated reading instruction in detail, the following description will give a brief overview, and then Chapters 4 through 8 will provide details of Ms. Palmer's decision-making and instructional routines.

The purpose of differentiated small-group reading lessons in Ms. Palmer's classroom is to allow the children to read a previously unseen text as independently as possible. In these lessons Ms. Palmer uses the **guided reading** approach and works with small groups of students who read at a similar level (Fountas & Pinnell, 1996). She uses leveled books matched to the instructional reading level of the students in each group so they have a minimum of new concepts, skills, and strategies to learn. The instructional reading level is the level at which students can orally read a text with 90 to 94 percent accuracy and with good comprehension (Fountas & Pinnell, 1996). During the sessions she provides scaffolding so the students can use the new skills and strategies successfully. Ms. Palmer directs the teaching focus and selects a text for each group that ensures maximum learning and success; in addition, she carefully observes student performance so she can provide support only as needed. This instructional strategy is designed to provide children the opportunity to work in their zone of proximal development (Vygotsky, 1978), as discussed in Chapter 1.

The children in Ms. Palmer's classroom are divided into six different reading groups of students with similar instructional reading levels. Each group meets with Ms. Palmer two to five times during the week, depending on the learners' needs. Group membership is flexible; this will change several times over the course of the year, since each child learns in a different manner and at a different rate. Each group of students is at a different level in their reading development, and so the texts and lesson focus will be different for each group. In other words, the lesson focus in differentiated reading instruction is determined by the developmental needs of the learners, not grade-level standards.

Today the children settle quickly into their center tasks and routines. After five minutes, Ms. Palmer calls five children to join her at the guided reading table (Exhibit 2.2). After some brief chatter about their literacy center work, Ms. Palmer pulls out a new text, Brenda Z. Guiberson's *Ocean Life* (2011), to introduce to the children. *Ocean Life* is a nonfiction book about life in the ocean. Ms. Palmer selected the book based on the text features, such as table of contents and glossary, which her monitoring of the students indicated she needed to review with this group. Another important factor was the text level; these children read at Guided Reading Level M, which corresponds approximately with the end of second grade (Fountas & Pinnell, 1996). As with most books at this level, the vocabulary is complex, the pictures do not strongly correlate with the text, and the print layout varies throughout the book. Finally, Ms. Palmer knew that the children would be interested in the topic; the class has been engaged in a unit of study centered on animal habitats. The ocean has been the topic of enthusiastic conversations with Ms. Palmer's first-graders.

After the children are settled at the table, Ms. Palmer asks the children to predict the genre of the book and what they may learn from reading it. Next, she explains that this book has a table of contents, like several big books that the class has read together recently. She asks the children to explain the purpose

EXHIBIT 2.2

Small-group reading table.

of the table of contents, and she elaborates and extends the responses as needed. The lesson continues with the children locating information to read, using the table of contents as a guide. Each child reads the text silently and participates in the small-group discussion that follows.

Since Ms. Palmer needs to meet with two or three groups each day, she keeps the lessons focused and short. After about 15 minutes, Ms. Palmer closes the lesson and asks the children to take the book and finish reading it independently before returning to their centers. The children in this group are reading above grade level, and Ms. Palmer is confident that with the lesson on using the table of contents, her students will be able to navigate the text successfully, based on their performance during the small-group meeting. She promises that they will discuss the new content the next time they meet for a small-group reading lesson.

The children leave the guided reading table, allowing Ms. Palmer to make a quick assessment of the other children working at the various learning centers. She reminds one child of the importance of staying focused during center time, and redirects her by helping her choose a different book to read. Ms. Palmer then calls her second group to the guided reading table as she pulls their books from the shelf. These six children will begin to read and discuss their first simple chapter book, a piece of realistic fiction identified as Guided Reading Level J, which is approximately equivalent to a beginning second-grade reading level. The book, *Henry and Mudge: The First Book* (Rylant, 1996), is a short chapter book with illustrations to support the readers. The vocabulary and storyline are simple and familiar, yet there are several characters for the readers to keep track of throughout the book, as is characteristic of books at Level J. Ms. Palmer introduces the readers to the characters and the organization of the book. She asks the children to predict events based on the title of Chapter 1 and dismisses them to read the chapter on their own. The group will meet again tomorrow to discuss the chapter before receiving their next reading assignment.

The third group consists of four children who meet with Ms. Palmer each day. They are currently reading below grade level. Ms. Palmer has selected a Level E text, which is slightly below their instructional level. Books at Level E are equivalent to an early first-grade reading level; they have several lines of text on each page, with some repetitive language to support the reader. Typically, there are detailed pictures on each page to support readers' developing decoding skills. Ms. Palmer chose *Who Is Coming?* (McKissak, 1986). This group needs practice with making inferences and reading fluently, and Ms. Palmer chose an easier text so that the children would not have to focus too much on decoding.

Shared Reading Experience

Upon completion of her final small-group reading lesson, Ms. Palmer gently touches the wind chimes hanging from her ceiling. The quiet music signals the end of differentiated group reading/literacy center time, and the children quickly begin to put materials away and gather on the carpet in the whole-group meeting space. One of the children exclaims, "It's time for shared reading!"

Shared reading was first introduced as an instructional strategy by Holdaway (1979). He described it as akin to a bedtime story, where a caregiver reads to and with a child, providing insights into how to read a text. In the primary grades, shared reading is usually conducted with the whole class, often with enlarged text, such as a big book, a poster, or projected text (see Exhibit 2.3). Enlarged text is essential to allow all participants to view the text as the teacher models reading strategies, highlights text features, describes print features, and teaches students about the process of reading. Teachers use grade-level standards, such as state standards or the CCSS, to determine the lesson focus in shared reading.

For today's shared reading lesson, Ms. Palmer has selected a big book about the coral reef to demonstrate how to determine the main idea of a text by summarizing key details. This teaching focus is based on CCSS RI.1.1. Ms. Palmer starts by introducing the book to the class, asking if the children can read the title chorally to her. The children do, and Emma offers that it looks like a nonfiction text, because the photographs are real. Ms. Palmer praises the prediction and elaborates on several text features (CCSS RI.1.5) that indicate that this is indeed a nonfiction book. Next, Ms. Palmer asks the children about the first page of the text, and Amos answers that this is the table of contents. The class has discussed this feature several times, but Ms. Palmer knows that several children are still a bit unclear about how to use it. After a brief review of the function of the table of contents, Ms. Palmer models how to locate the information on where to find coral reefs, and turns to these pages.

Ms. Palmer reads the three pages aloud to the class. After the reading, Ms. Palmer asks the children to turn and tell a friend about the type of place where somebody might find a coral reef, using only one sentence. She listens to the students' responses and then asks four volunteers to share their responses with the class. Ms. Palmer records each response on chart paper. She points out that, although the sentences are slightly different, the information contained in the four responses is nearly the same. Ms. Palmer explains that the students described the main idea of this section of text. She reads several more sections of the text, asking the children to discuss the main idea of each section. Ms. Palmer elaborates upon the students' responses as needed, but she allows the children to provide as much information as possible.

EXHIBIT 2.3

Shared reading on an interactive whiteboard.

Ms. Palmer conducts a shared reading lesson every day. She will continue to work with nonfiction text features until most of the children seem to be proficient in them. Then, Ms. Palmer will revisit nonfiction text features periodically throughout the year to ensure that the children can successfully navigate informational texts independently. Still, Ms. Palmer understands the importance of selecting informational and narrative texts from different genres and teaching various grade-level strategies and skills, as required by the school district's curriculum and the CCSS.

To transition to independent reading/individual conference time, Ms. Palmer again provides a statement of transfer. Similar to the statement of transfer that Ms. Palmer used after the interactive read-aloud, the statement of transfer that she uses after shared reading is designed to ensure that the children attempt to use the strategy that was modeled during shared reading. She asks, "What have we learned about what good readers can use to find the information they need or want to read in a nonfiction book? And about how good readers use it?" Asking this question allows Ms. Palmer to assess the students' understanding, and this statement of transfer also deepens their understanding because they will share their definition of the table of contents in their own language. Once the students respond by naming the table of contents and describing its use, Ms. Palmer adds, "Now it's your turn. If you have chosen a nonfiction book to read today during independent reading time, try using the table of contents to find the information that interests you most. When I meet with you for our conference, you can tell me how you used the table of contents."

Independent Reading/Individual Reading Conferences

Ms. Palmer dismisses the children from shared reading by naming different sea creatures, reminding them of an activity they completed in science class on the previous day. "Girls and boys, yesterday you chose a picture of your favorite sea creature to add to our bar graph. It is hanging by the door in case you don't quite remember which creature you chose. Please listen for the creature you placed on the graph. When I call that sea creature, take your independent reading books to a comfy place in the room. Remember to choose a place where you can concentrate and won't be tempted to talk to others. Now, if you placed an octopus on the chart, please find a good place to read." Ms. Palmer continues to call sea creature names until all of the students have found a quiet space to read.

Earlier in the school year, Ms. Palmer taught the children how to self-select appropriate texts based on their interest and purpose for reading. The classroom is well stocked with books, and they are organized by genre, which helps the students find the types of books that interest them most. In addition to printed texts, four tablets with ebooks are available for student use. Ms. Palmer has created a rotating list, allowing each child a turn with an ebook. When a child completes a book on the device, it is available for another student. In today's conferences, Ms. Palmer wants to assess whether the children have selected books appropriate to their reading levels and purposes. Ms. Palmer understands that sometimes students pick difficult-to-read books because they enjoy browsing the pictures. Other times, students select easier books, which allows them to apply the strategies and skills she has taught. In addition to discussing book selection with the students, Ms. Palmer is interested in assessing students' use of the table of contents, if any of the children have selected texts with this feature.

Each day Ms. Palmer meets with three or four children for individual conferences during independent reading time. She meets with most of her students on a rotating basis and is careful to meet with two of her students several times each week, since they are struggling readers and need extra support to maintain focus and comprehend what they read. Ms. Palmer's reading conferences are student-centered. This means that she begins the individual meetings with an open-ended question, such as, "What are you reading about today?" She then asks questions to prompt the reader to provide additional detail, discuss reading strategies and goals, or revisit the text selection process. When appropriate, Ms. Palmer uses this time to reinforce skills or strategies that she has taught during a whole-class lesson. For example, Ms. Palmer may reinforce the use of the table of contents with a student by asking, "Where might you look to find out the page where the author described turtles? Show me how to find that." However, this takes place only if a child has selected a book containing this feature, and if the child requires additional instruction in the use of the feature. Each conversation is responsive and is designed to encourage deep reading for meaning and pleasure.

Independent reading time also allows an additional opportunity for Ms. Palmer to assess students, both informally and formally. Prior to each conference, Ms. Palmer plans for a specific focus. At times she plans to elicit summaries or retellings of books, to determine whether students understand the gist of their texts. At other times Ms. Palmer asks key questions about topics, events, or characters in a text, to check general comprehension. She documents information regarding each student's comprehension with anecdotal records, which are short notes detailing her observations of the student's progress. Ms. Palmer then references these notes to inform her instruction. If it seems that a student does not have a deep understanding of a text, Ms. Palmer may take a brief running record. (See Chapter 5 for an explanation of running records.) This allows her to determine future small-group lesson teaching points and helps her assist the child in choosing an easier book, if necessary.

Writing Instruction: Writing Workshop

Clearly, Ms. Palmer devotes a large chunk of instructional time to teaching reading each day. Still, she realizes that reading and writing are reciprocal processes, so she plans and conducts daily explicit writing lessons and devotes a block of time to writing instruction each day, usually in the form of a writing workshop (Calkins, 1986; Graves, 1983). The workshop consists of explicit instruction delivered through a 10- to 20-minute mini-lesson, followed by a period of time provided for children to practice the new techniques independently. While children work on independent writing, the teacher provides differentiated instruction to small groups or individuals through writing conferences.

Mini-lesson

After the independent reading/individual reading conference component, Ms. Palmer once again invites all of the children to sit on the carpet in the whole-class meeting area. She picks up her marker and approaches the easel, and the children immediately recognize this cue for the beginning of the mini-lesson. Calkins (1986) describes a writing mini-lesson as a brief instructional session designed to demonstrate how proficient writers compose and record ideas. The mini-lesson is the teacher's opportunity to demonstrate skills and strategies that proficient writers use. This is similar to the purpose of the interactive read-aloud and shared reading experience included in Ms. Palmer's reading instruction. As she does with the IRA and shared reading, Ms. Palmer selects her teaching points based on district curriculum (reflecting the CCSS) and the needs of her students as determined by assessments. The content of the writing mini-lesson may include how to select a topic to write about, spelling strategies, grammar and punctuation rules, writing with voice, organizing ideas, or any other information needed to help students develop as writers.

Today, the focus of Ms. Palmer's mini-lesson is word choice. All eyes are on the easel as Ms. Palmer composes a message and explicitly explains how she will use interesting words to engage the reader. After writing several lines, she rereads what she has written. After stating, "I picked a flower for my mom," Ms. Palmer pauses. She puts her hand on her head and asks, "Can I write this sentence in a more interesting way?" After a few seconds, she says, "I plucked a purple tulip out of the garden. Wow, that's better. Can you see me doing that? Can you see the purple tulip, and me walking right over to pluck it out of the garden? Good writers use interesting, specific words to paint a picture, so their readers can visualize what they've written." Ms. Palmer crosses out the original sentence on the easel, repeats her new sentence, and writes it on the easel. As she writes the sentence, she invites the children to help her spell each word as best they can. This allows the children to practice spelling known and unknown words. After composing a second sentence, Ms. Palmer invites the students to offer ideas for revision, encouraging the children to help her use interesting words to improve her writing.

Independent writing

Once again, Ms. Palmer issues a statement of transfer to encourage her students to apply the strategy that she just modeled (use interesting words). "Good writers paint a picture for their readers by using interesting, descriptive words. Try this in the piece you are writing during our writing workshop. Reread one of your sentences and change the words to paint a picture for your reader. Off you go!" With this reminder, the children gather their writing folders and get started on their independent writing.

While the children are engaged in writing individual pieces, Ms. Palmer works with individuals or small groups to guide the children in their writing development. Similar to guided reading and individual reading conferences,

Ms. Palmer uses writing conferences to work with children in their zone of proximal development (Vygotsky, 1978). She uses assessments, such as a rubric or self-editing checklist, of current samples of the students' writing to determine which skills and strategies to focus on during these meetings. Ms. Palmer limits each conference to five to seven minutes, focusing on one or two teaching points to help her writers develop. This allows her to meet with four or five students each day, providing differentiated instruction for all of her students at least once over the course of two weeks.

CONCLUSION

The children in Ms. Palmer's classroom are engaged in many different types of reading and writing instruction throughout the course of a day. Differentiated small-group reading lessons are one essential component in comprehensive literacy instruction. The children will have several opportunities each week to engage in lessons that are personalized to meet their individual developmental needs and build their strengths. In addition, the students will engage in whole-class lessons designed to introduce and reinforce grade-level standards and expectations.

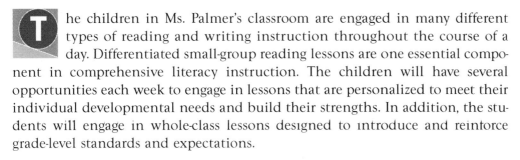

Practical Application

1. Preview three picture books. What types of comprehension strategies might you be able to demonstrate through an Interactive Read-Aloud with each book?

2. Ms. Palmer used books with varying levels of difficulty to teach her differentiated small-group lessons. Using the website www.scholastic.com/bookwizard/, compare and contrast books from five different text levels. How are the books similar? How are they different?

3. Ms. Palmer focuses her whole-class lessons on teaching points that are aligned with grade-level standards. However, differentiated instruction is not necessarily aligned with grade-level standards or expectations. Review the phases of literacy in Chapter 1 (Exhibit 1.2, pp. 5–6). Explain which phase of development would benefit from differentiated instruction with the following CCSS from first grade:

a. Reading Literature – R.L.1.5: Explain major differences between books that tell stories and books that give information, drawing on a wide reading of a range of text types.

b. Reading: Informational Text – R.I.9: Identify basic similarities in and differences between two texts on the same topic (e.g., in illustrations, descriptions, or procedures).

c. Reading: Foundational Skills – RF.1.1.a: Recognize the distinguishing features of a sentence (e.g., first word, capitalization, ending punctuation).

Recommended Resources

The following texts provide additional information on organizing the literacy block:

Calkins, L. (2001). *The art of teaching reading.* New York: Longman.

Calkins, L., Ehrenworth, M., & Lehman, C. (2012). *Pathways to the Common Core.* Portsmouth, NH: Heinemann.

Collins, K. (2004). *Growing readers: Units of study in the primary classroom.* Portland, ME: Stenhouse.

Dorn, L. J., & Soffos, C. (2005). *Teaching for deep comprehension: A reading workshop approach.* Portland, ME: Stenhouse.

Miller, D. (2013). *Reading with meaning: Teaching comprehension in the primary grades* (2nd ed.). Portland, ME: Stenhouse.

REFERENCES

Ankrum, J. W., Morewood, A. L., Bean, R., & Genest, M. (2008, Spring/Summer). Teacher talk: A close-up look at verbal scaffolds. *Michigan Reading Journal, 40* (3), 6–12.

Block, C. C., & Mangieri, J. N. (2003). *Exemplary literacy teachers.* New York: Guilford.

Calkins, L. M. (1986). *The art of teaching writing.* Portsmouth, NH: Heinemann.

Fountas, I. C., & Pinnell, G. S. (1996). *Guided reading: Good first teaching for all children.* Portsmouth, NH: Heinemann.

Graves, D. H. (1983). *Writing: Teachers and children at work.* Exeter, NH: Heinemann.

Guiberson, B. Z. (2011). *Ocean life.* New York: Scholastic.

Henkes, K. (1988). *Chester's way.* New York: HarperCollins Publishers.

Holdaway, D. (1979). *The foundations of literacy.* New York: Scholastic.

Lyon, G. R., & Weiser, B. (2009). Teacher knowledge, instructional expertise, and the development of reading proficiency. *Journal of Learning Disabilities, 42* (5), 475–480.

McKissak, P. C. (1986). *Who is coming?* New York: Scholastic.

Pinnell, G. S., & Fountas, I. C. (2011). *The continuum of literacy learning.* Portsmouth, NH: Heinemann.

Pressley, M., Allington, R. L., Wharton-McDonald, R., Block, C. C., & Morrow, L. M. (2001). *Learning to read: Lessons from exemplary first-grade classrooms.* New York: Guilford.

Rylant, C. (1996). *Henry and Mudge: The first book.* New York: Scholastic.

Sailors, M. (2013). Making literacy a "pervasive" part of a second grade classroom. *Pennsylvania Reads, 12* (1), 7–13.

Taylor, B. M., Pearson, P. D., Peterson, D., & Rodriguez, M. C. (2003). Reading growth in high-poverty classrooms: The influence of teacher practices that encourage cognitive engagement in literacy learning. *Elementary School Journal, 104* (1), 3–28.

Taylor, B. M., Pearson, P. D., Peterson, D. S., & Rodriguez, M. C. (2005). The CIERA School Change Framework: An evidence-based approach to professional development and school reading improvement. *Reading Research Quarterly, 40* (1), 40–60.

Vygotsky, L. S. (1978). *Mind in society: The development of higher psychological processes.* Cambridge, MA: Harvard University Press.

Wolfersberger, M. E., Reutzel, D. R., Sudweeks, R., & Fawson, P. C. (2004). Developing and validating the Classroom Literacy Environmental Profile (CLEP): A tool for examining "Print Richness" of early childhood and elementary classrooms. *Journal of Literacy Research, 36* (2), 211–272.

Classroom Context II

LITERACY INSTRUCTION IN A MIDDLE-LEVEL EXEMPLARY CLASSROOM

elcome to Mr. Metzgar's classroom. He has been teaching fifth grade for 12 years and, like Ms. Palmer in the previous chapter, he was nominated by his district's administrators and literacy specialists as an exemplary teacher of literacy. This means that Mr. Metzgar employs research-based effective instructional practices (see the box in Chapter 2), and as a result, the students in his classroom have higher-than-expected achievement in reading and writing.

As you read, consider how Mr. Metzgar organizes his physical space and time blocks, and how this organization enables him to differentiate reading lessons effectively during small-group instruction. How does Mr. Metzgar's teaching differ from Ms. Palmer's teaching, described in the previous chapter? How does Mr. Metzgar manage to monitor the progress of individual students?

THE LITERACY BLOCK

ike most teachers in an elementary school, Mr. Metzgar begins the school day with attendance, all-school announcements, and general classroom discussion about the day's events. The students are quite independent, so this routine lasts only about ten minutes, and then it is time for the students to prepare for their first subject, literacy.

Mr. Metzgar devotes approximately three hours each day to reading and writing instruction, in addition to the literacy integration he accomplishes in other subjects, such as science. He has organized this literacy block of time using a workshop approach, which consists of daily mini-lessons followed by independent or small-group work time (Calkins & Tolan, 2010). While the students independently read and write, Mr. Metzgar meets with individuals or small groups of students to differentiate instructional support. Exhibit 3.1 describes the instructional components included in Mr. Metzgar's literacy block.

The following sections describe Mr. Metzgar's literacy instruction. This is not the only way that teachers organize their literacy instruction, but this example provides an overview of effective literacy instruction in the middle grades. The remainder of the book will focus on the component of small-group differentiated reading instruction.

Mini-Lesson in Reading

The content of the mini-lesson varies over the course of the school year in Mr. Metzgar's room, based on the needs of the learners each year. However, the purpose for this block of time is consistent: Mr. Metzgar provides explicit whole-class lessons to help his students successfully comprehend increasingly complex texts. Like Ms. Palmer's district, his district's curriculum is based on the CCSS, so each whole-class lesson focuses on a specific standard. Mr. Metzgar models the implementation of skills and strategies with a variety of text sources, including

| | | | | EXHIBIT 3.1 |
| Components of literacy instruction. | | | |

COMPONENT	INSTRUCTIONAL FOCUS	GROUPING ARRANGEMENT	APPROXIMATE TIME FRAME
Reading instruction: mini-lesson	Comprehension Fluency Vocabulary	Whole class	20 minutes
Differentiated small-group reading instruction: book club	(Varies depending on strengths and needs of learners) Comprehension Vocabulary development Fluency practice Word study	Small groups and individuals (each group meets with teacher daily)	60 minutes
Interactive read-aloud	Comprehension Vocabulary	Whole class	10 minutes
Independent reading (individual reading conferences)	Comprehension	Individuals	30 minutes
Writing instruction: writing workshop Mini-lessons	Writing process and strategies Spelling Grammar	Whole class	20 minutes
Independent writing (while the teacher conducts small-group lessons and individual conferences)	Writing process and strategies Spelling Grammar (Varies depending on strengths and needs of learners)	Small group or individual	40 minutes
Whole-class sharing	Students share their writing or an interesting portion of text with the class	Whole class	10 minutes

novels, picture books, informational trade texts, and articles from online sites. The mini-lessons are short and focused, and they may take on characteristics of the interactive read-aloud or shared reading, both described in Chapter 2.

As the literacy block begins, Mr. Metzgar invites the students to the whole-class meeting space in the center of the room. This space is defined by a large rug, a comfortable chair, a small table with several texts on it, an interactive whiteboard on the wall, and an easel with chart paper (Exhibit 3.2). Similar to Ms. Palmer, Mr. Metzgar has learned that his students are generally more engaged in a mini-lesson if they are sitting near him. His fifth-graders often bring their chairs to the meeting space, where they can clearly see the text or screen as needed. Mr. Metzgar's demonstrations are highly interactive, and he often invites the students to share their perspectives and questions during the lesson. This allows Mr. Metzgar to assess the students informally and plan his next instructional moves.

Today's mini-lesson is part of a unit designed to help students determine the theme of a story by discussing how the characters respond to a challenge (CCSS RL.5.2). Mr. Metzgar has been reading *Because of Winn-Dixie* (DiCamillo, 2000) to the students for ten minutes each day after lunch. He starts by projecting a previously read section of the text on the screen and asking the students to read it silently and then talk to their partner about why they think it took the Preacher so long to talk to Opal about her mother. After the students talk for a few minutes, Mr. Metzgar asks volunteers to share their group's ideas.

> *Mr. Metzgar:* Julius, what did your group come up with? What might one theme of this book be?
>
> *Julius:* We thought that one of the main themes in the book is loneliness.
>
> *Mr. Metzgar:* Tell me more. Why do you think that?
>
> *Julius:* Well, first, when Opal came, she didn't have any friends. That's why Winn-Dixie was so important to her.
>
> *Lily:* Right! And the Preacher was lonely because his wife was gone and they just moved.
>
> *Julius:* And he was so lonely that he couldn't talk to Lily about her mom, that's why it took so long.

EXHIBIT 3.2   Whole-class meeting areas.

As the volunteers explain their ideas, Mr. Metzgar asks them to read a portion of the text or reference a previously read event to provide evidence for their answer.

This mini-lesson allows Mr. Metzgar to revisit a novel he is currently reading aloud to the class and reinforce the genre study on realistic fiction. Over the course of the school year, he carefully selects texts that represent various genres to ensure that the students can apply effective reading skills and strategies with texts of varying types and complexity. In addition, the focus of the mini-lesson changes over time, so that all students in the class have opportunities to develop their reading skills and meet the school's curricular requirements, based on the CCSS.

At the end of each mini-lesson Mr. Metzgar restates the main teaching point(s) of the lesson. Today he explains that by carefully analyzing how characters react in a book, the reader can begin to understand the overall theme. He asks the students to describe the emerging theme in the novel, recording their thoughts on a piece of chart paper. Mr. Metzgar ends the mini-lesson by asking the students to pay attention during independent reading to the way the characters in their self-selected books react to challenges. He suggests that they jot their ideas down in their reading journal, to share during a future mini-lesson.

This statement of transfer is meant to encourage the students to apply the strategy in their independent work.

Differentiated Small-Group Reading Instruction: Book Club

The fifth-graders are quite familiar with the routine, so when they hear Mr. Metzgar's statement of transfer they recognize this as a cue for transition. The students begin to organize for their assigned tasks and their book club meetings. "Book club" is the term that Mr. Metzgar uses to describe the differentiated small-group reading lessons that he conducts during the literacy block. Mr. Metzgar meets with two or three of his five book club groups daily, depending on how long each discussion lasts. While he meets with a small group, the other students are engaged in various literacy tasks. The students are aware that they need to complete assigned work by the end of the week, and the rest of the time can be devoted to reading their assigned novel or a self-selected novel. This week's assigned literacy tasks include practicing oral reading fluency with poetry, working as a group to write a summary of previously assigned reading, playing a vocabulary game in a small group, and reading independently. (Chapter 4 describes management activities in detail.) After a few brief reminders about his expectations for behavior and quality work, Mr. Metzgar dismisses the students to begin their independent work.

The purpose of differentiated small-group reading lessons in Mr. Metzgar's classroom is to provide the students with opportunities to engage in high-level discussions about books they read. As mentioned, the class is studying the genre of realistic fiction (RF), so about a week ago Mr. Metzgar provided several RF texts from which the students could choose. It is important that the books be at an appropriate level so that the students can understand the text; therefore, if any students are interested in selecting a text that is out of their range for understanding, Mr. Metzgar will guide them in making a better choice. Mr. Metzgar prepares a few essential questions to begin each group's discussion but allows the students to take the lead as they share insights gained from the text. The primary goal for these discussions is to deepen comprehension, so Mr. Metzgar is careful to keep the conversations on task, while ensuring that all the students participate.

Mr. Metzgar asks the first group to join him on the floor near the reading corner to discuss their novel, *Maniac Magee* (Spinelli, 1990). This book is labeled at Guided Reading Level W (Fountas & Pinnell, 1996), which is approximately equivalent to a mid-fifth-grade level. This book is a good fit for many of Mr. Metzgar's students because it contains important themes (e.g., racism, friendship) delivered with appropriate humor, which makes it an interesting book to discuss. As is expected for grades 3 and above, most students in this fifth-grade class are self-extending readers, so matching their precise instructional reading level is not a primary concern. More important, Mr. Metzgar wants to ensure that he provides all students with a meaningful example of realistic fiction that the students can read and comprehend.

Earlier in the week a student commented on several of the nicknames of the characters in *Maniac Magee*. Mr. Metzgar decided that this was an important topic to discuss with the small group, since the nicknames provide clues into the characters' personalities and events in the story. He now asks the group to list the nicknames and describe the meaning behind each name. Throughout the discussion the students discuss key features of each character and how the characters relate to the plot. Mr. Metzgar listens and records notes, so that he can follow up with key points. He wraps up the discussion by asking the students to consider how the nicknames define the characters and how others may define the characters through their nicknames. After about 15 minutes, the discussion ends and the students go to work on their assigned tasks.

Mr. Metzgar quickly walks around the classroom, checking in with individuals to ensure that they are engaged in their assigned tasks. He calls the next group to meet with him, and they gather on the floor with their novel. The students bring their individual copies of *Rules*, by Cynthia Lord (2006). Four of the five students in this group struggle to comprehend texts they read; therefore, Mr. Metzgar chose this sample of realistic fiction, which is labeled Guided Reading Level R (Fountas & Pinnell, 1996), with these students in mind. Because Level R correlates with a fourth-grade reading level, it is likely the students in this group will have an easier time decoding the words and comprehending the text. Still, it offers complex content (e.g., living with disabilities, friendships) for the students to grapple with and discuss.

As the students settle in, Mr. Metzgar asks each one to recap the previous day's reading, to ensure that each student has an understanding of the plot. He then reminds the students of the earlier whole-class discussion about the importance of paying attention to the way the characters react to challenges. Mr. Metzgar asks each student to take five minutes to find a section in the previously read portions of the book that illustrates how a character reacted to a challenge. As the students read their selected portions of the text to the group, Mr. Metzgar helps them decode difficult words, using each example as a teaching opportunity for the group. For example, when one student stumbles on the word *conversation*, Mr. Metzgar asks the student to think of a word that would make sense in the sentence. The student cannot, so Mr. Metzgar asks if anyone can help to decode the word. One student starts by showing the chunk *con*, and another notices *versa*. Mr. Metzgar praises the attempts and explains that there are actually four parts, separating *ver* and *sa*, and then shows several examples of words ending in *tion*. After the students determine that the word is *conversation*, they discuss what the word means and how they have previously used it or heard it used.

Although the students do stumble on a few words, this is rare and not the major focus of the lesson. After each student reads her or his portion of text, the group discusses the character involved, and Mr. Metzgar and the students compose an anchor chart—a poster that students can reference during subsequent lessons—to record how each character reacts to the challenges presented in the text. Each student shares one example before the lesson closes. Mr. Metzgar assigns the next chapter for independent reading, explaining that they will discuss character development at their next meeting.

When the discussion with the second group is complete, Mr. Metzgar asks the students to store their materials and resume their independent literacy tasks. After briefly circulating the room to check in with the other students, he calls a third group to meet with him. One of the group's members, Gabby, is bilingual. Her primary language at home is Spanish, though she speaks fluent English at school. Still, she is sometimes confused by figurative language, which can interrupt her comprehension of a text. Mr. Metzgar grouped her with two other transitional-level readers who read at approximately the same instructional level, Level O. Today's lesson focuses on introducing a new chapter book, *Amber Brown Is Feeling Blue*, by Paula Danzinger (1999). As Mr. Metzgar reads the title of the book to the children, they all giggle.

> *Mr. Metzgar:* What's so funny, why are you laughing?
>
> *Gabby:* How can you feel blue? That's a color, not a feeling.
>
> *Daniel:* That's right. That doesn't make sense!
>
> *Jake:* My mom once told me she felt blue, and she said it meant sad.
>
> *Mr. Metzgar:* That's right, Jake! Sometimes we can use the word *blue* to describe how we are feeling, like when we feel kind of sad. This is an example of figurative language. (Mr. Metzgar writes the phrase "figurative language" on a mini-whiteboard.) That means that the word or phrase doesn't mean exactly what it seems to say. Like feeling blue doesn't mean I look like a blueberry or I feel like the color, it means I'm sad. Another example of figurative language is when it rains really hard and we say, "It's raining cats and dogs!"
>
> *Students:* (everyone giggles)
>
> *Jake:* Cats and dogs?
>
> *Gabby:* Like raindrops from the sky?

Mr. Metzgar continues the brief discussion of figurative language by writing other examples on the mini-whiteboard and then introduces the first chapter of *Amber Brown Is Feeling Blue* to the students. He is careful to write each character's name on the mini-whiteboard and articulates clearly so that Gabby can practice the English pronunciation of unfamiliar names. Mr. Metzgar also provides explicit definitions of key vocabulary words found in the first chapter before he sends the group off to read, so that all of the students in the group can focus mainly on comprehension as they read the first chapter. As he dismisses the children, Mr. Metzgar asks them to jot down any unfamiliar words or examples of figurative language they come across while they read Chapter One. He adds that he will show them how to use context clues to figure out these words and phrases when they meet tomorrow.

Mr. Metzgar gives a five-minute warning by blinking the lights. The students know that they will hear him clap, signaling the end of small-group work. The group cleans up and departs for lunch and recess.

Interactive Read-Aloud

The students are usually chatty as they file into the classroom after lunch and recess. However, when Mr. Metzgar blinks the lights, the students quiet. They know it is time for the interactive read-aloud, and they are looking forward to hearing about Opal's adventures in the novel *Because of Winn-Dixie.*

Each day Mr. Metzgar reads from a chapter book for ten minutes. He varies the genre, so he can expose the students to various text types. He most often chooses a lengthy text so he can explicitly teach the students how to maintain interest and comprehend a text over an extended period of time. Mr. Metzgar also attempts to select texts that are highly engaging to the students, to support high-level discussions beyond the time devoted to the read-aloud. For example, after he reads Chapter 14 of *Because of Winn-Dixie* aloud, Mr. Metzgar states, "Back on page 96, Gloria Dump said that she learned the most important thing, adding that it is 'different for everyone. . . . You find out on your own. But in the meantime, you got to remember, you can't always judge people by the things they done. You got to judge them by what they are doing now.' I wonder what that means? What does that mean to you? Turn and tell the person sitting next to you." Mr. Metzgar listens to different pairs of students as they discuss this, engaging in the conversations to prompt students to elaborate their responses or link the sentences back to the characters and the different challenges they have faced in the book. After the brief discussion, Mr. Metzgar announces that they will read more tomorrow and that it is time for independent reading. The students groan, asking for one more chapter, and then scurry to get the books they've selected for independent reading.

Independent Reading/Individual Reading Conferences

One of the options for the students in Mr. Metzgar's class is to read self-selected novels while he meets with small groups. In addition, all students are required to read independently for 30 minutes per day after lunch. After he reads aloud to the whole class, Mr. Metzgar transitions to independent reading/individual conference time by repeating his statement of transfer. This will remind the students to attempt to use the skill or strategy that was introduced or reviewed earlier in the day. For example, "If you are reading fiction, think about how the characters are responding to challenges. How is this related to the emerging themes in the book?" Mr. Metzgar allows the students to find a comfortable place to read. Some scatter around the room, and several choose to remain in their seats.

Earlier in the year, Mr. Metzgar reviewed the process for self-selecting an appropriate book for independent reading. In addition, he regularly talks about the books he has read, sharing his methods for choosing books based on topics, authors, or genre. One principle that Mr. Metzgar shares with the students is that they should choose a book that engages them for an extended period of time, so that they will want to read it at school and at home. He also teaches the students the importance of understanding what they've read. Although he does not require a written summary at the end of independent reading time, he does suggest that students think about what they have read to monitor their own comprehension. Mr. Metzgar monitors the students' comprehension through individual conferences.

Each day Mr. Metzgar meets with three to five students for informal reading conferences while the others engage in independent silent reading. Each child's conference is different, based on the needs of the individual. Mr. Metzgar may focus on the major teaching point from the whole-class lesson; for example, the current grade-level teaching focus is on analyzing a character's response to challenge, based on the CCSS. However, the whole-class teaching point may not be appropriate for everyone. One of Mr. Metzgar's students, Marcus, has decided to read *Jane Goodall: My Life with the Chimpanzees*, an autobiography (Goodall, 1997). Mr. Metzgar discusses Marcus's choice with him, as well as the genre of autobiography. Throughout the discussion, Mr. Metzgar prompts for key facts, to ensure that Marcus is able to comprehend the information he is reading.

Regardless of the content of each discussion, Mr. Metzgar's reading conferences are student-centered. He begins each conference with the open-ended question, "What are you reading today?" and follows this with prompts for additional detail or a discussion of reading goals, if needed. He then responds to the student in an authentic, conversational fashion. These conferences allow Mr. Metzgar an additional opportunity to assess his students' reading comprehension, as well as differentiate teaching points for each child.

Writing Instruction: Writing Workshop

Each day two hours are devoted to reading instruction and independent reading in Mr. Metzgar's room. The remainder of the literacy block is devoted to explicit writing instruction. He often tells his students, "Strong writers must be strong readers first," and he has seen evidence of this in his classroom. During his daily writing lessons, Mr. Metzgar often references the high-quality literature used for reading instruction.

After the independent reading/individual reading conference portion of the day, Mr. Metzgar announces that it is time for the writing workshop. The students tuck their books into their desks and take out their writing folders. Mr. Metzgar begins the workshop with a quick status check: after he calls each student's name, the student reports what he or she will work on during the workshop time. Mr. Metzgar records the responses, so he can meet with individuals who request a teacher conference or seem to be in need of help to progress in their writing.

Mini-lesson

Next, Mr. Metzgar invites the students to the group meeting area for a mini-lesson, similar to the writing mini-lesson described in Chapter 2. The fifth-graders bring their folders and pencils to the meeting area, in case they need to jot something down; however, the students know the importance of listening and participating during this lesson. Mr. Metzgar selects the teaching focus based on the district curriculum, the CCSS, and the needs of his students as assessed through previous writing pieces that they have completed. The content of these mini-lessons may include strategies for revision or editing, how to conduct an effective peer conference, grammar, punctuation, considering audience and purpose, organizing ideas, genre writing, or other information needed to enhance the students' writing development. Of course, it is not necessary or possible to address all of these points in one mini-lesson; the teacher chooses a focus based on the students' needs.

Today's mini-lesson focuses on using technology to publish writing (CCSS W5.6). Over the past week Mr. Metzgar has helped each student select one short informational piece of writing to publish with Prezi presentation software. He begins the mini-lesson by asking students if they have used the software before. Grace, a student new to the school, explains that she used it at her previous school, so Mr. Metzgar invites Grace to demonstrate how to turn her manuscript into a presentation. Together, he and Grace show the students how they can publish their work with this software. Once the lesson is complete, Mr. Metzgar asks the students to find a sensible space to work on the project they reported to him before the mini-lesson. He adds, "If you are ready to publish, you may use a laptop from the cart to begin your Prezi. If not, remember to try this within the next two weeks." Mr. Metzgar plans to continue to demonstrate specific Prezi techniques each day for the next week during the mini-lessons.

Independent writing

Once the students are settled into their writing tasks, Mr. Metzgar begins to confer with students individually. Each meeting lasts approximately ten minutes, and the focus varies depending on the needs of each student. Some of the students have requested a meeting with him today, but others will have a conference with Mr. Metzgar because he has noticed that they are struggling with a technique or with a lack of focus. This is Mr. Metzgar's opportunity to work with students individually in their zone of proximal development to accelerate their writing development.

LITERACY INTEGRATION

Mr. Metzgar understands the importance of integrating literacy strategies into content-area instruction. It is essential for students to comprehend complex informational texts across the content areas, and this requires explicit teaching. Therefore, Mr. Metzgar intentionally weaves literacy instruction into his content-area lessons. The following example illustrates how Mr. Metzgar infuses science content with reading instruction.

Today when he teaches science, Mr. Metzgar assesses the students' prior knowledge about bodies of water. The students are seated in small groups at tables. Mr. Metzgar asks the students to discuss what they know about bodies of water with their groups. He monitors the discussions, posing questions at times to determine what the children know. For example, Mr. Metzgar asks one group if they know how many oceans we have on Earth. He asks another group if they can name any main bodies of water. After several minutes, Mr. Metzgar asks all of the students to turn their attention to the front of the classroom while he describes a visual display he created to introduce their new topic of study (Exhibit 3.3). After Mr. Metzgar explains how to read the visual display, he explains that this is "just one way to represent data visually."

Next, Mr. Metzgar reminds the students of the importance of using text maps to enhance their comprehension as they read about bodies of water. He starts by reviewing the definition of text map with the students. He explains that a text map is a type of graphic organizer that is used before and during reading. Mr. Metzgar reminds the students that they need to pay close attention to the visual displays in the text while they read. He then explains that the students will map their thinking onto the text by writing questions and comments about the content on sticky notes that they place on the text. Mr. Metzgar reminds the students of other text features, in addition to visual displays, that they have discussed previously in class, and he draws

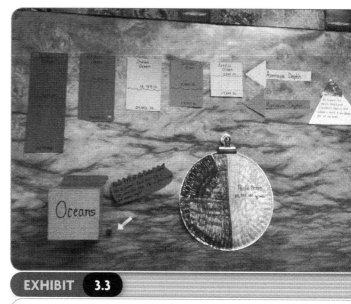

EXHIBIT 3.3

Bodies of water visual display.

their attention to the anchor charts on the wall (Exhibit 3.4). Mr. Metzgar explains that the students will collaborate in small groups. Each group will read an assigned text about a different body of water and complete an appropriate text map as a method for organizing their information. The next time they meet, each group of students will teach the rest of the class about their assigned body of water, using their text map as a guide.

Based on assessments conducted for literacy instruction, Mr. Metzgar is aware that the students do not all read and comprehend "on grade level." Several students read below the level expected for fifth-graders, and several read beyond that level. Therefore, Mr. Metzgar carefully assigns students to heterogeneous groups (i.e., mixed ability in text reading), so that all students can comprehend the material through their text-based discussions. In addition, he intentionally selects texts that will be readable for most students in the class. An instructional aide for students with learning difficulties provides additional support.

Each group receives a handout with a different graphic organizer to scaffold their reading of the assigned text (Exhibit 3.5). Mr. Metzgar confers with each group and with individuals to provide any needed support to enhance comprehension. For example, with one group Mr. Metzgar explains how to determine which information to record on the graphic organizer. With

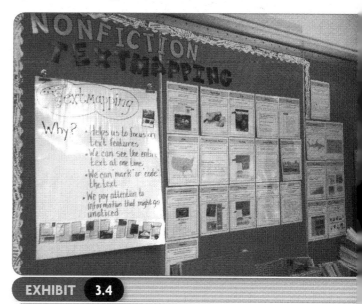

EXHIBIT 3.4

Text map anchor charts.

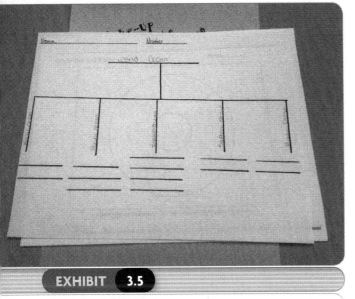

EXHIBIT 3.5

Example graphic organizer scaffolding handout.

another group he demonstrates how to read the pronunciation key in an article. This differentiated support enhances the students' engagement in the task, as well as their understanding.

The students work diligently on the assigned task for the remainder of the class period. Soon, Mr. Metzgar gives the five-minute warning: it is time to switch subjects. He announces that the students will present their information to the class the following day. It is now time to move into math instruction.

CONCLUSION

Mr. Metzgar's fifth-graders engage in many different types of reading and writing activities throughout the day. Because many are self-extending learners (see Exhibit 1.2), they operate in a largely independent manner. Still, Mr. Metzgar recognizes the need to provide explicit instruction in new strategies and skills, as well as differentiated small-group lessons in reading and writing each day. Just like in Ms. Palmer's classroom, each student has several opportunities each week to engage in personalized lessons, designed to meet the student's developmental needs and build his or her strengths. In addition, students engage in daily whole-class lessons that introduce and reinforce grade-level standards and expectations.

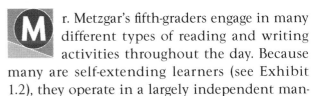

Practical Application

1. Conduct a search for the list of Newbery Medal–winning books. Select five titles and read reviews of the books on www.goodreads.com. Explain which book you would choose first to read aloud to a fourth-grade class, and why. Be sure to consider the developmental characteristics expected of most fourth-graders, listed in Exhibit 1.2.

2. Draw a picture of Mr. Metzgar's classroom. Describe how the different spaces in his classroom help to enhance his instruction.

3. How is Mr. Metzgar's teaching similar to Ms. Palmer's teaching? How is it different?

4. Describe three ways that Mr. Metzgar manages to monitor the progress of individual students.

Recommended Resources

The following texts provide in-depth information on organizing the literacy block and integrating reading instruction into the content areas.

Literacy Block

Allington, R. L. (2012). *What really matters for struggling readers: Designing research-based programs.* New York: Pearson.

Atwell, N. (2015). *In the middle: A lifetime of learning about writing, reading and adolescents* (3rd ed.). Portsmouth, NH: Heinemann.

Moses, L. (2015). *Supporting English learners in the reading workshop.* Portsmouth, NH: Heinemann.

Reading and Writing Project, http://readingandwritingproject.org/

Integrating Reading Instruction Into Content-Area Instruction

Bluestein, N. A. (2010). Unlocking text features for determining importance in expository text: A strategy for struggling readers. *The Reading Teacher, 63* (7), 597–600.

Duke, N. K. (2014). *Inside information: Developing powerful readers and writers of informational text through project-based instruction.* New York: Scholastic.

Dymock, S., & Nickolson, T. (2010). High 5! Strategies to enhance comprehension of expository text. *The Reading Teacher, 64* (3), 166–178.

Reading Rockets, www.readingrockets.org/reading-topics/content-area-literacy

REFERENCES

Calkins, L., & Tolan, K. (2010). *Guide to the reading workshop.* Portsmouth, NH: Heinemann.

Danzinger, P. (1999). *Amber Brown is feeling blue.* New York: Scholastic Press.

DiCamillo, K. (2000). *Because of Winn-Dixie.* Cambridge, MA: Candlewick Press.

Fountas, I. C., & Pinnell, G. S. (1996). *Guided reading: Good first teaching for all children.* Portsmouth, NH: Heinemann.

Goodall, J. (1997). *Jane Goodall: My life with the chimpanzees* (6th ed.). Washington, DC: National Geographic Society.

Lord, C. (2006). *Rules.* New York: Scholastic Press.

Spinelli, J. (1990). *Maniac Magee.* Boston: Little Brown.

Managing Small-Group
Reading Instruction

KEEPING ALL STUDENTS ENGAGED
IN LITERACY LEARNING

45

Mr. Waverly has just been hired to begin his first year of teaching first grade. Since only a few weeks of school remain before summer break, a future colleague, Mrs. Jones, invites him to observe her second-grade classroom.

Although Mr. Waverly will teach a different grade level, Mrs. Jones explains that many of the routines and classroom structures that she has in place will be helpful as he plans his classroom. He is amazed by the organization of Mrs. Jones's literacy block, particularly while she meets with each small group. Following the whole-class lesson, Mrs. Jones dismisses all of the students to different areas around the room, where they engage in various meaningful activities, until she calls a small group of students to meet with her. Students are given many authentic opportunities to extend their literacy development, including choral reading, independent reading, independent writing, and group projects.

Mr. Waverly sees clearly that the room is organized for small-group collaborative activities. In addition to the whole-class meeting area, there are several "learning stations" that stand out in Mrs. Jones's classroom. Exhibit 4.1 provides one example of a learning station. Five students are quietly writing at an area labeled "Writer's Corner," and Mr. Waverly notes that two of them are discussing methods for revision. Four students are listening to podcasts near the classroom library. Another group of three students is composing captions for a mural they painted earlier in the week. Seven students are reading independently in various places throughout the room. A group of five students is practicing fluency through a choral reading activity in the poetry area. The room is abuzz with literate conversations.

Mrs. Jones quietly walks around the classroom to praise the students who begin their tasks independently, answer questions for students as they begin new projects, and prompt students who are slow to start. The students know that once Mrs. Jones begins working with her first reading group, they will not be allowed to interrupt with questions.

Soon after her walkthrough, Mrs. Jones calls four students to her table to begin reading a new book together. After a brief book introduction, Mrs. Jones glances around the room. All of the students are engaged with their assigned tasks, though she notices a disagreement brewing about which poem to read chorally next in the poetry area. Mrs. Jones continues with her small-group lesson, and is pleased when the students resolve their conflict through a vote, as she modeled earlier in the year. A few minutes later a student from the Writer's Corner walks up to Mrs. Jones to ask if he may leave to get a drink of water. She simply holds her hand up and he walks away.

EXHIBIT 4.1

Example learning station.

A classmate reminds him, "Only emergency interruptions during small-group time!" Mrs. Jones continues her small-group lesson.

The students in Mrs. Jones's classroom are capable of managing themselves for the 20 or so minutes that she devotes to each small-group lesson. After she dismisses the students in her current reading group to resume their center work, Mrs. Jones walks around the classroom to monitor students and answer questions. Students are free to go into another literacy station at this time. Once the students are settled in their new areas, Mrs. Jones calls another small group to her table for a differentiated lesson.

How does Mrs. Jones organize these various activities? How do the students work effectively without teacher support? Mr. Waverly wonders where he should even begin. This chapter will provide insight and methods for managing student engagement while the teacher works with small groups on differentiated reading lessons.

BUILDING BACKGROUND: EFFECTIVE CLASSROOM MANAGEMENT

Mrs. Jones is clearly a master when it comes to classroom management. Research indicates that this is one characteristic of exemplary teachers of literacy (Block & Mangieri, 2003; Pressley, Allington, et al., 2001; Taylor, Pearson, Peterson, & Rodriguez, 2003). Research also suggests that high levels of student engagement increase student achievement in literacy (Baker, Dreher, & Guthrie, 2000); according to Taylor, Pearson, Clark, and Walpole (2000), the most accomplished teachers of literacy consistently engage over 95 percent of the class in literacy instruction and practice. This means that the students are active participants in meaningful reading and writing activities.

Effective teachers need to create opportunities for all students to apply and extend their learning, which in turn allows the teacher to meet with small groups and individuals as needed. However, managing multiple activities occurring simultaneously in a classroom filled with students is not an easy task. Schumm, Moody, and Vaughn (2000) found that many teachers simply avoid small-group instruction because they find it difficult to manage the other students in the classroom while they meet with small groups. In addition, according to novice teachers, classroom management is especially an area of concern as they begin teaching (Wideen, Mayer-Smith, & Moon, 1998). Classroom management for small-group instruction is complex; teachers must consider methods for creating a literate environment, time management, and effective strategies to encourage student engagement. Therefore, it is imperative to consider carefully the options for effective classroom management.

Managing Time in the Literacy Block

There is much to accomplish in the time allotted for daily literacy instruction each day. Teachers in the elementary grades typically devote 90 to 120 minutes to literacy instruction each day. This allotment allows ample time for the teacher

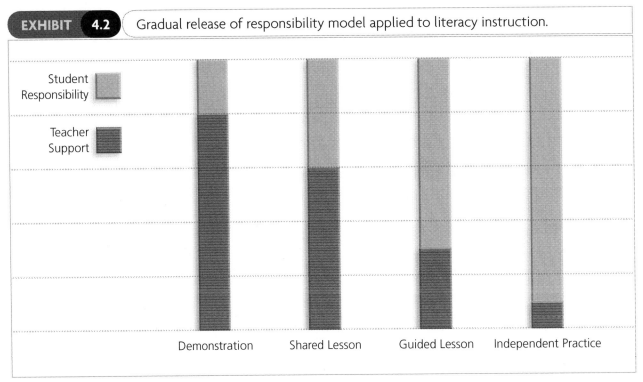

EXHIBIT 4.2 Gradual release of responsibility model applied to literacy instruction.

Student Responsibility

Teacher Support

Demonstration   Shared Lesson   Guided Lesson   Independent Practice

Source: Adapted from Pearson and Gallagher (1983).

to apply the gradual release of responsibility model (GRRM) of instruction (Pearson & Gallagher, 1983; Exhibit 4.2). This model of effective instruction begins with assessing student knowledge. Once it is determined that students require instruction in a new skill, strategy, or content area, the teacher demonstrates the new learning by assuming full responsibility for a task, in this case a literacy-related task. The teacher models, often through a think-aloud, the processes he or she uses to approach or complete a task, such as the application of the comprehension strategy of predicting in reading during a read-aloud. In subsequent lessons, the teacher invites students to participate in completing a task; in the example of applying a comprehension strategy, volunteers are invited to share their predictions while the teacher reads a text aloud. The next step is to release more responsibility to the learners by guiding individuals or small groups of students through the application of the modeled task. For example, the teacher might conduct a guided reading lesson with a small group of students, coaching them as they apply a strategy that was previously demonstrated. The final step of the process is to allow time for independent practice of the task. However, this does not happen in four simple reading lessons; this is actually a model of recursive instruction that cycles throughout the introduction and application of new skills and strategies across all content areas.

To accomplish the complex layers of teaching involved in the GRRM, teachers often integrate reading, writing, speaking, listening, viewing, and visually representing across the 90 to 120 minutes allotted each day. Time can be organized to allow teachers to plan various instructional strategies and grouping

	Sample daily literacy block schedule.		EXHIBIT 4.3	
INSTRUCTIONAL STRATEGY	**INSTRUCTIONAL FOCUS**	**LEVEL OF TEACHER SUPPORT**	**TYPICAL GROUPING ARRANGEMENT**	**APPROXIMATE TIME FRAME (DAILY)**
Interactive read-aloud	Reading Listening	High (demonstration with interactive discussion)	Whole class	10–15 minutes
Shared reading	Reading Listening Speaking	Moderate/high (teacher reads along with students)	Whole class	10–20 minutes
Guided reading	Reading Listening Speaking	Moderate/low (students read, teacher prompts as needed)	Small group	10–20 minutes per group; typically 30–60 minutes total
Independent reading	Reading	Minimal	Individual	10–30 minutes (may be during guided reading)
Independent and collaborative activities (e.g., centers)	Reading Writing Listening Speaking Viewing Visually representing	Minimal (students work independently or collaboratively)	Small group Individual	During guided reading
Modeled or interactive writing	Writing Speaking Listening Visually representing	High/moderate (demonstration with interactive discussion)	Whole class	15–20 minutes
Guided writing	Writing Speaking Listening Visually representing	Moderate (practice with teacher guidance)	Small group Individual	20–30 minutes in conjunction with independent writing
Independent writing	Writing Visually representing	Minimal	Individual	In conjunction with guided writing

arrangements that lend themselves to differing levels of teacher support. Exhibit 4.3 provides a sample daily literacy block schedule. Of course, times can be adjusted to meet the developmental needs of the learners, as well as the demands of the school and classroom schedule.

Managing the Physical Environment

To engage learners in the variety of instructional opportunities listed in Exhibit 4.3, it is essential to create a classroom that is conducive to various grouping arrangements and literacy activities. Careful planning is required when designing the physical arrangement of furniture and materials.

EXHIBIT 4.4 Whole-class meeting area.

EXHIBIT 4.5 Small-group meeting area.

EXHIBIT 4.6 Collaborative desk arrangement.

Although whole-class lessons are an essential element in effective literacy instruction, small-group instruction is another necessary component. The classroom environment must be carefully organized to allow students opportunities to meet in large or small groups with or without the teacher. A whole-class meeting space should be provided for modeled instruction, such as the interactive read-aloud or interactive writing. This space typically contains a large chair for the teacher with ample floor space for students to gather (Exhibit 4.4). It is usually located near a large screen (e.g., an interactive whiteboard) where the teacher can project images for use in modeling reading, writing, and viewing. In addition, an easel may be located here for modeling writing instruction or the creation of **anchor charts**. Students of all grade levels benefit from group meetings and modeled instruction; the close proximity to the teacher increases student engagement and participation, which in turn decreases behavior issues.

Many classrooms also feature an area designed specifically for the teacher to meet with small groups of students. This is where differentiated literacy lessons can occur. Such an area typically contains a meeting table, chairs for four to six learners and the teacher, and a storage area for needed materials (Exhibit 4.5). Placing the table near a set of shelves allows the teacher to store the books needed for reading lessons, small whiteboards and markers for modeled and guided word work, and paper and writing implements for guided writing lessons.

While the teacher meets with a small group of students, the other students must be actively engaged in meaningful activities to apply, extend, and enrich their learning. Some teachers provide meaningful literacy activities for students to complete at their desks. If this is the case, it is most helpful for the desks to be arranged in small groups, to encourage student collaboration (Exhibit 4.6). This arrangement maximizes space for the whole-class gathering area, as well. When possible, it is helpful to provide multiple areas around the room for such activities to take place. Specific examples are described in the section on literacy centers.

IMPLEMENTING AND MANAGING STUDENT ACTIVITIES

A thoughtfully arranged physical environment allows for the implementation of various instructional activities. The next sections detail several common approaches to managing student engagement in literacy practice; each can be differentiated to meet the needs of all learners. As you read this chapter, consider which of Tomlinson's (2000) four elements of differentiation, described in Chapter 1 (content, process, product, and learning environment), fit the activity. All of these planned activities are designed to enable the teacher to meet with small groups for differentiated lessons.

Literacy Centers

One approach that teachers commonly take to manage students during small-group instruction is known as **literacy centers**. Literacy centers are intentionally planned spaces in the classroom that allow students to work collaboratively or independently on literacy tasks. The teacher designs instructional activities in each center to reinforce and extend previously taught lessons based on learning standards (e.g., CCSS, state, or district standards) and the literacy curriculum. Tasks in literacy centers are most effective when they are open-ended in nature. In other words, while all students may work on the same (or a similar) task, students work at their own developmental level, based on their ability. For example, students may be required to select and read a text in the classroom library. Before this assignment is given, the teacher demonstrates how to select a "just right" text that is readable for each student (see Chapter 8). After much practice, students are then required to self-select a good-fit text for independent reading, read the text, and respond. Each student reads a different and appropriate text based on his or her individual strengths and interests. After reading their books, students are required to collaborate in an activity at the center. In this example, students may share the most interesting fact that they learned from the informational text they read. When the assignment is to select a narrative text, each student may describe the main character from her or his book.

In another example, after the teacher introduces the class to a comprehension strategy, such as visualizing, a small group of students in one center may practice this strategy by drawing a scene or building a model of a scene that they visualized after reading a story or passage. The students may later share their visualization with classmates to compare and contrast their drawings or models. It is usually expected that all students will visit this center at some point during the week to practice the strategy. In all cases, the teacher can differentiate the task to meet the varied needs of learners by guiding students in their selection of materials (differentiated content) and type of responses (differentiated product), or by providing additional support to students when needed (differentiated process).

If well planned, literacy centers can provide varied opportunities for students to practice literacy skills and strategies through authentic activities. As discussed above, small groups of students often work in collaboration on a center activity, allowing them to learn from one another. More knowledgeable students can help struggling learners extend their learning through apprenticeship as they deepen their own understanding. This is consistent with Vygotsky's (1978) theory of social constructivism; learners gain much from interaction and collaboration.

Although meaningful center activities are often collaborative in nature, they also require the learner to apply literacy skills and strategies independently. In the example above, students are required to read a text independently, reflect on their visualization, draw or build a representation, and then share with peers. In another example, students might read independently and then participate in a discussion with peers in the group who have read the same text. The classroom teacher might guide this discussion by providing specific prompts written on cards and placed in a box (Exhibit 4.7) or posted on a whiteboard. The following example is based on the novel *Sarah, Plain and Tall* (MacLachlan, 1985): "In her letter, Sarah explains that she has 'not been married, although I have been asked' (p. 9). What might you infer about the character (Sarah) based on this and other information revealed in the letter?" In this example, each participant in the center is responsible for reading the text independently and applying strategies that were taught in previous lessons. Independent practice is essential to all learning, especially in literacy (Duke & Pearson, 2002). However,

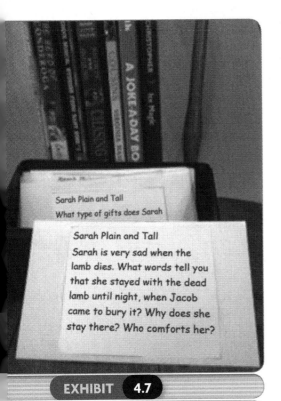

the assignment is not completed by independent work alone. The students are required to select and prepare a response to a prompt card independently to match the book they have read. Members of the group then collaborate as they share their inferences and learn from those of their peers. This activity deepens meaning and allows students to scaffold one another's understanding when needed.

In addition to providing opportunities for both collaborative and independent work, literacy centers allow students to gain valuable experiences in building problem-solving skills and taking responsibility for their learning. When students work with a small group to complete a task in a literacy center, they are encouraged to do so without teacher assistance. If they experience difficulty with a task, such as making an inference in the above example, they are encouraged to attempt first to solve the problem independently; if that fails, students are encouraged to seek help from a peer. Very young children are capable of applying similar problem-solving strategies. For example, when early learners are required to write a fact learned from listening to informational text, spelling difficulties may present a challenge. Students can lean on each other for support in their writing, rather than asking the teacher how to spell specific words. Similarly, English learners benefit from the support of peers, who may help them with vocabulary, syntax, or spelling as they attempt to write. Research has demonstrated that a common characteristic of exemplary teachers of literacy is that they foster independence and responsibility in their students (Pressley et al., 2001). When students are actively engaged in their own learning

EXHIBIT   4.7

Prompt cards used to guide student group literature discussions.

and can independently solve problems, teachers are free to tailor instruction to fit the needs of individuals and small groups of students.

Literacy centers also provide opportunities for content-area integration. With ever-increasing demands to introduce large amounts of specific content, it is difficult to teach the content in a deep and meaningful way. However, when students work in small groups to conduct a simple science experiment (e.g., does an object sink or does it float?) and then write about their observations, the students have the opportunity to apply both science and literacy knowledge and skills. The same can be true with math concepts, social studies, and nearly all content areas.

Providing students with varied authentic and meaningful opportunities to apply their developing skills and strategies decreases the occurrence of negative behaviors. When students are actively involved in tasks that they can successfully complete, they are less likely to be distracted and engage in inappropriate behaviors. Further, when all students are engaged in open-ended activities, they are less likely to rush to complete an assignment. As a result, the teacher is free to devote uninterrupted time to a small group or individual students.

Examples of literacy centers

When considering how to implement literacy centers, it is important to think about the number and types of centers to include in the classroom. The number of centers used in a classroom varies based on the teacher's preference, the developmental levels of the learners, and available materials. Specific tasks in centers can be aligned with the district's curriculum, state required standards (or CCSS), and the specific classroom theme or teaching focus. The main criteria for quality literacy centers include providing

- opportunities for authentic reading, writing, speaking, listening, viewing, and/or visually representing;
- engaging and open-ended activities; and
- tasks that can be completed without teacher assistance.

The following box offers a brief description of commonly used literacy centers. Descriptions are provided for classrooms in grades K and 1, grades 2 and 3, and grades 4 through 6.

Commonly used literacy centers

WRITING CENTER

Grades K–1

Materials: A table with 4 to 6 chairs; various supplies to write with, such as markers, crayons, colored pencils, chalk; various supplies to write on, such as paper of all sizes, mini-whiteboards, chalkboards; computers/laptops/tablet computers

Sample Assignments

- Draw a picture and write about it.
- Engage in free writing (students select topics and forms of writing).
- Respond to a direct prompt (such as, "Write a book of facts about the pilgrims").

  The focus can change with each unit of study.

Grades 2–3

Materials: A table with 4 to 6 chairs; various supplies to write with, such as pencils, pens, colored pencils; various sizes and types of paper; photographs, comic strips, wordless picture books; folders for keeping works in progress; computers/laptops/tablet computers; scaffolding handouts for different stages of the writing process (see Appendix A)

Sample Assignments

- Write a caption to go with each photograph in the box.
- Use your time in the writing center to continue a project from your writing folder.
- Conduct a peer conference with your writing buddy using the Peer Conference scaffolding handout (see Exhibit 4.8 for an example; Appendix A.1 contains a blank form).
- Choose one of your pieces and use the Self-editing Checklist handout to check your writing (see Exhibit 4.9 for an example; Appendix A.2 contains a blank form).

EXHIBIT 4.8

Example Peer Conference scaffolding handout.

Peer Conference

Author: _Claudia_

Conference Partner: _Ben_

Title of Piece: _Summer Fun_

Three things I liked about the piece:
(Explain why you liked each thing as well.)

1) You zeroed In on the small moment at the lake when you jumped in.

2) You described the action of jumping with descriptive words.

3) I could "feel" how cold the lake was because you described it well.

One wish:
(One suggestion for revision; to add clarity, detail, etc.)

You didn't have a full ending. You just wrote: the end.

EXHIBIT 4.9

Example Self-editing Checklist handout.

Name _Claudia_

_X_   I wrote the date at the top of my page.

_X_   I drew a beautiful picture. I colored it in.

_X_   I wrote about a **small moment**.

_X_   I wrote more than 5 sentences.

_?_   I wrote **no excuse** words correctly.
       most, I think.

_X_   I have punctuation at the end of each sentence.

_X_   I used capital letters at the start of each sentence and with special words.

Grades 4–6

Materials: A table with 4 to 6 chairs; various supplies to write with, such as pencils, pens, colored pencils; various sizes and types of paper; photographs, comic strips, wordless picture books; folders for keeping works in progress; computers/laptops/tablet computers; scaffolding handouts for different stages of the writing process (see Appendix A)

Sample Assignments

- Write three haikus in the writing center this week.
- Use your time in the writing center to continue a project from your writing folder.
- Conduct a peer conference with your writing buddy using the Peer Conference scaffolding handout (see Exhibit 4.8 for an example; Appendix A.1 contains a blank form).
- Choose one of your pieces and use the Self-editing Checklist handout to check your writing (see Exhibit 4.9 for an example; Appendix A.2 contains a blank form).

ABC OR WORD-BUILDING CENTER

Grades K–1: ABC Center

Materials: Table with 4 to 6 chairs; magnetic surface (e.g., easel, cookie sheet, or magnetic wall); assorted letter manipulatives, such as magnetic letters, letter tiles, letter cards; pencils, crayons, markers, chalk, wiki-sticks; paper, mini-whiteboards, mini-chalkboards, laminated paper, sandpaper; alphabet games, such as Scrabble, Banana-grams; alphabet books

Sample Assignments

- Sort the letters into two piles: straight lines/curvy lines.
- Match uppercase and lowercase letters with the letter magnets.
- Place each picture next to the matching letter tile.
- Make all the words you can that end in -*at*. Write the words on the whiteboard. When you are finished, read the whiteboard to a friend.
- Place the objects in alphabetical order, making a pile for each letter. Label each pile with the correct letter card.
- Trace letters (or words) on sandpaper.

Grades 2–3: Word Building

Materials: Table with 4 to 6 chairs; magnetic surface; assorted manipulatives, such as magnetic letters/words, letter/word tiles, letter/word cards; pencils, crayons, markers, chalk, paper, mini-whiteboards, mini-chalkboards, laminated paper for writing on; laminated poems; word games, such as Scrabble, Banana-grams

Sample Assignments

- Sort the words by spelling pattern (e.g., -*ou*, -*ow*).
- Build your spelling words with the letter tiles.
- Circle all of the words that end in -*er* on the laminated poetry cards.

- Write a list of all of the words you circled and read it to a friend.
- Play Go-Fish with the stack of homophone (words that are pronounced the same but have different meanings) word cards.

Grades 4–6: Word Building

Materials: Table with 4 to 6 chairs; magnetic surface; assorted manipulatives, such as magnetic letters/words, letter/word tiles, letter/word cards; pencils, crayons, markers, chalk, paper, mini-whiteboards, mini-chalkboards, laminated poems; word games, such as Scrabble, Banana-grams

Sample Assignments

- Sort the words by spelling pattern (e.g., *in-, un-, dis-*).
- Build your spelling words with the cards.
- Sort the word cards into piles with prefixes and suffixes.
- Play Concentration with the stack of synonym word cards.

BOOK NOOK OR CLASSROOM LIBRARY

Grades K–1

Materials: Books of all genres and reading levels; large pillows, chairs, or other comfortable seating. If located in a corner of the room, the area seems particularly cozy.

Sample Assignments

- Choose a book to look through or read to yourself.
- Choose an easy book to read. Practice reading it two times. Make an audio recording of your reading. Ask a friend in the Listening Center to listen to the recording and discuss how smoothly you read.
- Read a book. Draw a picture of the main character and write at least two sentences describing him or her.

Grades 2–3

Materials: Books of all genres and reading levels; large pillows, chairs, or other comfortable seating. If located in a corner of the room, the area seems particularly cozy.

Sample Assignments

- Choose a book to read to yourself.
- Read a chapter in a chapter book. Write a summary of the events of the chapter.
- Finish the book you are reading. Imagine the main characters are at recess with you. Write a conversation that might take place. Record a podcast of the conversation and share it with the class.

Grades 4–6

Materials: Books of all genres and reading levels; large pillows, chairs, or other comfortable seating. If located in a corner of the room, the area seems particularly cozy (see Exhibit 4.10).

Sample Assignments

* Choose a book to read to yourself.
* Read the next chapter in your book. Write a summary of the events of the chapter.
* Create a PowerPoint presentation to describe the changing events in the book.

LISTENING CENTER

Grades K–1

Materials: Any type of audio equipment will work: a CD or DVD player, an MP3 player, etc.; headsets or earbuds; audio texts and podcasts.

Sample Assignments

* Listen to at least two of the three nonfiction podcasts about the planets that are on each device. List all the facts that you learned about the planets.
* Listen to a friend's recorded reading and discuss how smoothly she or he reads.

EXHIBIT 4.10

Example class library.

Grades 2–3

Materials: Any type of audio equipment will work: a CD or DVD player, an MP3 player, etc.; headsets or earbuds; audio texts and podcasts.

Sample Assignments

* Listen to the podcast of *The First Thanksgiving*. The narrator will guide your reading of this article. Write your answer to each of the narrator's prompts in your literacy log.
* Select a short mystery. Predict who the culprit was and why this person committed the crime. Record your predictions at the required pauses.

Grades 4–6

Materials: Any type of audio equipment will work: a CD or DVD player, an MP3 player, etc.; headsets or earbuds; audio texts and podcasts.

Sample Assignments

* Select and listen to a podcast as a source for your animal research paper. Make note of animal facts while you are listening and include them in your paper.
* Listen to the poetry collection provided. Complete the response prompts in the center.

COMPUTER/TABLET CENTER

Grades K–1

Materials: Computers (2 or 3 desktop and/or 4 to 6 tablets); 4 to 6 chairs; printer if available; software

Sample Assignments

Students from the writing center will be using the computers this week.

- Choose your favorite vocabulary website from the menu and practice your high-frequency words.
- Use the LightSail app to practice reading for meaning. [Note: LightSail is used as an example; many apps are available for this purpose.]

Grades 2–3

Materials: Computers (2 or 3 desktop and/or 4 to 6 tablets); 4 to 6 chairs; printer if available; software

Sample Assignments

Students from the writing center will be using the computers this week.

- Choose your favorite vocabulary website from the menu and practice prefixes and suffixes.
- Select from the list of apps to practice writing strategies.

Grades 4–6

Materials: Computers (2 or 3 desktop and/or 4 to 6 tablets); 4 to 6 chairs; printer if available; software

Sample Assignments

Students from the writing center will be using the computers this week.

- Choose your favorite vocabulary website from the menu and identify important details in an informational article on the site.
- Select from the list of apps to practice writing strategies.

RESEARCHER'S LAB (SCIENCE CENTER)

This station integrates science and literacy.

Grades K–1

Materials: A table with 4 to 6 chairs or stools, clipboards, and various materials relevant to your current science unit

Sample Assignments

- Observe our special tree outside. Observe and record the changes in our tree since fall has started.
- Predict which objects on the table will sink or float. Record your predictions on the chart. Work with your group to test the predictions. Record what actually happened on your own sheet.

Grades 2–3

Materials: A table with 4 to 6 chairs or stools, clipboards, and various materials relevant to your current science unit.

Sample Assignments

- Use a magnifying glass to observe the objects on the table. Write a description of the details you notice with the magnifying glass.
- Browse through the informational books on plants. Use them to help you label the plant diagram with your group.

Grades 4–6

Materials: A table with 4 to 6 chairs or stools, clipboards, and various materials relevant to your current science unit.

Sample Assignments

- Work with your group to arrange the photographs from last week's science experiment in sequential order. Write a caption for each photo.
- Reread the article "The Earth's Water." Work with your group to complete the matrix on features of different bodies of water. If you finish early, select a book about water bodies to read from the table.

POETRY PLACE

Grades K–1

Materials: A large box filled with laminated poems printed on posters, tag board, or plain paper. Class favorites, as well as nursery rhymes, work well.

Sample Assignment

Pick a partner. Read your favorite poems to each other. Be sure to read with expression.

Grades 2–3

Materials: A large box filled with laminated poems printed on posters, tag board, or plain paper. Class favorites, as well as unseen poetry, work well.

Sample Assignment

Pick a partner. Read your favorite poems to each other. Be sure to read with expression.

Grades 4–6

Materials: A large box filled with laminated poems printed on posters, tag board, or plain paper. Class favorites, as well as unseen poetry, work well.

Sample Assignment

Pick a partner. Read your favorite poems to each other. Be sure to read with expression and proper phrasing.

VIDEO/PHOTOGRAPHY CENTER

Grades K–1

Materials: 2 or 3 small digital video cameras

Sample Assignment

Work with a partner. Take turns videoing each other reading on camera. Share your video during your reading conference with me.

Grades 2–3

Materials: 2 or 3 small digital video cameras

Sample Assignment

Conduct a peer conference with a piece from your writing folder. Video your conference. Share your video during your writing conference with me.

Grades 4–6

Materials: 2 or 3 small digital video cameras

Sample Assignment

Video your group doing readers theater with a text that you select from the table. Share your video with the class at the end of the day.

CREATION STATION

Grades K–1

Materials: Shelves filled with various art materials and donated scraps; a table with 4 to 6 chairs; an easel for painting. This works well near the classroom sink, if available.

Sample Assignments

- Use the materials on the table to create a unique project. Write a sentence (or story) about your creation.
- Create something with the provided materials. Write step-by-step procedures for making your creation.
- Follow the posted directions to create an insect. Does your insect look like the sample?

Grades 2–3

Materials: Shelves filled with various art materials and donated scraps; a table with 4 to 6 chairs; an easel for painting. This works well near the classroom sink, if available.

Sample Assignments

- Use the materials on the table to create a unique project. Write a story about your creation.

- Create something with the provided materials. Write step-by-step procedures for making your creation.
- Follow the posted directions to create a mystery object. Now look at the sample in the box. Does your object look like the sample? Why or why not?

Grades 4–6

Materials: Shelves filled with various art materials and donated scraps; a table with 4 to 6 chairs; an easel for painting. This works well near the classroom sink, if available.

Sample Assignments

- Use the materials on the table to create a unique project. Write a story about your creation.
- Create something with the provided materials. Write step-by step procedures for making your creation.
- Follow the posted directions to create a mystery object. Now look at the sample in the box. Does your object look like the sample? Why or why not?

READ/WRITE THE ROOM CENTER

Grades K–1

Materials: Long pointers (like those used for shared reading), clipboards, paper, pencils/pens/markers.

Sample Assignments

- Take turns with your partner to be the pointer holder. Start at the door, and point to and read the words and sentences on the charts and displays posted on the walls that you are able read.
- Take your clipboard around the room. Write all the words you know for objects in the room. Read them to a friend.

PROJECTOR/INTERACTIVE WHITEBOARD CENTER

Grades K–1

Materials: Projector (placed on the floor); interactive whiteboard; screen

Sample Assignments

- Practice writing all the words you know. Project them. Ask your friend to read them to you.
- Play high-frequency word Concentration on the interactive whiteboard with members of your group. When you are finished, you may read a book quietly.

Grades 2–3

Materials: Projector (placed on the floor); interactive whiteboard; screen

Sample Assignments

- Use the sentence strips on the projector to sequence the poems. Write and illustrate each completed poem in your poetry journal.

- Play the spelling game on the interactive whiteboard with your spelling partner.

Grades 4–6

Materials: Projector (placed on the floor); interactive whiteboard; screen

Sample Assignments

- Project several poems. Work with your group members and practice reading them chorally with proper phrasing and inflection.
- Select a vocabulary game to play on the interactive whiteboard. Work with all members of your group.

BIG BOOK CENTER

Grades K–1

Materials: Big books; these can be displayed near the book nook (or library).

Sample Assignments

- Read a familiar big book to a friend. Practice reading fluently.
- Choose a big book that you've never read. Take a picture walk first; then try to read the story.
- Search for words you know or search for our high-frequency words in the big books. Write down all the words you find.

Grades 2–3

Materials: Big books; these can be displayed near the book nook (or library).

Sample Assignments

- Read a familiar big book to a friend. Practice reading fluently.
- Search for homonyms (or antonyms, spelling words, etc.) in the big book. Write down all the words you find.
- Select one informational big book. Read the table of contents. Choose the section/chapter from the table of contents that you find the most interesting. Read the section/chapter, and write a summary (at least five sentences) to describe it.

BOOK BUDDY CENTER

Grades K–1

Materials: Individual book boxes (one for each student); easy or familiar texts for fluency practice

Sample Assignments

- Read the books in your book box silently.
- Read the books in your book box to a friend. Focus on phrasing/inflection/punctuation as you read.

Grades 2–3

Materials: Individual book boxes (one for each student); easy or familiar texts for fluency practice

Sample Assignments

- Read the books in your book box silently.
- Read the books in your book box to a friend. Focus on phrasing/inflection/punctuation as you read.

Grades 4–6

Materials: Individual book boxes (one for each student); easy or familiar texts for fluency practice

Sample Assignments

- Read the books in your book box silently.
- Read the books in your book box to a friend. Focus on phrasing/inflection/punctuation as you read.

Getting started with literacy centers

Although employing literacy centers is an effective method for managing small-group instruction, they are not necessarily easy for teachers to enact. Managing several activities simultaneously is complex and requires thoughtful planning, particularly when the teacher attempts this approach for the first time. Therefore, it is important to keep instructional activities simple for both the students and the teacher. That is not to say that the options should include rote or low-level activities. In fact, the open-ended activities in literacy centers should require the students to employ high-level thinking and application of skills and strategies that have been taught in previous lessons. Furthermore, the instructional activities must be focused, motivating, and engaging. The following discussion is designed to help novice teachers get started with literacy centers.

Designing for consistency and simplicity. Implementing too many center activities at one time can be overwhelming. This may be a new management system for both the teacher and the students. Therefore, easing into a routine is important. In the beginning of the school year, plan a small number of consistent literacy centers that can be used each week. For example, create four or five areas in the classroom to serve as the standard center areas. While the highlighted tasks in each center may change weekly, the name of the center and the materials within it should remain consistent. This allows students to become familiar with the routines in each center, leaving only the application of skills and strategies needed to complete a new task to be learned each week. Consider the examples provided in the preceding section. At each center, various activities can grow out of the consistently available materials and resources housed there.

It is helpful to provide a consistent space in the classroom for students to complete center activities. For example, a specific table may be identified as

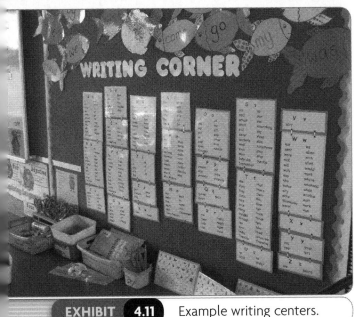

EXHIBIT **4.11**   Example writing centers.

the writing center (Exhibit 4.11). A small shelving unit or organizational bins may be placed on the table, allowing students easy access to materials. When teachers provide an assigned location for each center, it highlights the importance of the work to be done and allows ample space for student collaboration. This does not mean that a large classroom is required to employ literacy centers effectively. Small spaces can encourage cooperative teamwork.

Building the centers. Initially, it may be difficult to plan literacy centers because of a lack of materials, especially in the first year of teaching. Be assured, though, that you do not need to spend a great deal of money to stock literacy centers. At the beginning of the school year, many teachers simply provide the initial space, materials, and introductory activities. Students often help brainstorm additional activities to include in centers; these ideas can be effective and creative! Once an area is selected that will house each center, storage areas for materials can be obtained. Teachers should consider the available materials provided by the school, along with other materials that are easily accessible. For example, shelving and bins may be available from the school, or they may be purchased at large warehouse stores. It is also possible to find relatively new storage materials at garage sales. Exhibit 4.12 lists several donor websites where teachers can explore opportunities to obtain free classroom materials.

In addition, teachers can gather pencils, crayons, markers, chalk, mini-chalkboards, mini-whiteboards, tablet computers, magazine pictures (for writing prompts), paper of all sizes, and anything else that students can write with or write on. These items could be placed together in one area with a table, several chairs, and shelves or bins to hold the materials. Voila: a writing center!

Slowly establishing routines. For any classroom to run smoothly, routines are necessary with all activities. This is especially true with something as complex as literacy centers. If students do not understand where to access

	Sample donor websites.	EXHIBIT 4.12

ORGANIZATION	WEBSITE
AdoptAClassroom.org	www.adoptaclassroom.org
DonorsChoose.org	www.donorschoose.org
Edutopia	www.edutopia.org/free-school-supplies-fundraising-donation
Microsoft Educator Network	www.pil-network.com/resources/tools
ReadWriteThink (ILA and NCTE)	www.readwritethink.org/classroom-resources/lesson-plans/literature-circles-getting-started-9.html?tab=1#tabs

materials, how to work with other students (or independently) to complete activities, and how to clean up when they are finished, the classroom is likely to dissolve into chaos. Small-group instruction will be interrupted and ineffective. It is important to anticipate challenges that students may face. Clearly explain expectations for behavior by providing explicit models for each literacy task, as well as providing instructions for what to do once the task is complete. Practice routines for center time before starting literacy centers. The box on the following page describes possible routines to consider when introducing literacy centers, and Appendix A.3 provides a tip sheet of reminders based on these guidelines.

Even with students in the intermediate grades, it is helpful to introduce only one or two centers to students initially. Following the GRRM (Pearson & Gallagher, 1983), the teacher can invite all members of the class over to each center and introduce the students to the available materials, model appropriate use, and discuss expectations. If the center has an assigned task to complete, the teacher should model the procedures for completing it. Four or five students can then be invited to explore the materials and practice with one easy assignment, while the rest of the class reads quietly or observes the center workers. When the centers are first introduced, it is helpful to limit the time that students spend in one place to about 15 minutes. This will prevent students from losing interest or encountering too many challenges. This observation period would ideally be followed with a class discussion, led by the center participants, describing what went well in the center and any suggestions for improvement. Students who observe the centers in action might offer positive feedback and suggestions for improving productivity and behavior in the centers. Each subsequent day, the teacher may add an additional center and repeat the process, allowing different students to practice in the centers that have already been introduced. Eventually enough centers will be open so that all students can participate simultaneously.

While students practice collaborating in centers, the teacher serves as a guide and facilitator to ensure that students understand the expectations. As with all good teaching, however, this responsibility should be shifted to the learners. It is necessary for the teacher to stand back eventually and observe students as they work; this provides the learners with the opportunity to build independence. Center start-up does take time. It is common for teachers to devote four to six weeks to introducing students to the various routines and activities. This time investment is crucial to help teachers avoid the difficulties that arise when students are unsure of how to collaborate on student-centered activities.

Guidelines for literacy center routines

Knowing Where to Go!

Each time students are assigned to new centers, provide an explicit explanation of the centers. Introduce activities at a morning meeting, where all students gather around a chart or display of the week's centers. List the students' names next to the center activity so they can reference the task board or display to determine where they should begin working (Exhibit 4.13). As students become familiar with this routine, release responsibility to them; that is, allow the students to determine their starting point each day based on the display.

Center Rotation

Decide how many centers each student will visit each day; this is a matter of teacher preference. If students will visit only one center each day, simply change the display (explained above) to indicate where students work. However, if you require students to work in more than one center, explicitly describe the manner of rotation. For example, create a chart that lists students' names in one column, followed by two assigned centers (e.g., book nook and poetry area) to describe where they start (book nook) and where they go next (poetry area).

Accessing and Returning Materials

Introduce students to each of the centers and the materials available within each, to enable them to complete assigned tasks more independently. Explain where materials belong so that students can access them as needed and return them to their proper places for efficient cleanup.

Working with Others

For students of all ages, provide direction regarding the expectations for working with others. For example, in different lessons explain to students how to keep their voices at an acceptable level, how to help others without completing the other person's task, and how to offer constructive and positive feedback.

EXHIBIT 4.13

Example task board to guide students in moving between centers.

Seeking Help

Establish the common rule of effective classrooms: "Ask three before me." This means that if they need help, students should ask three peers for clarification prior to interrupting teacher conferences or small-group lessons.

What Do I Do When I Am Finished?

Off-task behaviors can be very disruptive to other activities occurring in the classroom. Regardless of your method for managing literacy tasks, it is vital that students always have something to work on once an assigned task is complete. Refer students to literacy activities (e.g., word games, reading texts, writing activities) that they may explore once an assigned task is complete, or simply allow students to read silently or browse texts quietly if they have extra time. The goal is simply to engage students in literacy activities.

Transitions

Students may get off task if they don't understand when to move from a center. Teacher preferences determine transitions. For example, if you assign students to complete tasks in several centers, you may allow the students to move freely as they finish each task, or you may provide a signal (e.g., ring a bell or blink the lights) when it is time to clean up an area and move to another task. You may also choose to provide a five-minute warning so that students may wrap up a task before cleaning up.

Where to Meet Following Cleanup

Clarify where students should meet once small-group lessons (and the accompanying literacy center activities) are complete. For example, invite students to gather at the whole-group meeting area for a recap of the day's literacy events, as well as directions for the next event on the agenda.

Providing authentic literacy opportunities. A primary purpose of literacy centers is to keep students actively involved in meaningful learning so that the teacher can work with individuals or small groups of students. Therefore, it is imperative that students be motivated to continue working in centers, rather than disrupting the class in any way. Simple worksheets and rote memorization activities will not keep learners on task long enough for the teacher to conduct an effective lesson with other students.

Students become proficient readers and writers by reading and writing, and center activities are most engaging when they are authentic and open-ended. Therefore, assignments that require students to read or write at their independent level are necessary. For example, in the writing center, kindergarten learners may be required to write about something they learned from a recent field trip. *All* students are capable of completing this task to some degree. Some may simply draw and color a picture of what they remember from the trip. Others may draw a picture and write letter-like forms next to it. Still other students may write words or sentences describing a specific event on the trip.

Similarly, second-grade students may be required to create a procedural podcast in the computer center. The students will compose and record directions for completing a task they select. Each student will compose a "how to" presentation, using vocabulary at his or her developmental level; if a student needs help, peers can lend a hand. All students in the class will have the opportunity to select and listen to a peer's podcast and follow the directions provided. As with the previous example, this open-ended activity allows each student to complete the task according to her or his ability. Although the task is the same for all students, the amount of support that is provided to complete the task is differentiated.

Reminding students no such thing as "I'm done!" Most teachers have encountered the problem of students rushing through an activity only to exclaim, "I'm done!" This creates opportunities for students to veer into "off limits" behaviors, disrupting others and the small-group lesson that the teacher is leading. Literacy centers work best when teachers make "I'm done" an impossible claim. When the literacy center is stocked with ample materials, teachers can provide suggestions for many additional activities in each center. Also, students can be encouraged to use the resources to read or write anything they would like upon completion of an assigned task. Careful planning such as this allows for open-ended application of literacy skills and strategies. For example, once students finish an assigned task in the writing center, they may choose any other materials in the center and write something else—anything else. Similarly, if students complete the assigned reading and response in the classroom library, they may browse any books for the remainder of the allotted time. Students who finish building assigned words in the word-building center may then write the word with pencils and then with markers. They may also create new words that they find in the room or know how to spell already.

Managing movement between centers. Methods for moving students between literacy center activities are just as varied as the teachers who implement them. The amount of control a teacher holds in the process will depend on each teacher's preference and comfort level. For example, some teachers determine the amount of time that all students will spend in a given center. When a signal is given, all students will move from one station to the next. A task board (Exhibit 4.13, p. 66) provides information so students know where to move next. In other classrooms, there might be a predetermined flow, such as a clockwise movement around the classroom, rather than a task board. Still other teachers simply provide students with a list of tasks to complete in a given amount of time. For example, the teacher might provide a menu of items and let the students individually pace their tasks throughout the week. This method is described more fully in the following **Classroom Snapshot.**

Classroom Snapshot

MRS. JONES'S LITERACY CENTERS: "TICKET WORK"

Wendy Jones, a second-grade teacher in Latrobe, Pennsylvania, refers to her literacy centers as "Ticket Work." The students in her classroom have assigned tasks and "choice" tasks to complete while Mrs. Jones meets with small groups. Every student in Mrs. Jones's class receives a "ticket" (Exhibit 4.14; Appendix A.4 contains a blank form) detailing the "Have-To's" and "Choices" for the week. The "Have-To" activities must be completed by the end of the rotation period (typically five days); once those tasks are complete, students are allowed to select "Choice" activities. Following are typical ticket tasks available to Mrs. Jones's students.

HAVE TO'S

Task: Browsing Box

Description: Mrs. Jones fills a large bin with teacher-selected texts and places it in a designated area. She selected books to correspond with either content-area themes or a specific genre study. Students browse through the books to select their "choice" text for the assigned task. Mrs. Jones designs the activities related to these books to support application of comprehension strategies that she has modeled in previous whole-class lessons. The texts that students use here vary in complexity and difficulty level; the activity is differentiated based on the students' reading level.

Example Activities

- Mrs. Jones places various books in the box, all of which have a similar problem-and-solution format. She assigns students a partner, and then they choose a book. They partner-read the story and then use a "story glove" to retell the story. This is a gardener's glove with each finger labeled: (1) who, (2) where, (3) problem, (4) then, and (5) solution.

- When the class was reading and exploring the genre of drama, Mrs. Jones compiled a collection of readers theater scripts. Some were familiar stories changed into scripts; others were new. Students chose two to read and then completed a scavenger hunt. For example, students were asked to find and copy a line the narrator said, find an example of stage directions, and list the characters and setting.

Task: Word Study

Description: Students play games and complete activities that provide practice with spelling and phonics patterns. Mrs. Jones introduced these skills previously during whole-class lessons.

EXHIBIT 4.14

Student ticket for assigned and choice tasks in Mrs. Jones's class.

Reading Ticket

Name Anna   Date March 31
Book Club Super sea Snails

Have-To's	Mon.	Tues.	Wed.	Thurs.	Fri.
Word Study	X				
Browsing Box				X	
Digging in the Dictionary			X		
Independent Reading				X	
Computer Time	X				
Guided Reading		X			X
Word Games			X		
Trash or Treasure		X			

Choices					
Independent Reading	X				X
Poetry Center			X	X	
Reader's Theatre		X			

CS

Example Activities

- Mrs. Jones creates interactive whiteboard activities for word sorts, matches, column sorts, and so forth for students to read and practice word patterns (e.g., sorting several words with –or patterns, or matching words and definitions, or sorting words into columns, such as –or words into one column, –ar words into another).

- Students use decodable texts and highlighter tape to find matching words, and then they record the matching words on a chart.

- Mrs. Jones makes word dominoes for an activity where students match sounds (e.g., two words with a long /o/, but one may be spelled /oa/ and the other /ow/).

Task: Word Building

Description: The focus in this task is vocabulary. Mrs. Jones conducts whole-class lessons to introduce grade-level-appropriate concepts such as prefixes, suffixes, synonyms, and antonyms. The practice games at this station enrich and extend these skills.

Example Activity: Expand-a-Word

Students choose a root word. They then choose from a variety of provided prefixes and suffixes. Students add the prefixes and suffixes to the root word and determine if each addition makes a new word. They then record only correct new words.

Task: Digging in the Dictionary

Description: This task provides skill practice for all students based on a whole-class lesson. For example, students learn about alphabetizing, using guide words, and reading pronunciation keys.

Example Activities

- At the beginning of the year, the focus is on ABC order. Students choose five words from a container and put them in ABC order. (Later in the year, the students select ten words.) They check with a partner before recording them. The activities involve high-frequency words or robust vocabulary words so that students see and use the words in various contexts.

- Later, students use the Digging in the Dictionary handout (see Exhibit 4.15; Appendix A.5 contains a blank form). Students choose a word from a list Mrs. Jones created and then locate it in the dictionary. They record the following for each word: page number, guide words, and definitions. On Fridays, students share five new words they learned during the week.

EXHIBIT 4.15

Sample Digging in the Dictionary handout.

Name Anna   Date May 16

DIGGING IN THE DICTIONARY

My word is Stow

I found my word on page 148

The guide words are Stour and Strain

My word means To put away, store.

My word is inquiry

I found my word on page 536

The guide words are inoculation and insert

My word means Request for information, matter of public interest

CS

Task: Independent Reading

Description: Mrs. Jones spends two to three weeks teaching the class how to choose a "just right" book—one that they can read, comprehend, and enjoy. Students learn about selecting the appropriate book for a specific purpose. Once they master text selection, students at this station self-select a text, read it, and write a journal entry about the reading.

Example Activities

- Students record the titles of the books they have read on paw prints; these are displayed on a board called "Leave Your Tracks," corresponding with the school district's wildcat theme.
- Mrs. Jones displays a chart where students can suggest a book for another student based on what they have read.

Task: Computer Time

Description: Students use various websites to practice online comprehension strategies and word study skills. Mrs. Jones matches the activity to the modeled instruction.

Example Activity

Various websites are used, depending on the instructional focus and student needs. Exhibit 4.16 provides a sample list.

Sample websites for students to explore.	EXHIBIT 4.16
WEBSITE	**DESCRIPTION**
Academic Skill Builders, www.academicskillbuilders.com	Many different free games across academic subjects. Great for word study skill practice.
PBS Kids, http://pbskids.org/arthur/games/index.html#1	Many options for students to practice comprehension strategies.
Jane Goodall, www.janegoodall.org/chimpanzees	Student-friendly website used to practice reading informational text and engaging in research.
Quia, www.quia.com/ba/41785.html	This game can be used to develop the strategy of inferencing.
Quia, http://www.quia.com/mc/94601.html	This game provides practice with determining cause and effect in a text passage.
Quia, www.quia.com/cb/258031.html	This game requires students to distinguish between fiction and nonfiction texts.
Kids Reads, www.kidsreads.com/authors	Students can connect with different authors and learn about their writing craft.
Internet for Classrooms, www.internet4classrooms.com/lang_elem_index.htm	Various games are provided for skill and strategy practice. Teachers can select the appropriate grade level and subject.
Speakaboos, www.speakaboos.com	Students can practice various reading strategies through games. This website is also available as an app for most devices.

CS

Task: Flip for Fluency

Description: This center is a favorite spot for Mrs. Jones's students to start their ticket work. Students practice independently orally reading and rereading short pieces of self-selected text.

Example Activity

With a partner, students practice re-reading a text while they record themselves with a Flip video camera. They then watch and critique as their partner rereads the same text, using the Fluency Checklist (Exhibit 4.17; Appendix A.6 contains a blank form). They then record themselves a second time. Mrs. Jones uses the second recording to assess each student's reading rate, phrasing, and expression.

Task: Listening Centers

Description: Mrs. Jones color-codes select texts for different groups of students. Each text is available in both print and audio. Students listen to the audio book while reading along with the print book.

Example Activity

Students choose their assigned texts, which are above their instructional reading level, and listen to the audio while they follow along in the book. Mrs. Jones asks the students to rate the stories they read. For example, she may ask, "Did you think it was good? Would you recommend it to others?" She then requires the students to explain why they have these opinions, supporting their reasons with evidence from the text.

EXHIBIT 4.17

Checklist of procedures for the Flip camera fluency activity.

☺ Flip Camera Fluency ☺

✓ Practice reading a text that is a good fit for you from the basket. Read the text out loud for the best practice. If you are stuck on a word, ask your partner to help you figure out what the word is.

✓ Then, have your partner use the flip camera to film you reading the text.

✓ Watch the video of yourself.

✓ Talk to your partner about the good things you saw and how you could improve your reading.

✓ Practice reading the text again.

✓ Have your partner use the flip camera to film you reading the text a second time.

✓ Watch the second video of yourself.

✓ Talk to your partner about these questions:

Did your reading improve the second time? Yes

What did you like best about how you read? it wus smoove

How did practicing your reading help you to sound better on the video? I sdtit like I wus tocuing.

Task: Guided Reading (Read with Mrs. J)

Description: This is Mrs. Jones's small-group differentiated reading instruction. She meets with each group once or several times per week depending on students' needs.

Example Activity

See the discussion in Chapter 2, pp. 22–24.

CHOICE TASKS

Task: Word Games

Description: Students play review games with a focus on basic skills, such as building compound words. This area also features word study games with which students are already familiar from previous "Have-To" work.

Example Activity

One favorite student activity is building compound words with ladybug wings (Exhibit 4.18; Appendix A.7 contains blank ladybug wings). Mrs. Jones has filled one basket with ladybugs and another basket with wings to place on the ladybugs' bodies. Each wing has a word, and the students place two wings (words) on each ladybug's body. For example, a student could place the words *base* and *ball* on a ladybug, to spell *baseball*.

EXHIBIT 4.18

Building compound words with ladybugs.

Task: Sentence Sorts

Description: Mrs. Jones stocks this area with laminated sheets of sentences. Students sort the sentences in various ways for phonics practice, grammar review, and editing practice.

Example Activity

Students use Trash or Treasure for phonics practice. For example, "treasure" might be sentences with words with the long /o/ sound; "trash" would be the sentences without the assigned sound.

Task: Independent Reading

Description: This task is similar to the "Have-To" task described on page 71.

Example Activity

Students can choose to read and respond to self-selected texts as often as they would like during the week, after their "Have-To" tasks are complete.

Task: Readers Theater

Description: In the area for this task, students can find various readers theater scripts in folders. The students self-select scripts and choose available classmates to practice fluency, phrasing, and comprehension.

Example Activity

Students work in a small group to practice reading the scripts of their choice.

Task: Poetry Center

Description: Mrs. Jones makes various poems available in printed form. Students choose poems to read on their own or with a friend.

Example Activity

At various times during the year, Mrs. Jones and her students hold Poetry Performance Times, during which students perform poems they have been practicing. The entire class acts as the audience.

CS

MRS. JONES'S LITERACY CENTERS IN ACTION

To get her students started on their ticket tasks, Mrs. Jones makes the following announcement: "All right, boys and girls. It is time for ticket work. Please take out your tickets and find the place where you need to start." Since this is mid-year, the students take only a few minutes to read their lists and select a station to begin their work. At the beginning of the school year, Mrs. Jones spent the first ten minutes after the modeled lesson performing a "status of the class" with the whole group. She called each student's name and asked, "How many ticket work tasks have you done this week?" and "What is your goal for today?" Mrs. Jones used to monitor the tickets daily to determine who would need reminders and support to complete their work. However, since she has slowly released responsibility for these tasks to her students, they are now independent; they know just what to do.

Chad wants to start with the Flip for Fluency station, but he is disappointed to find that there are already four students there. He glances around the room and selects the Browsing Box instead. Mari is finished with her "Have-To's" for the week, so she heads to the Poetry Center to read a favorite poem with her friend, Omar. Hadley missed the past two days of school, and her group will meet with Mrs. Jones first today. Hadley is planning to start with Word Building after small-group time, because she likes the games in that area.

Mrs. Jones watches as the students settle into their work. After five minutes, all the students are actively engaged in their tasks. The members of her first reading group for the day—Sam, Miles, Hadley, Kenzie, and Anya—have been notified, so they are at the reading table with their books, ready to discuss comparisons of what they read to the predictions they made. After a 20-minute small-group lesson, the students put their books and materials away and begin working on their ticket work. Sam and Kenzie join Chad and Marissa as they begin working at the Flip for Fluency station. Miles heads to the classroom library to hunt for a book for Independent Reading, while Anya joins Hadley at the Word Building area.

As the students settle, Mrs. Jones invites her next group to get their guided reading books and meet her at the reading table. Mari and Omar put their poems back in the box, grab their guided reading books, and join Mrs. Jones. Sarah had just finished her activity at the Computer station and was looking on her ticket work menu for another Have-To activity; instead, she heads to the reading table. Cora puts her Independent Reading text back on the shelf and helps Seth clean up his Word Building activity. Then together they join the group at the table. Only five minutes have passed, and the group is ready for its turn with Mrs. Jones. The rest of the students continue to work on their own ticket work activities.

Variations and Alternatives to Literacy Centers

Every teacher has unique preferences for and styles of classroom management techniques. Therefore, literacy centers may not be implemented exactly as the previous descriptions illustrate. In fact, literacy centers may not be the management choice at all. This section describes one teacher's alternative to traditional literacy centers, as well as some completely different methods for engaging learners in meaningful tasks while the teacher conducts small-group lessons.

Choice learning activities

Rather than creating consistent literacy centers in a classroom, some teachers allow students to self-select activities to engage in while the teacher instructs a small group. Tricia Stuck, a first-grade teacher from Grand Blanc, Michigan, adapted her method of managing students during small-group instruction from Cunningham and Allington's (2003) Open Centers. Instead of assigning her students to specific tasks in literacy centers, Tricia has designated a time each day as "choice learning time." While she instructs small groups for guided reading, the rest of the students in the class have the opportunity to engage in any literacy task they choose. The only restriction, besides acceptable behavior, is that students must engage in tasks where they are reading and/or writing. Tricia describes choice learning in her own words in the following **Classroom Snapshot.**

Classroom Snapshot

TRICIA STUCK'S CHOICE LEARNING ACTIVITIES

Tricia describes **choice learning time** in her own words:

My classroom offers many areas where the students can choose to go while I instruct a small group. These areas develop and change throughout the year, but every area contains reading and writing opportunities.

At the beginning of the year the students only have five choices during choice learning time, including the Writing Center, Listening Center, Classroom Library, Science Observatory, and Word Work. Later in the year these become the "anchor centers," and they are still open for students to explore. However, now the students are free to create their own choices (see Exhibit 4.19). They may work individually or collaboratively. My only limitation is that the students must be able to describe how their choice makes them a better reader and writer.

EXHIBIT 4.19

Tricia Stuck's choice learning task board.

Tricia's choice activities (listed above) are very similar to the basic literacy centers described previously. Tricia further clarifies this:

The areas have no set tasks. After a student selects an area, he or she goes into the area and selects materials to work with and projects to create. Each time I open a new area, I model project ideas; the students may choose to complete a similar project or not. For example, at the beginning of the year I modeled drawing and labeling in the writing area

CS

before I offered it as a choice area. Many students mimicked the practice when they initially visited the writing area. Now students are spending days and weeks in writing full-length stories in the writing area. The main focus is always to keep the students actively engaged in practicing literacy strategies. They cannot take on new learning if I am not there, so I keep the possibilities for practice open.

We need to rotate some popular areas, because everybody wants to start in these places. So, one group gets to choose first on Monday, another will choose first on Tuesday, and so on. This ensures that everyone gets to visit a favorite space at some point during the week. This year the most popular spaces include the writing area, listening area, and Science Observatory. Some newly created areas have emerged as very popular spaces, as well.

Exhibit 4.20 describes some newly created areas that have emerged as very popular spaces in Tricia Stuck's classroom.

EXHIBIT 4.20 Tricia Stuck's choice learning activity areas.

NEW AREA	DESCRIPTION
Post Office	This is an extension of the writing area. Students here use real stationery to write letters to friends and family members. After addressing envelopes students can add a "stamp" and deposit their mail in the classroom mailbox. Appointed students sort the mail and deliver those addressed to class members.
Art Area	This area consists of a table with shelves nearby, stocked with various art materials (e.g., colored paper, pencils, markers, crayons, glue, scissors, paints and paintbrushes, crafty objects such as sequins and confetti, and anything else the students donate). After students have a short period to explore the materials, "how to" books are added, such as *How to Draw Animals* or *How to Paint a Landscape*. Students can choose to follow directions, or just create their own masterpiece. All students write a description of their work to share with the class.
Publishing Area	This popular area is also an extension of the Writing Center. Students whose writing has developed into a book can illustrate it and choose a method for publication at this table. Students can choose various art supplies for illustrating from the shelves near this table. Mini-lessons for how to publish a book are presented to the whole class; many students use the techniques to publish their books in this area.
Computer Area	This area simply consists of three classroom computers. Students can work here individually or with a partner. Bookmarked sites are available for students to practice reading, writing, speaking, and listening through engaging games. Students may also choose to work on composing or publishing a book while they are here.

Tricia adds,

It definitely takes time to build up to independent rotation in these areas! At the beginning of the year I had to *teach* the students to be independent and to do *meaningful* things in each area. They initially chose to look at books and draw pictures only. To counter this, I presented a mini-lesson each day, where I shared

CS

appropriate ideas and provided suggestions. Each day, at the end of choice learning time, I required students to share with the class what they did. I praised creativity and independence, and other students grabbed onto the ideas. Now the students create their own choice learning tasks. It is very exciting!

Choice learning time makes it easy to pull students for small-group instruction. Students won't miss anything while they meet with me, because they can go back and pick up where they left off. I haven't had any discipline issues since I started with this method. Students are deeply engaged in reading and writing, and they create tasks that are of interest to them. They do not get "off task" and become a disruption.

While Tricia's technique is clearly quite similar to traditional literacy centers, it is also different. Instead of providing teacher-directed choices, Tricia allows students to be accountable for creating and selecting their own literacy application opportunities.

Independent work and silent reading

Teachers sometimes assign independent seat work (e.g., worksheets) for students to complete. This, too, can provide individuals with opportunities to practice skills and strategies taught in class during previous lessons. It is important, however, for teachers to provide students with authentic reading and writing applications to complete at their seats, not just rote practice. It is also vital for the assignments to be engaging. Finally, the students must be able to complete the work without teacher help. Meeting these three criteria with seat work can be challenging, so teachers must be diligent in planning such activities.

A more effective alternative to assigning worksheets is to assign all students to read independently while the teacher meets with a small group. The value in independent reading is that it is one way for students to apply reading skills and strategies to authentic texts. This approach works very well in some classrooms, particularly in the intermediate grades, where students may remain engaged in silent independent reading for periods long enough to allow the teacher to meet with groups. However, it is important to remember that whatever the students are assigned to do, they must stay actively engaged in meaningful tasks for the entire time the teacher is meeting with small groups. Some students are simply not capable of reading silently for long periods of time. Even the strongest readers will need explicit instruction in how to choose appropriate texts to read for the duration of the literacy block.

It is not uncommon for teachers to mix the two techniques described above. In other words, students work independently on assigned practice activities (e.g., handouts, games, or worksheets) and select books for independent reading when they finish. While these management ideas may prove effective for some students, the combination of seat work and independent reading often does not keep students actively engaged in literacy tasks long enough for extended learning, or for the teacher to provide effective small-group instruction. In addition, engaging in the same one or two activities day after day can quickly become monotonous. Another drawback is that these activities provide limited practice with authentic writing.

Literature circles

Harvey Daniels (1994) described a **literature circle** as a student-led discussion designed to enrich independent reading through collaborative conversations. In this structured activity, small groups of students sign up to read the same book, completing role sheets or jotting notes to use as scaffolds in subsequent collaborative conversations. Each member of the small group has a responsibility to read the assigned portion of text and participate in ongoing discussions. This is sometimes accomplished by assigning each participant a particular "role" for the discussion. Examples of discussion roles include, but are not limited to, the following: discussion director, summarizer, vocabulary wizard, illustrator, and connector. Each of the roles requires students to apply reading strategies that have been previously taught. It is important for students to rotate roles throughout the reading of a text so that they have multiple opportunities to practice different reading strategies and discuss books in various ways.

One positive outcome of literature circles is that students become deeply engaged in conversations, leading to thoughtful responses to texts. These rich text responses further enhance reading comprehension (Almasi, 1995). Research also demonstrates that literature circles can effectively increase comprehension in English learners (McElvain, 2010). Opportunities to discuss readings with a small group of students seem to benefit students because of the intimate nature of the discussion and the increased responsibility for participation. According to Peralta-Nash and Dutch (2000), students in the bilingual classroom they studied "learned to take responsibility for their own learning, and this was reflected in how effectively they made choices and took ownership of literature circle groups. They took charge of their own discussions, held each other accountable for how much or how little reading to do, and for the preparation for each session. The positive peer pressure that the members of each group placed on each other contributed to each student's accountability to the rest of the group" (p. 36).

Literature circles are considered practice and an application of strategies taught in previous whole-class or small-group (guided reading) lessons; they are not considered explicit instructional groups. Consequently, literature circles are often conducted as an instructional activity separate from guided reading group time. However, teachers of intermediate grades (4–6) may instruct their students to read and prepare for literature circles while guided reading groups are meeting with the teacher. Students will most likely meet with different peers in guided reading and literature circles, since the focus is different for each instructional arrangement. During literature circles, students read self-selected texts that they can easily comprehend without teacher help. In guided reading, students meet with the teacher to read and discuss texts at their instructional reading level. The teacher provides explicit instruction as needed to help the students through challenging parts of a book.

When used as a management technique for small-group instruction, literature circles provide an opportunity for students to read actively and independently, using a role sheet or handout as a scaffold at times. Once students complete their group's selected readings for the literature circle book, they become engaged in preparing to meet with their group to discuss the reading. This preparation is followed by a group discussion, ending with the group members determining the next portion to read. All of this can occur while the teacher meets with a small group of students in guided reading.

For example, when preparing his students to participate in literature circles, Mr. Myers, a fifth-grade teacher, introduces five different chapter books to his class through a brief Book Talk. Each of his students then selects the book he or she would like to read, with the number of students in each group limited to six. Jack and Claudia are the first students to sign up for *The Tale of Despereaux* (DiCamillo, 2003). Ruby showed some interest in the book, but Mr. Myers suggested a different novel for her, based on her interests. After several minutes, Mr. Myers announces that the students have two minutes to finalize their choices. In the end, Ben, Ella, and Andi join Jack and Claudia in what they quickly name The Tale of Despereaux (TTD) group. Over the course of the next several weeks, each student will take notes and/or complete a structured handout (i.e., role sheet) to prepare for the group discussion of an assigned portion of text. As students work independently to prepare for their next literature circle meeting, Mr. Myers meets with small groups to conduct differentiated reading lessons (i.e., guided reading). In fact, sometimes literature circle groups even meet to discuss their books quietly while Mr. Myers meets with small groups to conduct lessons.

CONCLUSION

t the beginning of the chapter, we read about Mr. Waverly and his questions about how to manage his classroom effectively during small-group instruction time. One answer is that there are various effective methods for managing students; each teacher has to find an approach that works with her or his personal teaching style. Literacy centers allow students to engage in multiple authentic activities designed to extend and enrich literacy skills and strategies. Although this approach is complex and requires careful planning, it is worth the effort to ensure that students have opportunities for meaningful reading and writing. Alternatives to literacy centers include choice learning activities, seat work, independent reading, and literature circles. Whatever the approach, the mandatory ingredient is that the students are actively engaged in reading and/or writing practice so that the teacher is free to meet with small groups or individuals to differentiate reading instruction.

Practical Application

1. Create and describe two different literacy centers to implement in your future classroom. Consider the space that will be needed and how it will be organized. Describe the furniture arrangement and material resources that will be housed in each center. Describe three or four activities that might be assigned in each center, and explain which of Tomlinson's (2000) four elements of differentiation (see Exhibit 1.1) may apply to each activity. If possible, share these centers in a field placement, using the guidelines for introducing centers in this chapter.

2. Research literature circles to learn more about how to implement this method. You may want to visit the following websites to learn more about literature circles:

- Definition of literature circles: www.literaturecircles.com/article1.htm
- Models for literature circles: www.lauracandler.com/strategies/litcircle models.php
- Overview of literature circles: www.litcircles.org/Overview/overview.html

Explain why you may (or may not) choose to use literature circles to manage the students in your classroom while you conduct small-group reading lessons.

Recommended Resources

The following sites offer practical information on how to manage your class while meeting with small groups:

Scholastic, Guided Reading, www.scholastic.com/teachers/2013/09/guided-reading-organization-made-easy

Scholastic, Reading Workshop, www.scholastic.com/teachers/article/classroom-management-reading-workshop

Teaching Channel, Guided Reading video, www.teachingchannel.org/videos/classroom-management-guided-reading

Tips for Teachers, Guided Reading, www.tips-for-teachers.com/guided%20 reading.htm#What%20are%20the%20other%20kids%20doing

REFERENCES

Almasi, J. (1995). The nature of fourth graders' sociocognitive conflicts in peer-led and teacher-led discussions in literature. *Reading Research Quarterly, 30,* 314–351.

Baker, L., Dreher, M. J., & Guthrie, J. T. (2000). Why teachers should promote reading engagement. In L. Baker, M. J. Dreher, & J. T. Guthrie (Eds.), *Engaging young readers: Promoting achievement and motivation* (pp. 1–16). New York: Guilford.

Block, C. C., & Mangieri, J. N. (2003). *Exemplary literacy teachers.* New York: Guilford.

Cunningham, P., & Allington, R. (2003). *Classrooms that work: They can all read and write.* Upper Saddle River, NJ: Pearson Education.

Daniels, H. (1994). *Literature circles: Voice and choice in the student-centered classroom.* Portland, ME: Stenhouse.

DiCamillo, K. (2003). *The tale of Despereaux.* Cambridge, MA: Candlewick.

Duke, N. K., & Pearson, P. D. (2002). Effective practices for developing reading comprehension. In A.E. Farstrup & S. Samuels (Eds.), *What research has to say about reading instruction* (pp. 205–242). Newark, DE: International Reading Association.

MacLachlan, P. (1985). *Sarah, plain and tall.* New York: HarperCollins Children's Books.

McElvain, C. E. (2010). Transactional literature circles and the reading comprehension of English learners in the mainstream classroom. *Journal of Research in Reading, 33* (2), 178–205.

Pearson, P. D., & Gallagher, M. (1983). The instruction of reading comprehension. *Contemporary Educational Psychology, 8,* 317–344.

Peralta-Nash, C., & Dutch, J. A. (2000, April). Literature circles: Creating an environment for choice. *Primary Voices K–6, 8* (4), 29–37.

Pressley, M., Allington, R. L, Wharton-McDonald, R., Block, C. C., & Morrow, L. M. (2001). *Learning to read: Lessons from exemplary first-grade classrooms.* New York: Guilford.

Schumm, J. S., Moody, S. W., & Vaughn, S. (2000). Grouping for reading instruction: Does one size fit all? *Journal of Learning Disabilities, 33* (5), 477–488.

Taylor, B. M., Pearson, P. D., Clark, K. F., & Walpole, S. (2000). Effective schools and accomplished teachers: Lessons about primary-grade reading instruction in low-income schools. *Elementary School Journal, 101* (2), 121–164.

Taylor, B. M., Pearson, P. D., Peterson, D., & Rodriguez, M. C. (2003). Reading growth in high-poverty classrooms: The influence of teacher practices that encourage cognitive engagement in literacy learning. *Elementary School Journal, 104* (1), 3–28.

Tomlinson, C. A. (2000, August). Differentiation of instruction in the elementary grades. *ERIC Digest.* Champaign, IL: ERIC Clearinghouse on Elementary and Early Childhood Education. (ERIC Document No. ED443572). Retrieved from http://www.education.com/reference/article/Ref_Teacher_s_Guide/.

Vygotsky, L. S. (1978). *Mind in society: The development of higher psychological processes.* Cambridge, MA: Harvard University Press.

Wideen, M., Mayer-Smith, J., & Moon, B. (1998). A critical analysis of the research on learning to teach: Making the case for an ecological perspective on inquiry. *Review of Educational Research, 68* (2), 139–178.

Starting With Assessment

BEGINNING WITH THE END IN MIND

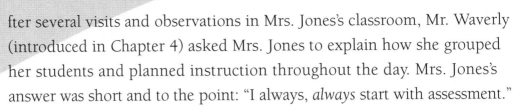

fter several visits and observations in Mrs. Jones's classroom, Mr. Waverly (introduced in Chapter 4) asked Mrs. Jones to explain how she grouped her students and planned instruction throughout the day. Mrs. Jones's answer was short and to the point: "I always, *always* start with assessment." Mr. Waverly recalled general information about literacy assessment from his pre-service teacher courses, but he also knew he needed to learn to conduct the specific assessments required by his new school district.

This chapter provides a brief discussion about assessments that are useful for informing reading instruction, but it is not intended to provide a comprehensive description of all literacy assessments. In the next chapter, examples will be provided of ways to use these assessments to inform and plan differentiated instruction. Like Mr. Waverly, you will also have some background knowledge and examples to reference in your future classroom, but you will need to learn to conduct specific assessments required by your school district.

While you are reading, consider the following questions: How can one possibly assign tasks without knowing what the students know and what they need to learn? What are some differences between assessment and testing? How do teachers determine which assessments to conduct?

BUILDING BACKGROUND FOR ASSESSMENT: WHAT AND WHY

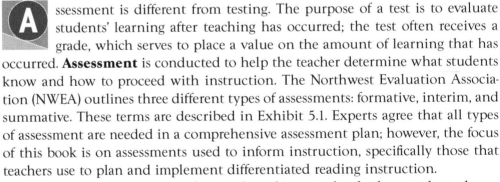

ssessment is different from testing. The purpose of a test is to evaluate students' learning after teaching has occurred; the test often receives a grade, which serves to place a value on the amount of learning that has occurred. **Assessment** is conducted to help the teacher determine what students know and how to proceed with instruction. The Northwest Evaluation Association (NWEA) outlines three different types of assessments: formative, interim, and summative. These terms are described in Exhibit 5.1. Experts agree that all types of assessment are needed in a comprehensive assessment plan; however, the focus of this book is on assessments used to inform instruction, specifically those that teachers use to plan and implement differentiated reading instruction.

Effective teachers start each year by taking stock of what students know before they start teaching. It is important to consider expectations: What do my students need to know based on the grade-level standards (e.g., CCSS, district, or state standards) and the district's curriculum? The next step is to determine students' current knowledge base. Some students may already be proficient in grade-level content, while others may not have the prerequisite skills for learning the new content. Exploring students' background knowledge before planning instruction is necessary to know what to teach, to whom to teach it, how to teach it, and when to teach it. Exhibit 5.2 illustrates the teaching cycle used by accomplished teachers.

Types of assessment.   **EXHIBIT 5.1**

TYPE OF ASSESSMENT	DEFINITION	EXAMPLES IN READING INSTRUCTION
Formative	Sometimes referred to as assessment *for* learning (Stiggins & Chappius, 2012), **formative assessment** is the planned process of gathering information (data) about students' abilities in order to inform instruction. Formative assessments are embedded in and linked to daily instruction and occur in an ongoing fashion throughout the academic year.	▪ Observations (e.g., checklists, running records) ▪ Questioning (e.g., teacher–student conferences, interviews) ▪ Independent application assignments
Interim	Sometimes called benchmark assessment, **interim assessment** is conducted at planned time points to measure an individual student's progress toward a specific goal. Interim assessment may be used to inform instruction, evaluate progress, or predict performance on summative assessments.	▪ Commercially or district-developed multiple-choice comprehension tests ▪ Dynamic Indicators of Basic Early Literacy Skills (DIBELS) ▪ Commercially published assessment kits (e.g., Fountas and Pinnell Benchmark Assessment System)
Summative	Also referred to as assessment *of* learning (Stiggins & Chappius, 2012), **summative assessment** (often *summative testing*) is conducted at the end of a unit of study or the end of a school year. These tests are used to evaluate the level of student learning over the course of study.	▪ State-level standardized tests ▪ National Assessment for Educational Progress (NAEP) ▪ End-of-unit test

As Exhibit 5.2 illustrates, assessment is the beginning of the teaching cycle, not simply a precursor to teaching. Once assessment data is gathered, teachers *analyze* the data to determine each student's learning strengths and needs. The next step is to *plan* the lesson, based on this analysis. At this point it is time to *teach* the lesson, and the process of assessing student learning begins as the lesson unfolds. Effective teachers constantly assess their students' understanding, often in the teaching moment; therefore, the cycle continues throughout the lesson. The focus of this chapter is to describe the assessments teachers use to inform small-group reading instruction. The rest of the teaching cycle will be addressed in subsequent chapters.

Opitz, Ford, and Erekson (2011) state that teachers must consider four questions before they begin to assess students:

1. What do I want to know about students' knowledge?
2. Why do I want to know this?
3. How can I best discover this information?
4. How can I use what I discover? (p. xiv)

EXHIBIT 5.2

The teaching cycle.

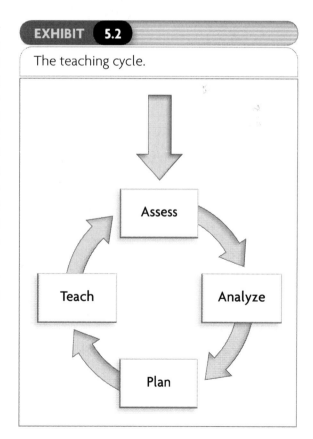

Asking these four questions encourages thoughtful reflection on the part of the teacher; rather than simply "testing" students, the teacher who asks these questions will think about what the students need to know, why that content is important to literacy development, which assessments might help to uncover the students' progress toward learning the needed content, and how to use the information to plan instruction. Think about the answers to the questions above while you read about each of the assessments in the next section. Appendix C.1 provides a form to help you use these questions to plan assessment.

ASSESSMENTS TO INFORM READING INSTRUCTION

The first question to ask when thinking about reading assessment is "What do I want to know about my students' knowledge?" Reading is a complex process that involves many types of knowledge, including concepts about print, letter knowledge, knowledge of words (e.g., word recognition, decoding skills, vocabulary), and text-level knowledge (e.g., comprehension). To build on the strengths of developing readers and meet their needs, teachers must discover what each student knows about each aspect of the reading process. Therefore, multiple assessments are used to inform reading instruction.

Comprehension is the primary goal of reading, but before assessing comprehension, it is important first to determine the instructional level at which a student can read—the level where comprehension can occur. As discussed in Chapter 2, the instructional reading level is the level at which the student orally reads a text with 90 to 94 percent accuracy *and* with good comprehension (i.e., at least 75 percent accuracy on text-based questions; Fountas & Pinnell, 1996). Teachers can use the following print, letter, and word knowledge assessments to help them determine where to begin the assessment of text-level knowledge.

Concepts About Print Assessment

If the answer to Opitz and colleagues' (2011) first question (What do I want to know about students' knowledge?) is *What my students know about how books and print work*, it is best to conduct an assessment of each student's **concepts about print (CAP)**. Based on research conducted in the 1960s, Marie Clay coined this term to describe the early understandings that emergent readers demonstrate (Clay, 1966, as cited in Clay, 1989). CAP include knowledge of book handling and orientation, directionality of print, literacy terminology (e.g., *word, letter, beginning, end, top, bottom*), punctuation marks, and spacing.

Why would a teacher want to know this information? At the beginning of the school year, many of the students entering kindergarten are emergent-level readers. It is essential for teachers of young students to know what each student knows about how print and books work before instruction begins. In addition, English learners with limited English proficiency may have developed literacy in their native language, but print concepts may be different in that language. For example, if learners do not understand that print moves from left to right in English books, it may be difficult to teach them to read words and sentences. Information gleaned from a CAP assessment will inform the teacher about the concepts on which to focus with the whole class (during the interactive read-aloud or shared reading) and with individuals, as well as which students are ready to move into more advanced skills and strategies instruction.

Teachers may conduct this assessment by using a standardized published version of the task, such as Clay's (2000) original version, or by asking students to demonstrate their understanding while they read a book. Exhibit 5.3 illustrates a teacher conducting this assessment. Appendix B.1 includes a version of this assessment. Teachers can also access a CAP assessment through the Teachers College Reading and Writing project at http://connect.readingandwritingproject. org/file/download?google_drive_document_id =0B3yKjAsMtuECVXFvM1NVZ1BJenc.

EXHIBIT 5.3

Assessing concepts about print.

CAP is often used as an interim assessment, providing baseline data in the first weeks of kindergarten, a mid-year check in January, and a summative assessment at the end of the year, if necessary. Note that once students move beyond the emergent stage of literacy development (refer to Exhibit 1.2), this assessment is no longer needed.

Letter/Sound Identification Assessment

Children enter kindergarten with varying amounts and types of knowledge. Some enter school knowing all of the letters and sounds, others enter with some knowledge of these items, and some students do not demonstrate understanding of any letters or sounds. English learners also come to the classroom with various amounts and types of knowledge, and their level of language proficiency will affect their understanding of the letters and sounds that make up English words. Therefore, it is important for teachers to ask, "What do my students know about letters and sounds?" and then assess the students' knowledge. This is quite a simple assessment task: the teacher shows an individual student all of the letters of the alphabet (uppercase and lowercase) in random order, recording the student's response to each. Exhibit 5.4 illustrates a teacher conducting this assessment with a young student. The teacher may ask the student to identify the letter, name the sound it typically makes, and ask if the student knows a word that starts with the letter. Standardized protocols for this assessment are available from Clay (2002) and Owocki (2010). Alternatively, teachers can access the assessment through Teachers College Reading and Writing Project, at http://readingandwritingproject.org/resources/assessments/running-records. A copy of the assessment is provided in Appendix B.2.

EXHIBIT   5.4

Administering a letter/sound identification assessment.

Like CAP, a letter/sound identification task may be used as an interim assessment (providing baseline data in the first weeks of kindergarten), a mid-year check in January, and a summative assessment at the end of the year, if necessary. Once the students have moved beyond the emergent stage of literacy development (refer back to Exhibit 1.2), this assessment is no longer needed. It may be necessary to conduct this assessment with struggling readers beyond the kindergarten year.

Qualitative Spelling Inventory

Another instrument that teachers often use to approximate the starting point for text-level reading assessments is a qualitative spelling inventory (QSI). A QSI is a research-based list of words selected to represent specific spelling combinations; the words are listed on a developmental gradient of increasing difficulty. Several publishers produce these inventories, which are commonly used to determine the developmental spelling level of individual students. The inventories are appropriate to use with students in grades K through 12.

Spelling inventories provide useful information about reading development, as well. Researchers have found that "students' spellings provide a direct window into how they think the system works" (Bear, Invernizzi, Templeton, & Johnston, 2012, p. 8). Because of this, a spelling inventory can predict a student's word-reading level (Bear et al., 2012). However, since the correlation between spelling level and word-reading level is not exact, a student's developmental spelling level determined from an inventory should be used only to *approximate the starting point* for a word recognition assessment (described in the next section).

After selecting a QSI, the teacher conducts the inventory like a traditional spelling test. The teacher reads each word and provides a sentence using the word, and the students record each word on a piece of lined paper. In analyzing the results, the teacher focuses on which spelling features are known and unknown, rather than which words are spelled correctly, to determine the student's developmental spelling level. For example, an inventory can show that a student is unfamiliar with some of the long vowel patterns. (Chapter 6 provides a more detailed analysis of a student's spelling inventory and Appendix B.8 provides a form for use in analyzing a student's spelling.) A student's developmental spelling level can be correlated with an approximate grade level for reading; this correlation will allow the teacher to select a word recognition inventory (described in the next section) at the appropriate level. The QSI assessment is typically conducted at the beginning of the year to provide baseline data, and again at the middle and end of the year to document students' growth and inform instruction.

Word Recognition Inventory

A word recognition inventory (WRI) is a common assessment for measuring a student's word reading ability. Teachers use WRIs, which are composed of graded (i.e., grade level) word lists, primarily to predict a student's text reading level. Additional information about a student's word analysis ability may be gained if the student does not recognize a word and, therefore, attempts to decode the word. According to LaBerge and Samuels (1974), if a student can read words automatically, cognitive resources are reserved for comprehension. Therefore, it stands to reason that if a student can accurately read words at a particular level from a graded word list, that student should be able to read and comprehend text at the same level. In fact, since text contains context cues at the sentence, paragraph, and passage level, students can often read text beyond the grade level of a word list they can accurately read. Students' performance on reading a word list can help the teacher select an appropriately leveled text to begin text reading and comprehension assessments.

A number of published word inventories are easily accessible for teachers. When selecting the list, it is important to consider the purpose for assessing students' word recognition. For example, one purpose is to determine the number of high-frequency words (i.e., words that commonly occur in text) that a student can read at a particular text level; in this case, the teacher would seek out a reputable graded sight word list. One of the most widely used word lists in the primary grades is the Dolch basic word list, first published by E.W. Dolch in 1936. Over time, the list has been divided into several graded word lists, the most advanced of which is grade 3. WRIs are available in many published comprehensive reading inventories, such as the *Basic Reading Inventory* (Johns, 2012), which is appropriate for use with students in grades K through 12. The Teachers College Reading and Writing Project provides graded word lists on its website for free download (http://readingandwritingproject.org/resources/assessments/running-records).

The WRI is administered to students individually. The teacher provides either a list of words or individual words printed on cards. Alternatively, the teacher may create a slide presentation containing one word per slide and present the words to the student on a tablet or other electronic device. As the student reads, the teacher notes both accurate responses and inaccurate attempts at each word. If the student becomes frustrated or misses several consecutive words, the teacher may stop the assessment. If the student successfully reads most of the words on a list, a higher-level list is provided. Each published WRI gives explicit directions and scoring guidelines, including the percentage of accurately read words required to move on to the next list. Once the student's word-reading level is determined, the teacher can use this information, along with information gathered from other assessments, to select the appropriate text reading level to begin the text reading and comprehension assessment.

Benchmark Text Reading Level Assessments

By using the assessments described above, teachers should be able to collect enough information to determine the text level at which to begin assessing each student's instructional reading level. Based on Betts' (1946) research on text levels, Fountas and Pinnell (1996) explain that when students read a text with 90 to 94 percent accuracy *and* good comprehension, they will have to work "hard enough" to learn new skills and strategies with teacher guidance, but not so hard that they will become frustrated and struggle to understand the text. Therefore, this is considered the *instructional reading level.*

Various educational publishing companies market benchmark texts, also referred to as informal reading inventories (IRIs). These are standardized reading level assessments, designed to guide teachers in determining each student's instructional reading level. Fountas and Pinnell (2006) define a benchmark text as "a reliable exemplar selected for each level on the gradient that you can use to determine a reader's level and to measure progress over time" (p. 86). Some publishers provide spiral-bound books containing short reading passages that are leveled according to grade-level equivalencies. Leslie and Caldwell's (2010) *Qualitative Reading Inventory-5 (QRI5)* and the *Basic Reading Inventory* (Johns, 2012) are two widely used examples. Both of these inventories also provide word lists and other assessments that teachers can use to help them gauge the appropriate level at which to start the text level assessment.

Other publishers provide kits containing small leveled books and scoring forms for the purpose of determining students' instructional reading level. Two popular examples are the *Developmental Reading Assessment, 2nd edition PLUS* (*DRA2+*; Beaver & Carter, 2015) and the Fountas and Pinnell *Benchmark Assessment System.* The texts in these assessments are not defined by grade level, but each system has its own gradient of text difficulty, which may be correlated to a grade level. For example, the *DRA2+* employs a mainly numerical leveling system. In this system, the simplest benchmark book is a pattern book, which is labeled Level A. After that, the numbering system begins, with Levels 1 and 2 representing simple texts appropriate for readers in the emergent phase of literacy development (see Exhibit 1.2). As the books in the *DRA2+* kit increase in complexity, their numerical text level increases.

Regardless of the leveling system, the process of determining an individual's instructional reading level is the same. Based on previously described assessments, the teacher decides the level at which to ask the student to begin oral reading. As the student reads, the teacher makes notes (i.e., takes a running record, explained later in this chapter) in a systematic way. This allows the teacher to calculate the student's rate of accuracy and fluency. Following the reading, the teacher asks the student several comprehension questions. If the student succeeds in reading the text or passage with 95 percent accuracy or better and with good comprehension, this is considered the student's independent reading level. The teacher asks the student to read texts at increasingly higher levels until a text is reached that the student reads with less than 90 percent accuracy or with poor comprehension. At this point, the teacher can estimate the student's instructional level as the last text read with 90 to 94 percent accuracy and good comprehension. Exhibit 5.5 summarizes this information.

As the table in Exhibit 5.5 illustrates, it is essential to consider the student's comprehension of the text when determining instructional level. Many benchmark assessments require readers to retell the story or the main elements of an informational text. Exhibit 5.6 contains a completed example of a retelling procedure and a comprehension questions form from the *DRA2+* assessment kit, and Appendix B.3 provides a blank generic retelling form.

After the *DRA2+* assessment is complete, the teacher can analyze the reader's comprehension by completing a comprehension rubric that is provided with each text. Exhibit 5.7 provides an example of the *DRA2+*'s comprehension rubric, and teacher scoring and analysis of a *DRA2+* rubic are discussed in Chapter 6.

Assessment of a student's benchmark text reading level is considered to be an interim assessment. At the beginning of the year this assessment provides baseline data; in other words, a starting point for instruction. Many districts collect benchmark text level data mid-year and at the end of the school year to track each student's reading progress. In addition, instructional reading level is one consideration for grouping students for small-group reading, which will be discussed in more detail in Chapter 7.

Retelling

A student's comprehension can be assessed through a retelling of a text. Generally, the text can be either read to the student or read by the student; however, for the purposes of differentiated reading instruction, it is important to assess the student's ability to comprehend a text that he or she has read. Retelling is part of the *DRA2+* assessment system, described above. However, a retell can be completed on any text, with a simple method described by Brown and Cambourne (1990). The teacher directs the student to read a text as many times as needed and then to tell the story (or the information in the text, in the case of

Reading performance and text levels.	EXHIBIT 5.5		
TEXT READING LEVEL DESIGNATION	**WORD-READING ACCURACY**		**COMPREHENSION LEVEL**
Independent Level	95% or above	AND	75% or above
Instructional Level	90–94%	AND	75% or above
Frustration Level	89% or below	AND/OR	74% or below

EXHIBIT 5.6 Example *DRA2+* retell procedure and comprehension questions.

Teacher Observation Guide   ***Chip to the Rescue***   Level 16, Page 4

3. COMPREHENSION

RETELLING

As the student retells, underline and record on the Story Overview the information included in the student's retelling. Please note the student does not need to use the exact words.

T: Close the book before the retelling, and then say: ***Start at the beginning, and tell me what happened in this story.***

Story Overview
Beginning
1. Chip the mouse and Dot the giraffe were good friends.
2. Some giraffes did not know why Chip and Dot were friends.
3. The giraffes thought Chip couldn't do anything because he was small.

Middle
4. The giraffes went kite flying and Dot asked Chip to go.   *Dot asked Chip to play*
5. The kites flew high in the sky.
6. The wind blew so hard that the kites got stuck in some trees.
7. The giraffes were sad. They could not get the kites out of the trees.
8. Chip got the kite strings out of the branches.
9. The giraffes cheered for Chip.   *The giraffes were happy when the kites were free.*

End
10. Chip could do things the giraffes couldn't do because he was small.

If the retelling is limited, use one or more of the following prompts to gain further information. Place a checkmark by a prompt each time it is used.

☐ *Tell me more.*
☑ *What happened at the beginning?*
☐ *What happened before/after* _____ (an event mentioned by the student)*?*
☐ *Who else was in the story?*
☑ *How did the story end?*

REFLECTION

Record the student's responses to the prompts and questions below.

T: ***What part did you like best in this story? Tell me why you liked that part.***
When the kites were free because everyone was happy.

MAKING CONNECTIONS

Note: If the student makes a text-to-self connection in his or her response to the above prompt, skip the following question.

T: ***What did this story make you think of?*** or ***What connections did you make while reading this story?***
112   *I am happy when I fix something.*

Example *DRA2+* comprehension rubric.   **EXHIBIT 5.7**

COMPREHENSION	INTERVENTION	INSTRUCTIONAL	INDEPENDENT	ADVANCED
Previewing	**1** Comments briefly about each event or action only when prompted or is uncertain	**2** Identifies and comments briefly about each event or action with some prompting	**3** Identifies and connects at least 3 key events without prompting; some relevant vocabulary	**4** Identifies and connects at least 4 key events without prompting; relevant vocabulary
Retelling: Sequence of events	**1** Includes 1 or 2 events or details (limited retelling)	**2** Includes at least 3 events, generally in random order (partial retelling)	**3** Includes most of the important events from the beginning, middle, and end, generally in sequence	**4** Includes all important events from the beginning, middle, and end in sequence
Retelling: Characters and details	**1** Refers to characters using general pronouns; may include incorrect information	**2** Refers to characters using appropriate pronouns; includes at least 1 detail; may include some misinterpretation	**3** Refers to most characters by name and includes some important details	**4** Refers to all characters by name and includes all important details
Retelling: Vocabulary	**1** Uses general terms or labels; limited understanding of key words/concepts	**2** Uses some language/vocabulary from the text; some understanding of key words/concepts	**3** Uses language/vocabulary from the text; basic understanding of most key words/concepts	**4** Uses important language/vocabulary from the text; good understanding of key words/concepts
Retelling: Teacher support	**1** Retells with 5 or more questions or prompts	**2** Retells with 3 or 4 questions or prompts	**3** Retells with 1 or 2 questions or prompts	**4** Retells with no questions or prompts
Reflection	**1** Gives an unrelated response, no reason for opinion, or no response	**2** Gives a limited response and/or general reason for opinion	**3** Gives a specific event/action <u>and</u> a relevant reason for response (e.g., personal connection)	**4** Gives a response and reason that reflect higher-level thinking (e.g., synthesis/inference)
Making connections	**1** Makes an unrelated connection, relates an event in the story, or gives no response	**2** Makes a connection that reflects a limited understanding of the story	**3** Makes a literal connection that reflects a basic understanding of the story	**4** Makes a thoughtful connection that reflects a deeper understanding of the story
Score	7 8 9 10 11 12 13	14 15 16 17 18	19 20 21 22 23 24 25	26 27 28

From *DEVELOPMENTAL READING ASSESSMENT SECOND EDITION* by J. Beaver and M. Carter. Copyright © 2015 Pearson Education, Inc., or its affiliates. Used by permission. All Rights Reserved.

nonfiction) so that someone who has not read it can enjoy or understand the text. The student can either write or speak the retell, depending on her or his proficiency in writing. Note that the student is not permitted to consult the text as he or she writes or narrates the retell.

Retellings provide information about what a child remembers about the content in the text, including story structure (e.g., characters, setting, plot) in narrative text or specific content in informational text. It is also possible to determine whether the reader can draw inferences from a text, based on the information provided in the retell. Teachers can even gather information about students' language development based on the way they speak or write about the text. Before a retelling can be used to assess comprehension, however, students must be taught how to write or orally retell a text. Otherwise, a student's lack of understanding about the information to include in a retell may be misinterpreted as a lack of reading comprehension. Appendices B.4 and B.5 contain sample rubrics that teachers can use to assess retellings for narrative and informational texts.

Fluency Measures

Fluency in reading refers to the ability to read text accurately, at an appropriate rate, and with proper expression. There is a correlation between fluent reading and comprehension; although fluency does not ensure comprehension, the use of proper expression in oral reading often indicates that the reader understands what he or she is reading (Price, Meisinger, Louwerse, & D'Mello, 2016). In addition, automatic word reading can facilitate comprehension, since the reader does not have to focus on decoding. Because fluency is considered a bridge between decoding and comprehension (Pikulski & Chard, 2005), teachers need to know their students' level of fluency, so that they may provide instruction as needed.

Assessing fluency can be complex, as it involves three constructs: accuracy, rate, and prosody (i.e., expression and intonation). In recent years, some educators have focused on the rate of reading, primarily because measuring a reader's speed is as easy as operating a stopwatch. However, to assess and then teach fluency effectively, teachers should use a comprehensive assessment tool. One of the most widely used comprehensive fluency assessments is the NAEP Oral Reading Fluency Scale (U.S. Department of Education, 2002). Exhibit 5.8 shows this scale, which can be viewed at the National Center for Education Statistics' website (http://nces.ed.gov/nationsreportcard/studies/ors/scale.aspx).

When a fluency scale is administered, such as the example in Exhibit 5.8, the student should read instructional-level text. It is not necessary to complete the rubric each time a student reads aloud; however, teachers should conduct periodic and scheduled assessments. Teachers often use a fluency scale as an interim assessment, documenting fluent reading performance at the beginning of the

EXHIBIT 5.8		NAEP Oral Reading Fluency Scale.
Fluent	Level 4	Reads primarily in larger, meaningful phrase groups. Although some regressions, repetitions, and deviations from text may be present, these do not appear to detract from the overall structure of the story. Preservation of the author's syntax is consistent. Some or most of the story is read with expressive interpretation.
	Level 3	Reads primarily in three- or four-word phrase groups. Some small groupings may be present. However, the majority of phrasing seems appropriate and preserves the syntax of the author. Little or no expressive interpretation is present.
Nonfluent	Level 2	Reads primarily in two-word phrases with some three- or four-word groupings. Some word-by-word reading may be present. Word groupings may seem awkward and unrelated to larger context of sentence or passage.
	Level 1	Reads primarily word-by-word. Occasional two-word or three-word phrases may occur—but these are infrequent and/or they do not preserve meaningful syntax.

year, at mid-year, and at the end of the academic year. In addition, if a student demonstrates a lack of oral reading fluency, the teacher may conduct the assessment more often (e.g., each month) to inform instruction for that student.

Interest and Attitude Inventories

When students are interested in what they are reading, they are generally more engaged in the task of reading, and their comprehension is enhanced (Cartwright, Marshall, & Wray 2016; Guthrie, Hoa, Wigfield, et al., 2007). Similarly, if students possess positive attitudes toward reading, they are likely to read more and comprehend more fully (Logan, Medford, & Hughes, 2011). Once an instructional reading level has been determined for each student, it is essential that the teacher assess the students' interests and attitudes. Not only will this help the teacher select appropriate texts for differentiated instruction, but this information also will be helpful in guiding young readers as they self-select texts for independent reading.

Since students' interests change over time, teachers most often use interest and attitude surveys as formative assessments to help them select texts for instruction. The simplest way to learn about students' interests is to ask them. Teachers may conduct informal interviews about topics that students like to read about, genre preferences, and when students like to read. Notes taken during these interviews can serve as formative assessments throughout the year. Johns (2012) includes an interest survey in his *Basic Reading Inventory*; similarly, Opitz and colleagues (2011) include interest and attitude assessments.

A commonly used tool for determining attitudes in reading was published by McKenna and Kear (1990). The Elementary Reading Attitudes Survey (ERAS) was created for teachers to use with students in grades K through 6. The survey may be administered to the whole class simultaneously; if it is given with the standard protocol, the teacher may compare the students' responses to national norms. The ERAS is available as a public-domain instrument, so it may be accessed online; one source is www.professorgarfield.org/parents_teachers/printables/pdfs/reading/writingsurvey.pdf. An example of a simple interest inventory is given in Appendix B.6.

Running Records

Reading is a cognitive process; that is, it occurs "in the head," and the process itself is impossible to observe directly. Still, it is possible to uncover information about a student's processing of text during reading. The **running record,** developed by Marie Clay, is a tool teachers can use to observe and document oral reading; it enables teachers to assess students' fluency, accuracy, and the application of strategies while reading. Running records may be conducted with benchmark-leveled text to determine a student's instructional reading level, which can help the teacher determine the starting point for small-group differentiated reading instruction. Running records are also used for the ongoing assessment of students' progress. According to Clay (2002), if "taken in a systematic way they provide evidence of how well students are learning to direct their knowledge of letters, sounds or words" (p. 49). This evidence provides invaluable information for teachers to use when planning differentiated lessons; therefore, running records are considered a formative assessment tool.

A simple way to describe running records is as a "shorthand" documentation of oral reading. As a student reads a selection of text, the teacher records each word, either on a blank piece of paper or a standardized form such as the one provided in Appendix B.7. The teacher uses standardized conventions to record the student's responses, which increases the reliability of the assessment. See Exhibit 6.6 for an example. Running records may be analyzed to determine the reader's accuracy rate, self-correction (of errors) rate, and the cue sources the reader uses or neglects (e.g., semantics, syntax, graphophonics; discussed below) when she or he makes a miscue, or reads a word that is different from the word in the text.

The process of reading is sometimes referred to as a three-cue system. Proficient readers access three sources of information when they read text: semantic information, syntactic information, and visual information. Running records allow teachers to analyze miscues in order to determine the type of information that students are using when they read. The semantic cue source refers to text meaning; in other words, does the miscue make sense in the sentence? It helps to think about this in terms of the whole story, the pictures on the page, and the reader's prior knowledge. A second cue source is syntax, which refers to language structure. Readers tap into oral language structures when they read. In other words, does the miscue sound like the way we would say it? Did the reader use a noun when a noun should be used in the sentence? Is the verb tense correct? Graphophonic information is the third cue source that readers use. This is the information contained in the print on the page, and is sometimes referred to as the visual information in the text. In other words, if the miscue was written, would it contain similar letters to the word on the page; does it look like the word on the page? Proficient readers integrate all three of these cue sources, and running records allow teachers to determine which cue sources a reader uses. When a reader demonstrates a pattern of neglecting a cue source, the teacher can provide instruction to address this. Exhibit 5.9 provides examples to illustrate the different types of cue sources.

EXHIBIT 5.9 Three cue sources.

CUE SOURCE	QUESTIONS TO ASK	EXAMPLE
Semantics (meaning)	Did the miscue make sense?	Child reads, "I put on my coat." The text states, "I put on my jacket." The picture on the page shows a child putting a jacket on. The child typically calls this garment a coat.
Syntax (structure)	Did the miscue sound right?	Child reads, "I put on my jeans." The text states, "I put on my jacket." Both the miscue and the word in the text are nouns, so the miscue "sounds right."
Graphophonic (visual)	Did the miscue look right?	Child reads, "I put on my shoe." The text states, "I put on my shirt." Both the miscue and the word in the text begin with *sh*, so they are visually similar.

Teachers use running records to group students in small groups for differentiated reading instruction. Typically, students are grouped with others at approximately the same instructional reading level; this ensures that each student will work within her or his zone of proximal development during the small-group lessons (Vygotsky, 1978; see Chapter 1 for an explanation of ZPD). Teachers also group students according to their learning needs and strengths. For example, students who neglect semantic cues (i.e., are not reading for meaning) when they make errors in instructional-level text, according to running record data, will be grouped with other students who make similar errors at nearly the same instructional level. For more information on running records, consult this site: http://readingandwritingproject.org/resources/assessments/running-records.

Assessing English learners

Contributed by Susan M. Sibert, Indiana University of Pennsylvania

Whether they are teaching in a rural, suburban, or urban setting, teachers will likely encounter English learners. The National Center for Education Statistics projects that the number of these students in U. S. public schools will probably increase annually, a trend that has been documented over the past decade. States and their school systems are required to provide English learner services and to report annually the academic progress of all English learners. The requirements are part of federal laws, including Language Instruction for Limited English Proficient and Immigrant Students, from Title III, a section of the No Child Left Behind (NCLB) legislation (see Chapter 1).

To support states and schools in complying with this law, a well-established, national educational consortium known as WIDA (named for the states originally involved: Wisconsin, Delaware, and Arkansas) was formed in 2003. The organization has evolved over the years, but its mission to support states in working with English learners and complying with federal mandates remains intact. An important part of that mission is providing assessment resources for compliance with identification of these students and reporting of student progress regarding English Language Proficiency (ELP).

When a child enters a school system and registers, the family is generally asked to share information on the languages spoken in the home. That information provides an important basis for identifying English learners. Students with home languages other than English are then assessed to determine their ELP. Many states use an assessment called the WIDA-ACCESS Placement Test (W-APT). The test is used to screen English learners new to a school system to ascertain their ELP. Assessment results help educators determine the placement and curriculum needs of these students. The important information derived from the assessment also serves teachers in formulating plans to instruct English learners.

The W-APT is an individually administered assessment based on the four domains of language: reading, writing, speaking, and listening. ESL teachers generally administer the assessment, but it can also be done by other educators, such as reading teachers, guidance counselors, school psychologists, or classroom teachers. The assessment places the student into one of six levels of language proficiency: (1) entering, (2) beginning, (3) developing, (4) expanding, (5) bridging, or (6) reaching. The W-APT is one component of WIDA's comprehensive assessment system.

Another component in WIDA's assessment system is a test called ACCESS for English learners. The assessment is based on ELP standards and assesses students in the four language domains indicated earlier. The ACCESS assessment is part of Title III of NCLB, mentioned earlier, which requires states to report the annual academic progress of English learners. Although many states use the assessment to assess the language proficiency of kindergarten through grade 12 students who are English learners, it also serves educators at the local level by providing data on the annual language proficiency progress of English learners and on programmatic efficacy.

Classroom teachers welcoming English learners will find the W-APT results valuable as they begin planning instruction. However, the results of the assessment may not be available on the first day the students arrive in the classroom. Furthermore, teachers will need additional curriculum-based data to plan effective, individualized lessons. They will want to conduct some basic literacy assessments of their own to gain understanding of students' current language and literacy levels. A starting point for this type of baseline assessment is a benchmark text-reading-level assessment, i.e., a basic informal reading inventory. Many commercial IRIs are available (see the References on p. 102 for examples). Select an inventory with assessments suitable for preprimer through twelfth grade, so that it can serve as a common assessment for many students of varying levels throughout the school. Assessments should begin with basic letter identification and sounds and then move to word lists and finally comprehension passages. For English learners, it may be necessary to start with word lists several grade levels below the generally recommended two grade levels. The information derived from the results of the IRI will provide valuable and immediate curricular and instructional direction. Teachers can use the IRI results in conjunction with the W-APT results, once available.

As mentioned previously, English learners are a diverse group of students. Some may demonstrate difficulty in developing literacy skills in English, some may not. In addition to the IRI, the other assessments described earlier in the chapter will help teachers pinpoint the developmental level of literacy of each child in the classroom, allowing them to plan appropriate small-group reading instruction. If an English learner has sustained difficulty reading in the second language, the classroom teacher should consult with the English learner resource teacher regarding the possible sources of difficulty (English language proficiency at the word or sentence level, difficulty reading in the first language, cultural incongruence or novel concepts as topics, etc.).

REFERENCES

No Child Left Behind (NCLB) Act of 2001, 20 U.S.C.A. § 6301 et seq. (West 2003).

U.S. Department of Education, National Center for Education Statistics (2015). *The Condition of Education 2015 (NCES 2015-144).*

WIDA (n.d.). Retrieved from https://www.wida.us/index.aspx.

FINDING TIME TO CONDUCT ASSESSMENTS

Clearly, teachers have much to consider when planning for instruction, and there are many assessments to conduct prior to that planning. Sometimes teachers view assessment as an additional obligation that interrupts teaching time. It is important to remember that assessment is a part of the teaching cycle, not an addition to the teaching cycle. When teachers believe this to be true, they plan for assessments just as they plan for other components of teaching. The following vignette demonstrates how Mr. Waverly integrates assessment into his instruction.

Classroom Snapshot

MR. WAVERLY'S INTEGRATION OF ASSESSMENT AND INSTRUCTION

BEGINNING OF THE YEAR

Based on advice from his colleague Mrs. Jones, Mr. Waverly carefully organizes his classroom environment according to guidelines similar to those provided in Chapter 4. He has decided that literacy centers will be the best management technique for him to use, so he devotes time in his literacy block to introduce and practice centers for the first two weeks of school. While the students are at centers, Mr. Waverly observes, offers reminders, and instructs students as necessary as they learn the routines. Since his students are in third grade, they seem to adapt to the routines quickly. Beginning in the third week of school, while the students work on their center activities, Mr. Waverly meets with individual students at the guided reading table to conduct assessments. It is a slow start; Mr. Waverly is still learning to conduct some of the assessments, and the students are still learning not to interrupt him when he is at the small-group instruction table. Still, with practice, patience, and persistence, Mr. Waverly is able to complete and analyze all of the district-required assessments before the deadline in the sixth week of school.

Six weeks may seem like an incredibly long time to gather assessment data; however, time is necessary to collect the invaluable information upon which instruction is based. This doesn't mean that students do not receive reading instruction for six weeks; Mr. Waverly conducts whole-class lessons based on the CCSS adopted by his state and district curriculum. For example, he begins the literacy block each day with an interactive read-aloud (described in Chapter 2), to demonstrate strategies that effective readers use and to discuss high-quality literature with the students. He also conducts lessons with text projected on a large screen during shared reading (also described in Chapter 2), so that all students can practice specific skills and strategies. In addition, students work in small groups on literacy tasks at their centers while Mr. Waverly conducts reading assessments.

In fact, the reading assessments start to inform his instruction before Mr. Waverly has completed all of them. As he analyzes the spelling inventories, for example, Mr. Waverly notices that most of the students misspelled *shines* and *wishes,* by omitting the *h.* He uses this information during shared reading, when he is reading a text projected on the screen. He explains that *s* and *h* work together to make a new sound, *"sh."* He then asks the students to circle the words that contain the digraph *(sh)* and read the words aloud. This is one of many mini-lessons he conducts to gather additional information to determine how many lessons the students need in this skill.

The information that Mr. Waverly gathers from assessments at the beginning of the year serves as baseline data. He uses this information to group the students and to determine the content to teach the whole class, small groups, and individuals. In the whole-class lesson, Mr. Waverly delivers grade-level content based on standards and curriculum. As previously mentioned, teachers need assessment data to know how much of the grade-level-required content is known and the depth to which they will need to teach it. In the example of Mr. Waverly's spelling discovery, this information helps him to meet CCSS RF.1.3: "Know and apply grade-level phonics and word analysis skills in decoding

CS

words. a. Know the spelling-sound correspondence for common consonant digraphs." Since the assessment demonstrates that most of the students do not know about the digraph, Mr. Waverly is aware that this should be the focus of a whole-class lesson.

Mr. Waverly also uses assessment data to determine the content for individual and small-group instruction. For example, four of his students demonstrated confusion about long vowel patterns on the spelling inventory, which means they may encounter difficulty when reading words with long vowel patterns. These students may see the word *made* in a text but read it as *mad,* because they are familiar with short vowel patterns but not long vowel patterns. Mr. Waverly plans to group these students together for spelling instruction so he can focus on that skill, in addition to the whole-class lesson on digraphs. The spelling inventory isn't the only assessment that is used in this way; teachers should use all of the assessments discussed in this chapter to inform teaching decisions.

ONGOING MONITORING

It should be clear at this point that instruction is most effective when it is informed by assessment. As illustrated in Exhibit 5.2, assessment must be conducted constantly and continuously to ensure that instruction meets the needs of individuals. Mr. Waverly manages his assessment schedule in different ways to suit the needs of his students and his own teaching preferences. For interim assessments (e.g., benchmark text reading level), he often suspends small-group instruction for several days in order to conduct assessments. On these days, similar to the beginning of the year in Mr. Waverly's classroom, the students complete literacy tasks either independently or at centers while he conducts individual assessments. When assessments can be completed with the whole class (e.g., QSI), he replaces one whole-class lesson (e.g., interactive read-aloud or mini-lesson) with the assessment.

Monitoring individual student progress with formative assessments is another essential component of the teaching routine. One way that Mr. Waverly, as well as other teachers, schedules these assessments (e.g., running record, comprehension discussion, fluency scale) is to conduct them prior to calling the first small group to the guided reading table each day. If he assesses one or two students each day, he will be able to monitor five to ten students each week. Another method Mr. Waverly uses for assessing all students is to suspend small-group instruction one or two days per month. On these days, instead of instructing small groups, he meets with individuals to conduct necessary assessments on a rotating basis.

CONCLUSION

Reading is a complex process, involving various skills and strategies. To be effective in teaching students to read, teachers must be adept in conducting and analyzing multiple assessments. This chapter provided descriptions and examples of various assessments that teachers can use to inform their reading instruction. The chapter emphasized the fact that assessment is a part of the teaching cycle, not separate from it.

Practical Application

1. Answer the following questions, which were posed at the beginning of the chapter:

What are some differences between assessment and testing?

How do teachers determine which assessments to conduct?

2. Complete the table below:

STUDENT KNOWLEDGE	HOW CAN I BEST DISCOVER WHAT THEY KNOW (WHICH ASSESSMENT SHOULD I USE)?	WHAT KIND OF LEARNING TASKS CAN I PLAN FOR SMALL GROUPS TO SUPPORT THIS CONTENT?
Knowledge of letter sounds		
Ability to recognize words		
Degree of fluency in reading		
Instructional reading level		
Degree of comprehension at instructional reading level		

Recommended Resources

Concepts About Print Assessment, Reading and Writing Project, http://connect.readingandwritingproject.org/file/download?google_drive_document_id=0B3yKjAsMtuECVXFvM1NVZ1BJenc

Elementary Reading Attitudes Survey, www.professorgarfield.org/parents_teachers/printables/pdfs/reading/writingsurvey.pdf

NAEP Oral Reading Fluency Scale, National Center for Education Statistics, http://nces.ed.gov/nationsreportcard/studies/ors/scale.aspx

Northwest Evaluation Association, www.nwea.org

Running Records, Foundational Assessments and Benchmarks, Reading and Writing Project, http://readingandwritingproject.org/resources/assessments/running-records

REFERENCES

Bear, D. R., Invernizzi, M., Templeton, S. R., & Johnston, F. (2012). *Words their way: Word study for phonics, vocabulary, and spelling instruction* (5th ed.). Upper Saddle River, NJ: Pearson.

Beaver, J., & Carter, M. (2015). *Developmental Reading Assessment, 2nd edition PLUS.* Upper Saddle River, NJ: Pearson.

Betts, E. A. (1946). *Foundations of reading instruction: With emphasis on differentiated guidance.* New York: American Book.

Brown, H., & Cambourne, B. (1990). *Read and retell: A strategy for the whole-language/natural learning classroom.* Portsmouth, NH: Heinemann.

Cartwright, K. B., Marshall, T. R., & Wray, E. (2016). A longitudinal study of the role of reading motivation in primary students' reading comprehension: Implications for a less simple view of reading. *Reading Psychology, 37* (1), 55–91.

Clay, M. M. (1989). Concepts about print in English and other languages. *The Reading Teacher, 42* (4), 268–276.

Clay, M. M. (2000). *Concepts about print: What have children learned about printed language?* Portsmouth, NH: Heinemann.

Clay, M. M. (2002). *An observation survey of early literacy achievement* (2nd ed.). Portsmouth, NH: Heinemann.

Dolch, E. W. (1936). A basic sight vocabulary. *The Elementary School Journal, 36* (6), 456–460. Retrieved from http://www.jstor.org/stable/995914.

Fountas, I. C., & Pinnell, G. S. (1996). *Guided reading: Good first teaching for all children.* Portsmouth, NH: Heinemann.

Fountas, I. C., & Pinnell, G. S. (2006). *Leveled books K-8: Matching texts to readers for effective teaching.* Portsmouth, NH: Heinemann.

Guthrie, J. T., Hoa, A. L. W., Wigfield, A., Tonks, S. M., Humenick, N. M., & Littles, E. (2007). Reading motivation and reading comprehension in the later elementary years. *Contemporary Educational Psychology, 32,* 282–313.

Johns, J. (2012). *Basic Reading Inventory: Pre-primer through grade twelve and early literacy assessments* (11th ed.). Dubuque, IA: Kendall Hunt.

LaBerge, D., & Samuels, S. J. (1974). Toward a theory of automatic information processing in reading. *Cognitive Psychology, 6* (2), 293–323.

Leslie, L., & Caldwell, J. S. (2010). *Qualitative reading inventory* (5th ed.). Upper Saddle River, NJ: Pearson.

Logan, S., Medford, E., & Hughes, N. (2011). The importance of intrinsic motivation for high and low ability readers' reading comprehension performance. *Learning and Individual Differences, 21,* 124–128.

McKenna, M. C., & Kear, D. J. (1990). Measuring attitude toward reading: A new tool for teachers. *The Reading Teacher, 43* (9), 626–639. Retrieved from http://www.jstor.org/stable/20200500.

Northwest Evaluation Association (n.d.). *Purposes of assessment.* Retrieved from http://www.nwea.org/assessment-literacy/assessment-literacy-101/purposes-assessments.

Opitz, M. F., Ford, M. P., & Erekson, J. A. (2011). *Accessible Assessment: How 9 sensible techniques can power DATA-DRIVEN reading instruction.* Portsmouth, NH: Heinemann.

Owocki, G. (2010). *The RTI daily planning book, K–6.* Portsmouth, NH: Heinemann.

Pikulski, J. J., & Chard, D.J. (2005). Fluency: Bridge between decoding and reading comprehension. *The Reading Teacher, 58* (6), 510–519.

Price, K. W., Meisinger, E. B., Louwerse, M. M., & D'Mello, S. (2016). The contributions of oral and silent reading fluency to reading comprehension. *Reading Psychology, 37* (2), 167–201, DOI: 10.1080/02702711.2015.1025118.

Stiggins, R. J., & Chappius, J. (2012). *An introduction to student-involved assessment for learning* (6th ed.). Upper Saddle River, NJ: Pearson.

U.S. Department of Education (2002). *NAEP–Oral Reading Fluency Scale.* Institute of Education Sciences, National Center for Education Statistics, National Assessment of Educational Progress (NAEP), Oral Reading Study.

Vygotsky, L. S. (1978). *Mind in society: The development of higher psychological processes.* Cambridge, MA: Harvard University Press.

Analyzing the Assessments

USING DATA TO DESIGN
DIFFERENTIATED INSTRUCTION

r. Waverly (the first-grade teacher featured in Chapters 4 and 5) followed the advice from Mrs. Jones and conducted assessments early in the year so that he could determine his teaching focus and grouping arrangements. Over the first several weeks of school, Mr. Waverly learned to conduct and analyze all of the reading assessments required by the school district. The results are considered baseline data, because they represent the starting point of learning for each student for the academic year. Mr. Waverly organized the student data from the assessments into the table in Exhibit 6.1. Appendix C.2 contains a blank form for use in compiling data, with an "Other" column for additional assessments.

EXHIBIT 6.1

Mr. Waverly's baseline data.
(The spelling pattern—the focus of instruction—and genre are set in *italics.*)

STUDENT	QUALITATIVE SPELLING INVENTORY (QSI)	WORD RECOGNITION INVENTORY (WRI)	BENCHMARK TEXT READING INSTRUCTIONAL LEVEL (*DRA2+*)	NAEP ORAL READING FLUENCY SCALE	INTEREST INVENTORY/ OBSERVATIONS
Michael	Late Letter Name–Alphabetic *Short Vowel*	Preprimer	8	Nonfluent Level 2	Sports Animals *Realistic fiction*
Emma	Early Within-Word Pattern *Long Vowel*	Grade 1	12	Fluent Level 3	Sea creatures Animals *Nonfiction*
Anna	Late Letter Name–Alphabetic *Short Vowel*	Primer	16	Fluent Level 3	Sports Space *Fantasy*
Gabi	Early Within-Word Pattern *Long Vowel (CVCE)*	Preprimer	6	Fluent Level 2	Sea creatures Countries Maps *Realistic fiction*
Finn	Early Within-Word Pattern *Long Vowel (CVCE)*	Grade 1	12	Fluent Level 4	Plant life Animals *Mysteries*
Amos	Early Within-Word Pattern *Long Vowel Blends*	Preprimer	8	Fluent Level 3	Sea creatures Animals *Realistic fiction*
Hadley	Late Letter Name–Alphabetic *Digraphs*	Primer	12	Nonfluent Level 2	Sea creatures Countries Maps *Nonfiction*
Sam	Early Within-Word Pattern *Long Vowel (CVCE)*	Grade 2	20	Fluent Level 3	Horses Animals *Mysteries*

Continued **EXHIBIT 6.1**

Chad	Early Within-Word Pattern *Long Vowel*	Grade 3	30	Fluent Level 4	Sports *Mysteries*
Katelyn	Late Letter Name–Alphabetic *Short Vowel*	Preprimer	10	Nonfluent Level 2	Sports Animals *Nonfiction*
Amelia	Late Letter Name–Alphabetic *Short Vowel*	Grade 1	14	Fluent Level 3	Sea creatures Computers *Nonfiction*
Anderson	Late Letter Name–Alphabetic *Digraphs*	Preprimer	10	Fluent Level 3	Weather Vehicles Sea creatures *Realistic fiction*
Jacob	Late Letter Name–Alphabetic *Short Vowel*	Primer	14	Fluent Level 3	Sports Animals *Fantasy*
Rosy	Late Letter Name–Alphabetic *Digraphs*	Grade 1	18	Fluent Level 4	Dance Sea creatures *Fantasy*
Maggie	Late Letter Name–Alphabetic *Short Vowel*	Grade 1	16	Fluent Level 4	Sea creatures Space *Realistic fiction*
Nicholas	Early Within-Word Pattern *Long Vowel (CVCE)*	Grade 3	30	Fluent Level 3	Countries Maps Animals *Nonfiction*
Noah	Early Within-Word Pattern *Long Vowel (CVCE)*	Grade 1	10	Fluent Level 3	Sports Sea creatures *Nonfiction*
Ben	Early Within-Word Pattern *Long Vowel*	Grade 3	20	Nonfluent Level 2	Sports Computers *Nonfiction*
Abby	Early Within-Word Pattern *Long Vowel (CVCE)*	Primer	12	Nonfluent Level 2	Sports Animals *Fantasy*
Jordan	Early Within-Word Pattern *Long Vowel (CVCE)*	Grade 3	30	Fluent Level 4	Sea creatures Animals *Realistic fiction*
Alexandra	Early Within-Word Pattern *Long Vowel (CVCE)*	Grade 3	28	Fluent Level 3	*Realistic fiction*
Julia	Late Letter Name–Alphabetic *Digraphs*	Grade 3	18	Fluent Level 3	Sea creatures Animals *Nonfiction*

Mr. Waverly then used a literacy assessment correlation chart (see Exhibit 6.2; also presented in Appendix C.3) to correlate the information from the various assessments to determine the students' approximate instructional reading level and literacy stage of development.

The rest of this chapter describes how Mr. Waverly gathered and interpreted this information and used it to plan his reading instruction.

EXHIBIT 6.2 Literacy assessment correlation chart.

GRADE LEVEL	DEVELOPMENTAL SPELLING LEVEL (QSI)	WORD RECOGNITION (WRI)	TEXT LEVEL (DRA2+)	TEXT LEVEL (FOUNTAS & PINNELL)	LITERACY STAGE
K	Emergent	n/a	A,1	A	Emergent
K.5			2	B	
1.0	Early Letter Name–Alphabetic	Preprimer 1	3	C	
1.1		Preprimer 2	4	D	
1.2	Middle Letter Name–Alphabetic	Preprimer 3	6–8	E	Early
1.4	Late Letter Name–Alphabetic	Primer	10	F	
1.5	Late Letter Name–Alphabetic		12	G	
1.7	Early Within-Word Pattern	Grade 1	14	H	
1.8			16	I	
2.0	Middle Within-Word Pattern	Grade 2	18	J	Transitional
2.3			20	K	
2.6	Late Within-Word Pattern		24	L	
2.9			28	M	
3.0		Grade 3	30	N	
3.3	Early Syllables & Affixes		34	O	
3.6			38	P	
4.0		Grade 4			
4.3			40	Q	
4.6	Middle Syllables & Affixes			R	Self-Extending
				S	
4.8			44	T	
5.0		Grade 5		U	
5.3	Late Syllables & Affixes		50	V	
5.6				W	
6.0		Grade 6	60	X	
6.5				Y	
7.0	Early Derivational Relations	Grade 7	70	Z	
7.3					
7.6					
8+		Grade 8	80		

ASSESSMENT 1: QUALITATIVE SPELLING INVENTORY

Mr. Waverly started his assessment collection with a qualitative spelling inventory taken from *Words Their Way* (Bear, Invernizzi, Templeton, & Johnston, 2012). This assessment, introduced in Chapter 5, is easily conducted with the whole class in a short period of time, so Mr. Waverly felt that it would be the logical first assessment for the first week of school. The QSI provides insight into each student's knowledge of how words work, which may predict the ability to decode new words. As a result, a student's spelling stage often correlates loosely to the student's stage of reading development (Bear et al., 2012). Therefore, Mr. Waverly can use this data as one piece of information to guide his choice of the level of text to begin assessing his students' reading ability, as will be discussed later in this chapter. Exhibit 6.3 describes the various levels of spelling development represented on this spelling inventory.

Description of spelling stages (Bear et al., 2012).   **EXHIBIT 6.3**

SPELLING STAGE (TYPICAL GRADE RANGE)	DESCRIPTION	EXAMPLE	
		WORD	STUDENT APPROXIMATION
Emergent (Pre-K–Grade 1)	Children in this stage may scribble, write random letters, or represent words with a single letter/sound.	cat	c
		dog	D
Letter Name–Alphabetic (K–Grade 2)	Children write words by representing sounds with letters. This starts with initial, dominant, and final consonants and then incorporates vowel representations.	cat	ct
			cat
		boat	bt
			bot
		sheep	sep
			shep
Within-Word Pattern (Grades 1–4)	Children in this stage start to use vowel patterns when spelling words. It is not uncommon for learners to overgeneralize patterns and confuse the application of certain spelling combinations.	deer or dear	der
			dere
		make	mak
			maik
		wait	wate
		drink	jrenk
Syllables and Affixes (Grades 3–7)	Students in this stage spell most short and long vowel patterns correctly. However, these students often need instruction in spelling multi-syllabic words, specifically with prefixes, suffixes, doubling consonants, and vowels at the syllable break.	flapping	flapping
		visitor	visiter
		action	actshun
Derivational Relations (Grade 4–Adult)	Spellers in this stage write primarily with conventional spellings. Errors, although rarely made, are the result of misunderstanding the relationship of prefixes and suffixes to the base of a word.	soften	soffen
		pneumonia	numonia
		comparable	compareable

EXHIBIT 6.4) Example analysis of Nicholas's spelling inventory.

Name: Nicholas   Grade: 1st

WORD	EMERGENT	ALPHABETIC	WITHIN-WORD PATTERN	SYLLABLES + AFFIXES	DERIVATIONAL RELATIONS
1. fan	✓	✓			
2. pet	✓	✓			
• • •					
10. shine			✓		
11. dream			grem		
• • •					
24. tries			thris		
• • •					

Words Spelled Correctly: 9/26   Spelling Stage: Early Within-Word Pattern

Nicholas misspelled two blends in words. He is working in the Early Within-Word Pattern stage.

The QSI itself took 20 minutes to conduct, and then Mr. Waverly took the inventories home to analyze. Throughout this chapter we will use Nicholas, one of Mr. Waverly's students, as the example. Exhibit 6.4 shows an example of a simplified analysis of Nicholas's spelling inventory, and a blank form is provided in Appendix B.8. See *Words Their Way* (Bear, Invernizzi, Templeton, & Johnston, 2012) for the Primary Spelling Inventory Feature Guide, the tool Mr. Waverly used in his analysis of his students' spelling. Because Nicholas misspelled two blends in words, he is considered to be working in the Early Within-Word Pattern stage of spelling (refer back to Exhibit 6.3).

ASSESSMENT 2: WORD RECOGNITION

fter analyzing the spelling inventory, Mr. Waverly met with each student individually to administer his district's word recognition assessment, a word recognition inventory based on the Dolch graded word lists. Since

Mr. Waverly was working with individuals, he made sure that the other children were fully engaged in their literacy center work before he began; this allowed him to meet with several students each day for about one week. He used the spelling inventory he administered earlier to select the word list to start with for each child. Since each spelling level corresponds to a grade-level reading equivalent (see Exhibit 6.3), Mr. Waverly selected the list that correlated with the beginning level of each child's spelling level grade range. For example, Nicholas's spelling stage was Early Within-Word Pattern (Exhibit 6.1). This developmental spelling stage is "typical" in grades 1 through 4 (Exhibit 6.3) and correlates with a grade 1 reading level (Exhibit 6.2). Therefore, Mr. Waverly began by asking Nicholas to read the grade 1 word list. Nicholas was very successful, reading all of the words accurately, in fact, Mr. Waverly was surprised to see that Nicholas accurately and quickly read the words through the grade 3 word list (Exhibit 6.5).

The correlation between the assessments is not always perfect, so Mr. Waverly used the spelling assessment as a starting point and adjusted by selecting additional reading lists depending on each student's performance. This means that when a student read one list successfully, Mr. Waverly asked the student to read the next higher grade-level list. Nicholas was able to read 38 (or 95 percent) of the words on the grade 3 word list accurately.

> **EXHIBIT 6.5**
>
> Nicholas's word recognition assessment.
>
> **Third Grade Dolch Sight Word List Assessment**
>
> | | | |
> |---|---|---|
> | about ✓ | grow ✓ | own ✓ |
> | better ✓ | hold ✓ | pick ✓ |
> | bring ✓ | hot ✓ | seven ✓ |
> | carry ✓ | hurt ✓ | shall ✓ |
> | clean ✓ | if ✓ | show ✓ |
> | cut ✓ | keep ✓ | six ✓ |
> | done ✓ | kind ✓ | small ✓ |
> | draw ✓ | laugh l-a-g | start ✓ |
> | drink ✓ | light ✓ | ten ✓ |
> | eight ✓ | long ✓ | today ✓ |
> | fall ✓ | much ✓ | together ✓ |
> | far ✓ | myself m-m- | try ✓ |
> | full ✓ | never ✓ | warm ✓ |
> | got ✓ | only ✓ | |

ASSESSMENT 3: TEXT READING LEVEL

If a student can accurately and automatically read 70 percent or more of the words on a given word list, a text written at the correlating grade level should be manageable for the child to read (Leslie & Caldwell, 2011). In fact, with context clues or pictures in a text, a child who successfully reads a certain graded list would likely be able to read a book written at or even above the next higher grade level. Therefore, the word recognition assessment provided another piece of information to help Mr. Waverly decide what text level to use as a beginning point for assessing each child's overall reading and comprehension ability.

Based on the results from the word recognition assessment for each child, Mr. Waverly selected a book from the benchmark text reading level assessment used in his school district (see Chapter 5). Mr. Waverly's district uses the *Developmental Reading Assessment, 2nd edition PLUS (DRA2+; Beaver & Carter, 2015)* for the purpose of assessing each student's text reading and comprehension ability. As mentioned above, Nicholas read the third-grade equivalent of the district's word recognition inventory at an acceptable (with at least 70 percent accuracy) level. This means he should be able to read text leveled at approximately *DRA2+* levels 38 through 44 successfully; this is the range equivalent to one grade level above his word-reading ability (see Exhibit 6.2). Mr. Waverly used the level 38 benchmark book because he predicted that Nicholas would be successful, based on his word-reading results. Nicholas did indeed read the level 38 book with 92 percent accuracy; however, Nicholas scored low on the comprehension portion of the *DRA2+* assessment, indicating that this particular level 38 book was not a good fit for Nicholas to read and comprehend. Next, Mr. Waverly chose a level 34 benchmark book to determine if Nicholas might demonstrate a higher level of comprehension. Nicholas read the second book with 94 percent accuracy and poor comprehension, indicating that level 34 may also be too difficult for Nicholas to read successfully.

As a result, Mr. Waverly asked Nicholas to read the level 30 benchmark text, which Nicholas read with 93 percent accuracy, misreading only 14 of the 207 words in the text. A sample of a running record for Nicholas's reading of the level 30 text is provided in Exhibit 6.6. Since Nicholas did not make an attempt to read the word *throughout*, Mr. Waverly read it to him and marked the text with *T* for told; this counts as one reading error. In the same line, Nicholas substituted the word *nice* for the word *trying*; this error seemed to make sense, but the words are not visually similar. As discussed in Chapter 5, by analyzing the words Nicholas reads differently from the words in the text, Mr. Waverly can determine which cue sources Nicholas uses: semantic, syntactic, or visual (see Exhibit 6.7).

Since Nicholas made relatively few uncorrected errors, and most of his errors made sense in the context of the text, Mr. Waverly deduced that Nicholas

---

EXHIBIT   6.6   Sample of Mr. Waverly's running record of Nicholas's reading.

Page 4

Throughout the summer, Annie had been trying ~ *nice*

to talk Lia into joining the Blasters. Now Lia, who *WOW*

used a wheelchair, was happy she could help

the team.

Annie leaned over to hug her friend. "Oh, Lia!" she *lended*

said. "I'm so excited!"

After practice, Annie, Lia, and their friend Nick *playing*

walked home together.

		EXHIBIT 6.7

Analysis of Nicholas's running record for the cue sources he uses.

TEXT	STUDENT RESPONSE	EXPLANATION
Throughout	No response; Nicholas sat silently.	The teacher told Nicholas the word and marked the word with T. This counts as one error.
trying	nice	When Nicholas read the sentence, he predicted the word *nice* would fit: "Throughout the summer, Annie had been nice." This makes sense up to this point and even seems acceptable after finishing the sentence (semantic cue source). Still, the word *nice* does not look like the word *trying*, which indicates that Nicholas was not monitoring the visual information.
who	wow	Nicholas read, "Now Lia wow used a wheelchair…" This miscue does not make sense or sound right (semantic and syntactic cue sources).
leaned	lended	Nicholas read this sentence as "Annie lended to hug her friend." When he read "Annie lended," Mr. Waverly noticed that the sentence structure was incorrect and the word did not make sense in the context of the story (semantic and syntactic cue sources). Still, the word *lended* was visually similar to *leaned* (visual cue source).
over	This word was omitted and Nicholas read on.	Omitting the word *over* was not particularly disruptive to the story; however, it showed that Nicholas was not carefully monitoring the visual information in this sentence.
practice	playing	This substitution makes sense, fits the sentence structure, and is visually similar to the word in the text (semantic, syntactic, and visual cue sources).

was understanding the text. Nicholas answered the comprehension questions, provided with the *DRA2+* text, following the reading (Exhibit 6.8). Mr. Waverly recorded some of Nicholas's oral responses on the form when Nicholas seemed to lose the ability to focus on the questions because it took him so long to write his responses. Nicholas demonstrated adequate comprehension on the level 30 text, scoring at the instructional level for comprehension according to the rubric provided with the text (Exhibit 6.9, p. 113). As a result, Mr. Waverly recorded this level as Nicholas's instructional reading level in the data table (Exhibit 6.1).

ASSESSMENT 4: ORAL READING FLUENCY

M r. Waverly's primary responsibility during the text level assessment was to record each student's text reading and comprehension for later analysis. He also recorded brief notes about each student's fluency, using the NAEP Oral Reading Fluency Scale (explained in Chapter 5) as a framework. Once he determined a student's instructional reading level, he completed the Oral Reading Fluency Scale (ORFS) for that text and recorded it in his data

EXHIBIT 6.8 Sample of Nicholas's *DRA2+* comprehension assessment.

| Student Booklet | *The Blasters* | Page 2 |

AFTER READING

SUMMARY

Write a summary of this story in your own words. Include the important characters, events, and details from the beginning, middle, and end of the story. You may use the book and the words below to help you write your summary.

In the beginning, Lia founed her ferened.

Next, The team woked hor toether!

Then, nik got hert!

After that, the team got rede to play!

In the end, The to team's got tide.

| Student Booklet | *The Blasters* | Page 3 |

You may use the book to answer the following questions.

LITERAL COMPREHENSION

List 3 things that Coach Dave said in his pep talk to the team.

Coach Dave's Pep Talk
1 Try your best.
2 Have fun!
3 Work together

INTERPRETATION

Why do you think Nick got so angry during the game? thay wunnot yeting soors!

REFLECTION

What do you think is the most important message in this story? Try your best, winning isn't the most important thing. Just have fun!

Tell why you think this message is important. Because it is good to try your best

Reread what you have written to make sure your answers are the way you want them before you hand in your booklet.

table (Exhibit 6.1). While Nicholas read the level 30 text, he grouped the words into meaningful phrases and responded appropriately to the punctuation on the page. He read at a natural pace, but his reading lacked expression. As a result, Mr. Waverly recorded Nicholas's fluency at a level 3 on the ORFS (Exhibit 6.10, p. 114).

ASSESSMENT 5: INTEREST INVENTORY

The first-grade team in Mr. Waverly's school collaborated to create an interest inventory they could use with their students (Exhibit 6.11; see Appendix B.6 for a blank form), which Mr. Waverly also administered at the beginning of the school year. This simple questionnaire required students to rate certain topics (e.g., sea creatures, sports) on a scale with a sad face, a neutral face, or a happy face. In addition, Mr. Waverly closely observed students during independent reading time, when they were able to self-select books to

	Nicholas's *DRA2+* comprehension rubric.	**EXHIBIT 6.9**

Student: Nicholas   Date: October 20

COMPREHENSION	INTERVENTION	INSTRUCTIONAL	INDEPENDENT	ADVANCED	SCORE
Use of text features	**1** Very little or no description of the setting and character(s)	**2** Partial description of the setting and character(s); general statements	**3** Accurate description of setting and character(s) with some specific details	**4** Effective description of setting and character(s) with specific details	1
Questioning/ prediction	**1** Unrelated predictions or no response	**2** At least 1 reasonable prediction related to the text	**3** At least 2 reasonable predictions that go beyond the text read aloud	**4** Three thoughtful predictions that go beyond the text read aloud	3
Scaffolded summary	**1** 1–2 events in own language and/or copied text; may include incorrect text	**2** Partial summary; generally in own language; some important characters/ events; may include misinterpretations	**3** Summary in own language; includes most of the important characters' names, some details, and many of the important events in sequence from the beginning, middle, and end	**4** Well-organized summary in own language; includes all important characters' names, specific details, and all important events from the beginning, middle, and end	2
Literal comprehension	**1** Little information from the text and/or incorrect information	**2** Partial information from the text; may include misinterpretation	**3** Information from the text that accurately responds to question(s) or prompt(s)	**4** All important information from the text that effectively responds to question(s) or prompt(s).	4
Interpretation	**1** Limited or no understanding of important text implication(s)	**2** Partial understanding of important text implication(s); little or no detail	**3** Understands important text implication(s); relevant supporting details	**4** Insightful understanding of important text implication(s); important supporting details	2
Reflection	**1** Insignificant or unrelated message or event, no reason for opinion or no response	**2** Less significant message or event and general reason(s) for opinion	**3** Significant message or event and a relevant reason for opinion	**4** Significant message or event and reason(s) for opinion that reflect higher-level thinking	2
Score	6 7 8 9 10 11	12 13 14 15 16	17 18 19 20 21 22	23 24	14

browse. He recorded each child's topics of interest, along with the genres each seemed to favor, in the data table (Exhibit 6.1). Mr. Waverly will use this information when he forms his small groups and selects texts for the students to read during small-group lessons. He believes that if he selects texts on topics that interest his students, they will be motivated to read the books.

EXHIBIT 6.10 (Nicholas's performance on the Oral Reading Fluency Scale.

Student: Nicholas   Date: Sept. 20

Fluent	Level 4	Reads primarily in larger, meaningful phrase groups. Although some regressions, repetitions, and deviations from text may be present, these do not appear to detract from the overall structure of the story. Preservation of the author's syntax is consistent. Some or most of the story is read with expressive interpretation.	
	Level 3	Reads primarily in three- or four-word phrase groups. Some small groupings may be present. However, the majority of phrasing seems appropriate and preserves the syntax of the author. Little or no expressive interpretation is present.	X
Nonfluent	Level 2	Reads primarily in two-word phrases with some three- or four-word groupings. Some word-by-word reading may be present. Word groupings may seem awkward and unrelated to larger context of the sentence or passage.	
	Level 1	Reads primarily word by word. Occasional two-word or three-word phrases may occur, but these are infrequent and/or they do not preserve meaningful syntax.	

EXHIBIT 6.11

Nicholas's interest inventory.

Name Nicholas   Date 9/7

Interest Inventory

How much do you like each topic?

	☺	☺	☹
animals	X		
sea creatures		X	
sports		X	
space			X
countries around the world	X		
plant life			X
computers		X	
weather			X
trucks and cars		X	

What is your favorite sport? Soccer
What is your favorite animal? dog
What is your favorite book? Owen

ANALYZING AND USING THE ASSESSMENT DATA

A s he finished the data table shown in Exhibit 6.1, Mr. Waverly noticed the wide range of instructional reading levels represented in his class. One student in his class had an instructional reading level of 6 (*DRA2+*), three read at an instructional level of 30 (*DRA2+*), and the remaining students read at various levels in between. Mr. Waverly summarized this information in the graph displayed in Exhibit 6.12.

Next, Mr. Waverly discussed the range of reading levels represented in his class with Mrs. Jones. She reminded him to be cautious in his conclusions, since the results provide only a limited view of each child's reading ability. In other words, Mr. Waverly should use all of the baseline data that he collected only as a starting point for grouping and instruction. Once he begins to teach the students during small-group instruction, Mr. Waverly will frequently conduct informal and formal assessments so that he can monitor each student's developmental progress. This will provide Mr. Waverly with the information he needs to change instructional groupings as needed throughout the year, so that he can meet the specific needs of each student.

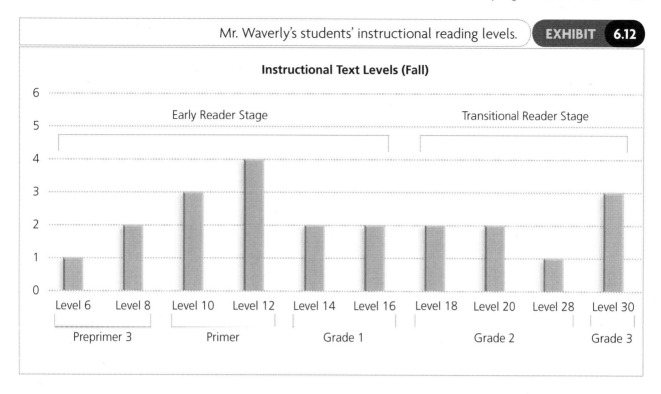

Mr. Waverly's students' instructional reading levels.   EXHIBIT 6.12

Planning for Whole-Class Reading Instruction

Because the students are varied in their strengths, needs, and interests, Mr. Waverly's class is described as a *heterogeneous* group; that is, the group is made up of children of mixed ability in reading and writing. Knowing the approximate stage of literacy development of each child is important; however, Mr. Waverly does need to make decisions about what to teach to *all* learners during whole-class reading lessons. When Mrs. Jones and Mr. Waverly compared the instructional reading levels in Exhibit 6.12 to the literacy assessment correlation chart shown in Exhibit 6.2, they noticed that the majority of Mr. Waverly's class (14 students) seems to be composed of early readers (i.e., DRA2+ levels 6–16); the remaining eight students seem to be in the transitional phase of literacy development (levels 18–40). Just over half of the class is reading at grade level (levels 6–16), and the remainder of the children are reading above grade level for the beginning of first grade.

Mr. Waverly will be sure to model teaching points that are appropriate for early and transitional learners (Exhibit 1.2) and based on the CCSS during his whole-group lessons, such as during the interactive read-aloud and shared reading each day (see Chapter 2 for brief descriptions of these literacy activities). He will also use the data from his interest inventory to select high-interest texts for these lessons. For example, since many students indicated an interest in animals and/or sea creatures, Mr. Waverly will select nonfiction books on these topics when he teaches his units on text features and text structures of informational texts. He also has noticed that most of the class did not choose mysteries as a genre they liked. To increase their familiarity with and interest in this genre,

Mr. Waverly is planning to conduct a genre study on mysteries during the time slotted for interactive read-aloud each day. He will start with the Cam Jansen series, by David A. Adler, because the characters are relatable and the simple stories allow the students to identify characteristics of the mystery genre easily.

When he selects texts for some whole-class instructional activities, such as interactive read-aloud, Mr. Waverly will not need to be concerned about meeting the reading level of all of his students since he will read the text to the students. He often selects texts that are complex enough to address the grade-level standards. However, when selecting a text for other activities, such as shared reading, during which students often read along, Mr. Waverly often chooses texts at a level where most of the students can read many of the words. Teachers may also choose texts that are slightly above the level of most students in the class, since the group reads the text together, which allows the teacher—and some students—to lend support if a word poses difficulty for certain students. After considering the range of instructional levels in his class (Exhibit 6.12), Mr. Waverly decided it would be best to select books in the range of *DRA2+* levels 12 through 18 for most of his shared reading lessons. Of course, he can choose books outside of this range, if necessary. For example, he may select a higher-level text and read more of it to the students if the book fits his teaching point better than a lower-level text.

Planning for Differentiated Reading Instruction

Once Mrs. Jones and Mr. Waverly discussed the assessment data in terms of whole-class reading instruction, they looked at the data for each child. Exhibit 6.13 is taken from the original data chart (Exhibit 6.1) to illustrate how Mr. Waverly recorded Nicholas's scores. From the data, it is clear that Nicholas can read and comprehend text well above grade level. Beginning first-graders typically have an instructional reading level of *DRA2+* 6 through 10; *DRA2+* level 30 is approximately a third-grade reading level. As explained earlier, Nicholas's strength is that he reads for meaning with appropriate phrasing and fluency. His comprehension is generally good, though he could add more detail when answering comprehension questions. Mr. Waverly may place Nicholas in a group with Chad, Jordan, and Alexandra, because they read at nearly the same instructional level.

Still, Mr. Waverly will need to consider the skills and strategies for which the children require additional support. For example, if Chad required support in fluency, he would not have been a good fit in a group with Nicholas, who is a fluent reader. However, Chad *is* a fluent reader (level 4), so this was not an issue. In addition, Mr. Waverly will need to consider the genre and topic that would fit the students best when he determines his grouping arrangements. Nicholas enjoys books about other countries, as well as books about animals. Although he prefers nonfiction texts, Mr. Waverly will likely choose other types of texts to round out Nicholas's reading repertoire. This type of grouping arrangement is considered homogeneous, because the group members share similar needs. Small-group lessons, such as guided reading, are typically conducted with homogeneous groups so that the teacher can focus the instruction on the specific developmental needs of the group members.

STUDENT	QUALITATIVE SPELLING INVENTORY (QSI)	WORD RECOGNITION INVENTORY (WRI)	BENCHMARK TEXT READING INSTRUCTIONAL LEVEL *(DRA2+)*	NAEP ORAL READING FLUENCY SCALE	INTEREST INVENTORY/ OBSERVATIONS
Nicholas	Early Within-Word Pattern *Long Vowel (CVCE)*	Grade 3	30	Fluent Level 3	Countries Maps Animals *Nonfiction*

Nicholas's assessment scores.   **EXHIBIT 6.13**

HETEROGENEOUS VERSUS HOMOGENEOUS GROUPS

Most classrooms are composed of heterogeneous groups of children; this means that the students have different ability levels and interests. In this section, the term *ability* refers to students' instructional reading level. Since whole-class reading lessons (i.e., shared reading, interactive read-aloud) are based on grade-level curriculum, they are delivered to the heterogeneous group. However, heterogeneous grouping is not limited to whole-class instruction. Students can be grouped with others of varying ability for independent application activities, such as literacy centers. Literature circles present another opportunity for students to work with peers with varying reading levels; if texts are chosen that all students in the group can read and comprehend, rich discussions can take place with all members of the group participating. See Chapter 4 for explanations of literacy centers and literature circles.

The above paragraph provides examples of independent activities that allow students to work in heterogeneous groups. It is also possible for teachers to group children of different ability to work on specific areas of need. For example, five children in Mr. Waverly's classroom—Michael, Hadley, Katelyn, Ben, and Abby—require work on fluency, so he may group the children together to provide a mini-lesson on reading words in phrases. This would require each child to bring an instructional-level text to the table for practice. Some observers would label this group as homogeneous, in the sense that all participants share a specific need (fluency instruction).

For the most part, teachers group children homogeneously based on instructional reading level for small-group differentiated instruction. This allows teachers to instruct students near their zones of proximal development, where the most effective learning takes place (Vygotsky, 1978). However, as explained in the case of the fluency grouping, instructional reading level is not the only condition for grouping; students with similar needs (e.g., focus on vocabulary, fluency, or comprehension) and similar instructional reading level may be grouped together, so that the teacher can tailor lessons and meet the students' specific needs.

Students learn at different rates, so it stands to reason that individual participants in reading groups will not progress simultaneously. Group membership, therefore, is not static. For example, Nicholas may improve in comprehension more quickly than the other members of his group. Since he previously demonstrated the ability to read words in higher-level text, once he can also demonstrate comprehension at a higher level, Nicholas will be ready to read more challenging texts. If the other members of his group are not ready for such a move, Mr. Waverly may meet with Nicholas individually to engage in deeper conversations based on appropriately complex texts. Effective teachers move their students to new groups as frequently as needed to fit their developmental needs (Wilkinson & Townsend, 2000).

CONCLUSION

Effective teachers conduct various assessments in the first four to six weeks of each academic year, quite like Mr. Waverly did. Although the specific assessments will vary across grade levels and school districts, the intent is generally the same: to collect enough data to inform instruction. In reading, this means that teachers need to conduct developmentally appropriate assessments that provide insight into students' word-level competencies (i.e., decoding and word identification) and text-level competencies (i.e., comprehension and fluency). Once the assessment data is collected, the teacher can analyze the data to determine grouping arrangements for small-group lessons and to select texts for the whole class and small groups. This data can also inform teachers about the focus of instruction, which will be discussed in the next chapter.

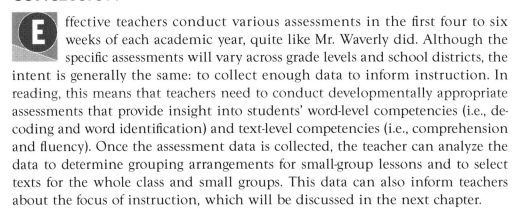

Practical Application

1. Use the data in Exhibit 6.1 and the information in Exhibit 6.2 (literacy assessment correlation chart) to answer the following question: Based on Anna's instructional reading level, which students are similar to her in reading level and correlated phase of literacy development?

2. Imagine that Exhibit 6.1 is your data chart. How would you group the students? Create the groups by listing the names of the members in each group, and for each group explain why you placed the students together.

3. What generalization can you draw about the spelling knowledge of most of the children in Mr. Waverly's class? Use the information in Exhibit 6.1 to support your answer.

Recommended Resources

For a more complete discussion of running record analysis, refer to the following resources:

Clay, M. (2000). *Running records for classroom teachers.* Portsmouth, NH: Heinemann.

Gunther, J. Ongoing assessment for reading: Running records, www.learnnc. org/lp/editions/readassess/1.0

Reading A–Z, https://www.readinga-z.com/helpful-tools/about-running-records/

Reading and Writing Project, http://readingandwritingproject.org/resources/ assessments/running-records

Reading Recovery, http://readingrecovery.clemson.edu/index.php/reading/ formative-assessment

Teacher Sites, http://teachersites.schoolworld.com/webpages/JD'Ippolito/files/ running%20records.pdf

REFERENCES

Bear, D. R., Invernizzi, M., Templeton, S.R., & Johnston, F. (2012). *Words their way: Word study for phonics, vocabulary, and spelling instruction* (5th ed.). Upper Saddle River, NJ: Pearson.

Beaver, J., & Carter, M. A. (2015). *Developmental Reading Assessment, 2nd edition PLUS*. Upper Saddle River, NJ: Pearson.

Leslie, L., & Caldwell, J. (2011). *Qualitative Reading Inventory–5*. Boston: Pearson/Allyn & Bacon.

Vygotsky, L. S. (1978). *Mind in society: The development of higher psychological processes*. Cambridge, MA: Harvard University Press.

Wilkinson, A. G., & Townsend, M. A. R. (2000). From Rata to Rimu: Grouping for instruction in best practice New Zealand classrooms. *The Reading Teacher, 53* (6), 460–471.

Planning the Lesson Focus

s. Shaw: Veronica, tell us about one connection you had with a character in this chapter.

Veronica: I moved here last year, and Opal is living in a new town. It can be lonely when you don't have friends yet.

Ms. Shaw: So you could really understand how lonely Opal felt? How did that help you understand her character or the plot?

Veronica: Well, since Opal was lonely, I think she really wanted to keep Winn-Dixie. That's why she worked so hard to keep him. That's why she talked her dad into him!

The above transcript represents a portion of a text discussion from one of Ms. Shaw's small-group reading lessons. The focus of the discussion is the assigned book *Because of Winn-Dixie*. Ms. Shaw just started teaching fifth grade; she was hired at the same time as Mr. Waverly, the first-grade teacher who was introduced in Chapter 4. Like Mr. Waverly, Ms. Shaw has benefited from Mrs. Jones's experience and mentoring. Once her assessments were complete, Ms. Shaw met with Mrs. Jones for help in forming her instructional reading groups. As the year progressed, Ms. Shaw learned to plan small-group lessons based on the students' needs and interests, as indicated by assessments. The focus of this chapter will be the various factors that teachers consider when determining the content and structure of small-group differentiated reading lessons. Specifically, we will look closely at how Ms. Shaw grouped her students, what she taught them during a sample week, and why she made these decisions.

Just like all of the teachers discussed in previous chapters, Ms. Shaw began collecting assessment data at the beginning of the school year. As mentioned before, assessment is a critical first step in good teaching. Exhibit 7.1 illustrates Ms. Shaw's data table; see Chapters 5 and 6 for an explanation of each assessment and its use. In her chart, Ms. Shaw uses various colors to indicate the current grouping arrangements for reading instruction; these will be explained later in the chapter. (In Exhibit 7.1 the groups' colors are labeled since the chart is reproduced in black and white.)

EXHIBIT 7.1 Ms. Shaw's data table.

STUDENT NAME	QSI	INSTRUCTIONAL READING LEVEL (DRA 2+)	WRI (AREA OF NEED)	COMPREHENSION RUBRIC (OVERALL)	NAEP ORAL READING FLUENCY SCALE	INTEREST INVENTORY
[THE YELLOW GROUP]						
Gabriella	Within-Word Pattern	24	Decoding multi-syllabic words	Instructional	Nonfluent Level 2	Historical fiction Animals
Sarah	Within-Word Pattern	30	Decoding multi-syllabic words	Advanced	Fluent Level 3	Animals Realistic fiction
Wade	Within-Word Pattern	30	Decoding multi-syllabic words	Instructional	Fluent Level 3	Sports fiction Sports biography

Continued.   **EXHIBIT   7.1**

[THE BLUE GROUP]						
Samantha	Within-Word Pattern	38	Proficient	Advanced	Fluent Level 4	Sports Historical fiction
Charlie	Syllables & Affixes	40	Proficient	Independent	Fluent Level 4	Historical fiction Biography
Veronica	Within-Word Pattern	40	Proficient	Instructional	Fluent Level 3	Nonfiction Biography
Liam	Within-Word Pattern	40	Proficient	Instructional	Fluent Level 3	Historical fiction Biography
Marlee	Syllables & Affixes	44	Proficient	Instructional	Fluent Level 4	Biography Historical fiction
[THE ORANGE GROUP]						
Max	Within-Word Pattern	44	Proficient	Advanced	Fluent Level 4	Airplanes/flying Sports
Lily	Syllables & Affixes	44	Proficient	Advanced	Fluent Level 4	Nonfiction Sports
Julia	Syllables & Affixes	50	Proficient	Independent	Fluent Level 3	None
Ellie	Syllables & Affixes	50	Proficient	Independent	Fluent Level 3	Realistic fiction Animals
Josh	Syllables & Affixes	50	Proficient	Independent	Fluent Level 4	None
Ben T.	Syllables & Affixes	50	Proficient	Independent	Fluent Level 3	Realistic fiction Sports
[THE WHITE GROUP]						
Connor	Syllables & Affixes	50	Proficient	Instructional	Fluent Level 3	Realistic fiction Space
Ben M.	Derivational Relations	50	Proficient	Instructional	Fluent Level 3	Realistic fiction Animals
Emma	Syllables & Affixes	50	Proficient	Instructional	Fluent Level 4	Fantasy Historical fiction
Skylar	Syllables & Affixes	60	Proficient	Instructional	Fluent Level 3	Realistic fiction Space/universe
Myranda	Derivational Relations	60	Proficient	Instructional	Fluent Level 3	Fantasy Realistic fiction
Tia	Syllables & Affixes	60	Proficient	Instructional	Fluent Level 3	Fantasy
[THE GREEN GROUP]						
Jacob	Syllables & Affixes	50	Proficient	Advanced	Fluent Level 4	Realistic fiction Fantasy
Mari	Derivational Relations	50	Proficient	Instructional	Fluent Level 4	Realistic fiction
Harrison	Derivational Relations	60	Proficient	Independent	Fluent Level 4	Sports
Derek	Derivational Relations	70	Proficient	Independent	Fluent Level 4	Prehistoric life Fantasy
Mark	Syllables & Affixes	70	Proficient	Advanced	Fluent Level 4	Fantasy
Anna	Derivational Relations	70	Proficient	Advanced	Fluent Level 4	Realistic fiction

CLASSROOM PROFILE

s. Shaw organized her data table according to ability so that she could easily see the full range of reading levels in her classroom. To do this, she considered the students' instructional reading level, comprehension level, and performance in oral reading fluency. Average fifth-graders are expected to read at *DRA2+* level 44 at the beginning of the school year and *DRA2+* level 50 at the end of the school year (Exhibit 7.2). Ms. Shaw noted that the majority of the students in her class were categorized as self-extending readers, according to her assessments; this is exactly where fifth-graders are expected to be in their literacy development (see Exhibit 7.2, extracted from Exhibit 6.2 on p. 106). This is important, because whole-class lessons are designed to meet grade-level standards and curriculum. However, as in Mrs. Jones's class, the assessment results also revealed that several students are categorized as "below grade level" readers, and several other students are categorized as "above grade level" readers. This is the reason that Ms. Shaw, like all other teachers, needs to differentiate her instruction through small-group lessons.

Through carefully executed small-group reading lessons, Ms. Shaw can provide extra support in literacy development for the students who read below the expected level for their grade; she can also provide enrichment for the students who read beyond the expected level. Further, Ms. Shaw can provide additional support for those reading at grade level, deepening their understanding of reading skills and strategies and helping them move to the next stage of literacy development.

GROUPING STUDENTS

nce Ms. Shaw listed her students by reading ability, she decided how to group the students for small-group instruction. As mentioned, she uses various colors to indicate the five different reading groups.

The Yellow Group

Instructional reading level (i.e., the *DRA2+* level at which the student can read with 90 to 94 percent accuracy and good comprehension) is one key consideration; it is, however, not the only consideration in planning reading groups. If Ms. Shaw considered only instructional reading level, for example, the Yellow Group would consist of only two students, Sarah and Wade, and Gabriella

EXHIBIT 7.2	Grade-level expectations for Ms. Shaw's class.				
GRADE LEVEL	**DEVELOPMENTAL SPELLING LEVEL**	**WORD RECOGNITION**	**TEXT LEVEL (DRA2+)**	**TEXT LEVEL (FOUNTAS & PINNELL)**	**LITERACY STAGE**
5.0	Middle Syllables & Affixes	Grade 5	44	T	Self-Extending
				U	
5.3	Late Syllables & Affixes		50	V	
5.6				W	

		The Yellow Group.				EXHIBIT 7.3
STUDENT NAME	QSI	INSTRUCTIONAL READING LEVEL (DRA 2+)	WRI (AREA OF NEED)	COMPREHENSION RUBRIC (OVERALL)	NAEP ORAL READING FLUENCY SCALE	INTEREST INVENTORY
Gabriella	Within-Word Pattern	24	Decoding multi-syllabic words	Instructional	NonFluent Level 2	Historical fiction Animals
Sarah	Within-Word Pattern	30	Decoding multi-syllabic words	Advanced	Fluent Level 3	Animals Realistic fiction
Wade	Within-Word Pattern	30	Decoding multi-syllabic words	Instructional	Fluent Level 3	Sports fiction Sports biography

would have to meet with Ms. Shaw alone (Exhibit 7.3). However, both level 24 and level 30 indicate that students are transitional learners (see Exhibit 6.2, p. 106), and Sarah, Wade, and Gabriella all need additional support with decoding multisyllabic words and fluency. In addition, Gabriella is an English learner. Ms. Shaw knew that Gabriella would have opportunities to practice conversational English through meaningful text discussions with this group of transitional readers. Therefore, Ms. Shaw grouped these students together.

The Blue Group

Ms. Shaw placed five students together in the Blue Group (Exhibit 7.4). The members of this group represent three different *DRA2+* text levels, ranging from level 38 to level 44. Still, Ms. Shaw placed these students together because they all demonstrated proficiency in word recognition (i.e., accurate word reading and good decoding skills) and comprehension at their diagnosed text reading level. Further, all of the students indicated that they enjoyed reading historical fiction, biographies, or both. This will make it easy to find books that will interest all five students during the small-group lessons. In addition, none of these students indicated on their interest inventory that they read fantasy books. Since Ms. Shaw is planning a whole-class unit on this genre, she believes she may need to provide extra support during that unit for these five students, and grouping them together will make that easier to accomplish. One member of the group, Marlee, demonstrated an instructional reading level of 44, similar to the students in the Orange Group, described below; however, her comprehension was scored at the instructional level (i.e., adequate comprehension) on the comprehension rubric, whereas the members of the Orange Group demonstrated stronger overall comprehension (i.e., these students were identified at the independent and advanced levels on the comprehension rubric; see Exhibit 5.7). Marlee, like Gabriella, is an English learner. The school's English as a Second Language (ESL) specialist informed Ms. Shaw that Marlee is proficient in reading French, her first language. However, her comprehension lags a bit when she reads English because she often doesn't understand words with multiple meanings. As a result, Ms. Shaw placed her in the Blue Group, to provide slightly easier texts for Marlee until she builds her English vocabulary.

EXHIBIT 7.4	The Blue Group.

STUDENT NAME	QSI	INSTRUCTIONAL READING LEVEL (DRA 2+)	WRI (AREA OF NEED)	COMPREHENSION RUBRIC (OVERALL)	NAEP ORAL READING FLUENCY SCALE	INTEREST INVENTORY
Samantha	Within-Word Pattern	38	Proficient	Advanced	Fluent Level 4	Sports Historical fiction
Charlie	Syllables & Affixes	40	Proficient	Independent	Fluent Level 4	Historical fiction Biography
Veronica	Within-Word Pattern	40	Proficient	Instructional	Fluent Level 3	Nonfiction Biography
Liam	Within-Word Pattern	40	Proficient	Instructional	Fluent Level 3	Historical fiction Biography
Marlee	Syllables & Affixes	44	Proficient	Instructional	Fluent Level 4	Biography Historical fiction

The Orange Group

Ms. Shaw placed six students together to form the Orange Group (Exhibit 7.5). All six students read at DRA2+ level 44 or 50 at the instructional level and have independent or advanced comprehension scores on the comprehension rubric. Two members of the Orange Group, Julia and Josh, indicated on the interest inventory that they do not like to read, adding that they do not have a favorite genre. However, since Ms. Shaw knows that Julia plays soccer and Josh is an avid baseball player, she decides to select informational and realistic fiction books about sports for the first several texts, which should pique the interest of all of the readers in this particular group.

EXHIBIT 7.5	The Orange Group.

STUDENT NAME	QSI	INSTRUCTIONAL READING LEVEL (DRA 2+)	WRI (AREA OF NEED)	COMPREHENSION RUBRIC (OVERALL)	NAEP ORAL READING FLUENCY SCALE	INTEREST INVENTORY
Max	Within-Word Pattern	44	Proficient	Advanced	Fluent Level 4	Airplanes/flying Sports
Lily	Syllables & Affixes	44	Proficient	Advanced	Fluent Level 4	Nonfiction Sports
Julia	Syllables & Affixes	50	Proficient	Independent	Fluent Level 3	None
Ellie	Syllables & Affixes	50	Proficient	Independent	Fluent Level 3	Realistic fiction Animals
Josh	Syllables & Affixes	50	Proficient	Independent	Fluent Level 4	None
Ben T.	Syllables & Affixes	50	Proficient	Independent	Fluent Level 3	Realistic fiction Sports

The White Group

Ms. Shaw noticed that the six students in the White Group (Exhibit 7.6) all read slightly above grade level for the beginning of fifth grade, but all scored at the instructional level for comprehension on the comprehension rubric. Although "instructional level" indicates adequate comprehension, when Ms. Shaw took a closer look at each student's comprehension assessment, she noted that they scored at the intervention level for interpretation of the text (Exhibit 7.7). This meant that all of these students would benefit from additional support in drawing inferences. In addition, most of the students in this group indicated that they enjoy reading fantasy books or books about space. Ben M. listed realistic fiction and animals as his favorite types of books; however, because he is close friends with Emma, Ms. Shaw thought he would enjoy some exposure to fantasy books, as well. In addition, Ben M. may be able to share his expertise about animals and realistic fiction with the group when Ms. Shaw selects those types of books for the group to read.

The Green Group

The final group in Ms. Shaw's class is composed of her six strongest readers. All of the students in the Green Group (Exhibit 7.8) read above grade level, although

The White Group.   **EXHIBIT 7.6**

STUDENT NAME	QSI	INSTRUCTIONAL READING LEVEL (DRA 2+)	WRI (AREA OF NEED)	COMPREHENSION RUBRIC (OVERALL)	NAEP ORAL READING FLUENCY SCALE	INTEREST INVENTORY
Connor	Syllables & Affixes	50	Proficient	Instructional	Fluent Level 3	Realistic fiction Space
Ben M.	Derivational Relations	50	Proficient	Instructional	Fluent Level 3	Realistic fiction Animals
Emma	Syllables & Affixes	50	Proficient	Instructional	Fluent Level 4	Fantasy Historical fiction
Skylar	Syllables & Affixes	60	Proficient	Instructional	Fluent Level 3	Realistic fiction Space/universe
Myranda	Derivational Relations	60	Proficient	Instructional	Fluent Level 3	Fantasy Realistic fiction
Tia	Syllables & Affixes	60	Proficient	Instructional	Fluent Level 3	Fantasy

Interpretation component of the *DRA2+* comprehension rubric.   **EXHIBIT 7.7**

COMPREHENSION	INTERVENTION	INSTRUCTIONAL	INDEPENDENT	ADVANCED
Interpretation	1 Little or no understanding of important text implication(s)	2 Partial understanding of important text implication(s); little or no detail	3 Understands important text implication(s); relevant supporting details	4 Insightful understanding of important text implication(s); important supporting details

EXHIBIT 7.8 The Green Group.

STUDENT NAME	QSI	INSTRUCTIONAL READING LEVEL (DRA 2+)	WRI (AREA OF NEED)	COMPREHENSION RUBRIC (OVERALL)	NAEP ORAL READING FLUENCY SCALE	INTEREST INVENTORY
Jacob	Syllables & Affixes	50	Proficient	Advanced	Fluent Level 4	Realistic fiction Fantasy
Mari	Derivational Relations	50	Proficient	Instructional	Fluent Level 4	Realistic fiction
Harrison	Derivational Relations	60	Proficient	Independent	Fluent Level 4	Sports
Derek	Derivational Relations	70	Proficient	Independent	Fluent Level 4	Prehistoric life Fantasy
Mark	Syllables & Affixes	70	Proficient	Advanced	Fluent Level 4	Fantasy
Anna	Derivational Relations	70	Proficient	Advanced	Fluent Level 4	Realistic fiction

their instructional reading levels range from DRA2+ level 50 to level 70. Still, most of the students in this group read with excellent comprehension and fluency. Mari scored at the instructional level on the comprehension rubric, but because she has demonstrated her love of reading and a high level of confidence during whole-class reading activities, Ms. Shaw felt that she would work well with this group of students. Just to be sure, Ms. Shaw will choose realistic fiction texts (Mari's favorite genre) for the first couple of lessons, so that Mari can be engaged in a familiar style of reading. Also, Ms. Shaw will watch Mari closely during small-group lessons, to be sure she is comfortable with the books and the group members and is developing at nearly the same rate as the others.

Grouping Changes

It is important to note that membership in these groups is temporary. Since students learn at different rates, groups change as often as necessary. For example, Gabriella moved from the Yellow Group to the Blue Group during the course of the year. Ms. Shaw started teaching students in small groups in October, once the students were able to operate independently while she worked with each small group. By the end of November, Gabriella demonstrated proficiency in decoding multisyllabic words and could read at DRA2+ level 38 at the instructional level. Since the other members of the Yellow Group needed additional support with decoding, Ms. Shaw moved Gabriella into the Blue Group. Several other students were moved into different groups throughout the course of the year, so that by year's end, all of the groups were completely different from the chart provided in Exhibit 7.1.

DETERMINING LESSON FOCUS

As mentioned in Chapter 1, effective teachers differentiate the content of lessons (Tomlinson, 2000). There are various pieces of information to consider when planning content for small-group lessons; these fall into the categories of addressing students' developmental needs and addressing standards.

Addressing Developmental Needs

The primary consideration in planning content for small-group instruction is the developmental needs of the learners, that is, what the students are able to do in the group independently, and what they need to do next to progress in their development. Overall, the students in Ms. Shaw's room demonstrated competencies in two phases of development: transitional and self-extending. Exhibit 7.9 is an excerpt from Exhibit 1.2, listing the expected competencies (i.e., what the child can do) for students operating in each stage of development. It is likely that a student will demonstrate some, but not all, of the competencies listed in a phase. Competencies that a student does not meet are considered needs. For example, if a

---

Competencies of transitional and self-extending learners.   **EXHIBIT 7.9**

LITERACY STAGE: TRANSITIONAL

Typical Grades: 1–3

DRA2+ Levels: 18 to 40

Description: Readers at this stage are able to use various reading strategies independently. They are able to decode most words automatically and, therefore, can devote more attention to comprehension and fluency.

Learner Characteristics (reading)

- Asks questions before, during, and after reading
- Summarizes accurately with appropriate detail
- Cites evidence from text in summary and retell
- Describes character, setting, problem, and solution
- Determines main idea and important details
- Forms and describes an opinion about text
- Accurately distinguishes fact from fiction
- Connects texts to other texts
- Draws inferences based on prior knowledge and information in text
- Automatically cross-checks (e.g., checking pictures to confirm word reading) and self-corrects
- Begins to solve unknown words by using syllables or meaningful word parts (e.g., root words, prefixes, suffixes)
- Independently looks for known parts of words to read unknown words
- Applies analogous thinking to read unknown words (e.g., I can read *cheek* and I can read *air;* I can use parts of those words to read *chair.*)
- Reads orally with appropriate expression and pauses based on context and punctuation

LITERACY STAGE: SELF-EXTENDING

Typical Grades: 3+

DRA2+ Levels: 40 to 80+

Description: Students integrate all cue sources fluently, smoothly, and automatically. They are capable of maintaining comprehension and fluency across complex texts from various genres and with various structures.

Learner Characteristics (reading)

- Intentionally compares what is read to prior knowledge
- Integrates information from the text and prior knowledge to make inferences and draw conclusions
- Applies knowledge of text structures, literary devices, and literary elements to evaluate, interpret, and respond to texts
- Interprets and responds to various (i.e., diverse, multicultural, informational, and time period) texts
- Maintains interest, comprehension, and fluency throughout long texts
- Reads independently for a variety of purposes and genres; identifies purpose for reading
- Has automatic word identification skills
- Recognizes and remembers robust vocabulary words
- Respectfully listens and responds to others' opinions about a text
- Automatically adjusts reading rate to meet the demands of the text

student operating in the transitional phase of literacy development demonstrates the ability to summarize a text independently but does not cite evidence from the text in the summary, that particular competency has not been met. The classroom teacher should plan instruction to address that specific need (e.g., citing evidence from the text when summarizing) during a small-group or individual lesson. If a child does demonstrate all of the competencies in a phase, the teacher will focus instruction on the next phase of literacy development.

Addressing Standards

When they determine focus of lessons, in addition to considering the developmental needs of the learners, teachers also consider grade-level standards and curriculum, which are the basis for whole-class lessons. For example, the Common Core State Standards provide descriptions of key competencies that students must master at each grade level. The school where Ms. Shaw works has a standards-based curriculum; in other words, her state has adopted the CCSS, and each grade level's reading curriculum is based on the standards. Exhibit 7.10 illustrates one CCSS standard that Ms. Shaw focused on during the first week in October, when she started her small-group lessons. This standard concerns determining the main idea of informational texts, and it may be addressed through nearly any informational text that is complex enough to have multiple key details to support the main idea.

To address this standard, Ms. Shaw reviewed how to determine the main idea of an informational text with the whole class during the first several weeks of school. She accomplished this through several mini-lesson sessions (see Chapter 4 for a description of mini-lessons). By the first week of October, the focus of Ms. Shaw's mini-lessons shifted to identifying two or more main ideas in a text and providing supporting details. At the beginning of this week, Ms. Shaw demonstrated this skill through a think-aloud as she read an informational article about the coral reef, which was projected on the large screen in her room. Ms. Shaw asked the students to read the text silently as she read it aloud and verbalized her thinking. As she read, Ms. Shaw stopped occasionally to express her interest in the facts in the text, demonstrate her surprise when appropriate, and predict what she thought the author's main ideas were on each page. Next, Ms. Shaw reread portions of the text aloud and used a marker to highlight key details that supported the main idea. At the end

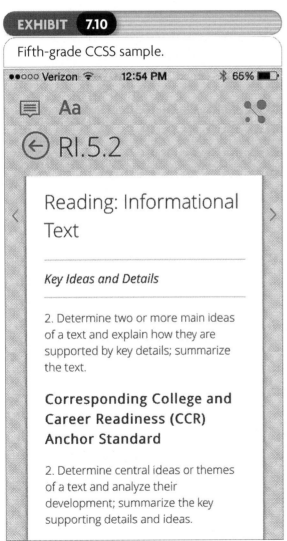

EXHIBIT 7.10

Fifth-grade CCSS sample.

●●○○○ Verizon 🔒   12:54 PM   ⚡ 65% ▭

💬 Aa

← RI.5.2

Reading: Informational Text

Key Ideas and Details

2. Determine two or more main ideas of a text and explain how they are supported by key details; summarize the text.

Corresponding College and Career Readiness (CCR) Anchor Standard

2. Determine central ideas or themes of a text and analyze their development; summarize the key supporting details and ideas.

Source: Screenshot from Common Core app, MasteryConnect.

of the lesson, Ms. Shaw asked volunteers to share what they felt the author's two main ideas of the text were, and she recorded all of the responses on chart paper to display in the classroom. As the week progressed, Ms. Shaw asked the students to work in heterogeneous small groups to identify main ideas and key details in similar nonfiction texts and share them with the whole class to discuss. All of this occurred during the whole-class mini-lesson time.

During the same week, Ms. Shaw met with each of her homogeneous small groups for differentiated instruction; this occurred after the mini-lesson was complete each day. (A sample daily schedule is included in Chapter 3.) The accompanying **Classroom Snapshot** outlines the focus of the lesson plan for each of Ms. Shaw's small groups.

Classroom Snapshot

MS. SHAW'S SMALL-GROUP LESSON PLAN FOCUS

Ms. Shaw planned the content of her small-group lessons based on the needs of the learners, so each small-group lesson was, of course, different from the other groups' lessons. However, when possible Ms. Shaw tied the lessons to the whole-class lessons, for coherence. Following are descriptions of the focus of each small-group lesson during the first week of October:

YELLOW GROUP (*DRA2+* levels 24 to 30)

Student strengths: Good comprehension

Student needs: Decoding multisyllabic words

Instructional focus: Identifying main idea and key details in nonfiction text

> *Rationale:* Students demonstrated difficulty in identifying main idea in whole-class lessons. I plan to reteach this topic to prepare students to identify multiple main ideas and support with key ideas.

Instructional focus: Decoding multisyllabic words (chunks)

> *Rationale:* Students demonstrated difficulty in decoding these words. I plan to introduce the strategy of using known word parts (chunks) rather than reading letter by letter.

Instructional focus: Rereading to improve fluency

> *Rationale:* All three students could benefit from instruction in reading fluency, particularly in noticing punctuation.

BLUE GROUP (*DRA2+* levels 38 to 44)

Student strengths: Good/excellent comprehension, proficient decoding

Student needs: Citing evidence from the text to support the main idea

Instructional focus: Identifying more than one main idea

> *Rationale:* Students in this group enjoy biographies, so nonfiction is familiar. All were successful in identifying at least one main idea in group lessons. Reviewing this strategy will provide students with the opportunity to apply this skill in instructional level text (e.g., *DRA2+* levels 38 to 44) for reinforcement.

Instructional focus: Citing evidence from the text to support your answer (e.g., support the identified main idea)

> *Rationale:* The CCSS require students to be able to cite evidence from the text to support conclusions drawn from a text (CCSS RI.5.1). These students have demonstrated the ability to identify a main idea but have struggled to support this with evidence from the text.

ORANGE GROUP (*DRA2+* levels 44 to 50)

Student strengths: Excellent comprehension, proficient decoding

Student needs: Prosody—reading with expression (3 members)

Instructional focus: Identifying multiple main ideas and support with key details

> *Rationale:* Students will have the opportunity to apply the whole-class lesson in instructional-level text (i.e., *DRA2+* level 44). They will read the text independently and then bring their books to the small group for discussion about the main idea and details. While the students are reading their books independently, I will use the time to listen to each student read a small section of the text. (Begin with books about sports to increase engagement.)

Instructional focus: Reading with expression (prosody)

> *Rationale:* Three students—Julia, Ellis, and Ben T.—demonstrated they need support in this area. I will draw on the strength of other students to model this. During the post-reading discussion, I will ask Josh, Max, and Lily to read select portions of the text aloud to demonstrate reading with expression.

WHITE GROUP (*DRA2+* levels 50 to 60)

Student strengths: Reading above-grade-level texts with instructional-level comprehension; good phrasing

Student needs: Drawing inferences; reading with expression to enhance fluency

Instructional focus: Drawing inferences in text

> *Rationale:* These students demonstrated adequate comprehension in above-grade-level texts. All can independently identify multiple main ideas and key details in texts, which was the focus of the whole-class lesson. Therefore, I do not need to revisit this with the students during small-group lessons. However, all students in this group struggle to draw inferences at times. This high-level strategy is required for readers at the self-extending level.

Instructional focus: Reading punctuation

> *Rationale:* The students in this group read accurately; however, most do not pause or stop at punctuation. Instead they read through it, which affects prosody and can affect comprehension.

CS

GREEN GROUP (*DRA2+* levels 50 to 70)

Student strengths: Good to excellent comprehension, proficient fluency

Student needs: No apparent needs

Instructional focus: Discussing theme and exploring how characters respond to challenge (realistic fiction novel)

> *Rationale:* These students demonstrated excellent comprehension in above-grade-level texts. All can independently identify multiple main ideas and key details in texts. Therefore, I will let the group choose a high-interest realistic fiction text from the library; I plan to lead them in explorations of theme and how characters respond to challenges (CCSS R.L.5.2) to deepen their comprehension of complex texts.

PLANNING THE STRUCTURE OF THE LESSON

According to Tomlinson (2000), the manner in which content is presented—the *process* of teaching—should be differentiated to meet the needs of learners (see Chapter 1). The lesson structure is considered the instructional process; therefore, teachers need to consider the structure of each small-group lesson to ensure that students are engaged and learning. No one "recipe" exists for how to organize an effective small-group lesson; each lesson is tailored to the group members who participate. Just as the content and focus of the lesson is designed to meet the needs of the individuals in the group, the structure of each small-group lesson is designed to meet the needs of its members and capitalize on their strengths. When planning the structure of differentiated instruction, effective teachers consider the level of support to provide to students. In cases where students are struggling to develop efficient reading processes, teachers often plan for predictable routines and high levels of support through prompting and questioning. When students are advanced readers, the teacher often allows the students to lead the discussion and the routines for the lesson. Three commonly used structures are guided reading, book club, and literature circles, introduced in Chapters 2 through 4.

Guided Reading

The Yellow Group, for example, is composed of students who are reading below the expected grade level; therefore, Ms. Shaw provides a high level of support to the readers during small-group instruction through a structure similar to Fountas and Pinnell's (1996) guided reading lessons (see Chapter 2). Guided reading lessons are carefully structured and closely tied to the instructional reading level of the group members. During these lessons, Ms. Shaw typically provides an introduction to a short text, including a description of the characters and plot; when the text is informational, she provides an overview of the content. The introduction also includes an explanation of the key teaching point(s). Ms. Shaw then typically requires students to read the text independently during the lesson, while remaining present to lend any needed support. Although emergent and early readers in earlier grades often whisper-read the text aloud, transitional readers, such as the members of the Yellow Group, most often read the text silently. While the students read, Ms. Shaw often asks one student to read a portion of the text aloud to her, to assess the student's accuracy and fluency. Also, if any student experiences difficulty in reading the text during the time allotted, Ms. Shaw provides on-the-spot prompts to help the student problem-solve and continue reading. Following the reading, the small group engages in a discussion about the content of the story or informational text. At this time Ms. Shaw reinforces the teaching points that she presented before and during the reading. For example, after today's lesson, Ms. Shaw leads a discussion about the main idea of the text, asking the students to provide details to support it. She also reminds the students to apply the chunking strategy for decoding unknown words in their independent reading. The students often finish an entire book or chapter of a book in one lesson; therefore, Ms. Shaw introduces a new text daily.

Most guided reading lessons take the form of teacher-led discussions of a text, centering on a particular skill or strategy that was previously introduced through whole-class mini-lessons. In addition, if a need unique to the group (based on assessments and the students' developmental level) becomes evident, the teacher designs the lesson to address this need. Ms. Shaw followed this format with the Yellow Group. Recall that Ms. Shaw's instructional focus for this group was decoding multisyllabic words and identifying main ideas and key details.

The following is an excerpt from a mini-lesson on decoding from one of Ms. Shaw's post-reading discussions with this group:

Ms. Shaw: This is the tricky chunk that's in there. That c-h. How does it sound in the word *machine?*

Students: Shhhhhh.

Ms. Shaw: It kind of sounds like an s-h, doesn't it?

Sarah: Yeah. It sounds alike but it's spelled differently. It's like a homophone or…

Ms. Shaw: Yes, kind of…

Gabriella: People think there's an s-h in my middle name; it's Charlotte.

Ms. Shaw: But it's not there, is it? So we've discussed before how letters sometimes sound different when they are in certain combinations. And you have to think about that, because I noticed a lot of you, when you were reading those sentences, you were saying "He also loved…," and when I worked with Wade he was saying "match… mach" using the typical *ch* sound. And then he got stuck because the ending didn't sound right. So Wade had to think about what happened and what would make sense in that sentence.

Wade: It was *machine!*

Ms. Shaw: Right! *Machine;* and that c-h combination actually comes up quite a bit. I brainstormed some words that you can look at when that c-h sounds a little bit different. Look at this word. (Ms. Shaw writes the word *chef* on the whiteboard.)

Sarah: That's *chef!*

Ms. Shaw continued the lesson by providing other words, not contained in the text, that are spelled with the c-h combination. The lesson was not limited to decoding strategies, however. Ms. Shaw also led the students in a conversation where students could practice identifying the main idea and key details:

Ms. Shaw: Find an important detail for me. Remember it's more than just what you liked; think about something that's really interesting. (Pause) Because, remember when we read *Life in the Coral Reef* with the whole class, we talked about what was important and what was interesting, what stands out.

Sarah: I think this is kind of important.

Ms. Shaw: Okay. Sarah, why don't you get us started? Tell us what important part you found.

Sarah: I'll read it. "Jacques got many awards for his work. He died in 1997. The world said a sad goodbye to the man who loved the sea."

Ms. Shaw: Ohh… so that was interesting, wasn't it? Jacques got lots of awards for all of those things that he did. That does seem like an important detail.

In previous whole-class and small-group lessons Ms. Shaw had modeled and discussed the importance of locating important information to support the main idea, and she simply reinforced these skills by allowing the students to practice them with guidance during this lesson.

Book Club

For later transitional readers and self-extending readers, Ms. Shaw, like many teachers, organizes small reading groups in a format similar to book clubs, as described by McMahon and Raphael (1997). Book clubs were developed as small-group student-led discussions within a teacher-created instructional context. The intent of book clubs is for students to use developmentally appropriate texts to practice previously taught strategies in their independent reading. Students read assigned portions of text silently and independently, away from the group lesson. The group meets periodically with the teacher, who provides support as necessary, to discuss key points in the text.

During book club meetings, Ms. Shaw often initiates the discussion, allowing the students to determine the direction of the conversation as long as it is relevant, meaningful, and educational. For example, if her intent is to discuss character development, she may pose a question about a character and then allow the students to proceed with the discussion. This may lead to an interesting discussion about the developing theme. As long as the conversation deepens comprehension for the group members, Ms. Shaw facilitates discussion in this new direction. The structure of the book club lesson is less predictable than a traditional guided reading lesson, since the students lead the discussion. However, Ms. Shaw does intentionally guide the students to specific planned teaching points, and she clarifies misunderstandings as needed. This is different from literature circles (introduced in Chapter 4 and discussed further later in this chapter), where the teacher does not participate in the discussions.

At the beginning of the school year, Ms. Shaw used the book club format with most of the groups, because the students required a moderate amount of support to solidify their reading strategies. The following is an excerpt from one such lesson that Ms. Shaw conducted with the Blue Group to reinforce the whole-class lesson about identifying a main idea. She chose realistic fiction for this group to extend their interest beyond biography and historical fiction.

Ms. Shaw: Okay. When I read the assigned chapter in *Stone Fox* [Gardiner, 1980], it reminded me of something that you told me you were doing in media class.

Samantha: We were watching the movie *Balto*.

Ms. Shaw: And isn't that the story of a sled dog?

Samantha: Yeah, Balto was the… I think he was the leader of that team.

Veronica: The lead dog.

Samantha: Yeah. He was the lead dog.

Charlie: I don't think the other dog, Stelle, ever existed.

Samantha: Yeah. Steele wasn't a real dog. That was just in that movie called *Balto*.

Ms. Shaw: Okay, so tell me this. We're talking about three different texts, the movie *Balto,* the book *Balto,* and *Stone Fox*. The book *Balto* did explain about Steele being a made-up character. Let's get back to *Stone Fox*. What were you saying about Balto being the lead dog?

Samantha: I also heard that the lead dog always has to be the smartest and the strongest.

Ms. Shaw: Tell me why.

Samantha: Usually 'cause he has… well, he has to be smartest because he has to know how to make the dogs do what he needs them to do.

Liam: Like when to take a break or when to keep going.

Charlie: Like when to take a break, which way to turn… and so the musher can trust him the most.

Ms. Shaw: Do you think this might be one of the main ideas, Charlie?

Charlie: Yes, I think so!

Ms. Shaw: How so?

Charlie: I think the author was trying to show how careful the musher has to be with the dogs.

Veronica: You can't have your lead dog… you can't have your lead dog step in water or anything because then their paws will freeze and they won't be able to move again.

Ms. Shaw: This chapter gave a lot of information about taking care of the dogs.

Marlee: There's a whole page of it.

Veronica: Right there. They put these little things around their paws to protect them.

This discussion illustrates how Ms. Shaw initiated the conversation and later brought it back around to the teaching point of the lesson: main idea. Still, the students were the primary participants in the conversation, sharing their insights about what they read and how it connected to a movie they watched. This discussion allowed Ms. Shaw to assess and deepen the students' comprehension.

In addition, when Ms. Shaw mentioned "one of the main ideas" of the chapter, she was beginning to reinforce the previous whole-class lesson on multiple main ideas in a text.

Literature Circles

The final structure Ms. Shaw uses during her small-group lessons is a modified version of literature circles (Daniels, 2001). (See Chapter 4 for a brief explanation of literature circles.) In traditional literature circles, the teacher does not participate at all. When she introduces this format to her students, Ms. Shaw designates a portion of the text for the group members to read, and each student is assigned a task to complete with the support of role sheets that Ms. Shaw adapted from Daniels' book. However, as the year progresses, Ms. Shaw removes this scaffold and the students lead the discussion without the role sheets. Because she uses this lesson format with the most capable readers (i.e., self-extending learners), Ms. Shaw limits her participation in the discussion to times when the students need clarification or if they get off task. This format is different from Ms. Shaw's book clubs; she lends much less support during the literature circle discussions.

When Ms. Shaw began her small-group lessons in October, the students in the Green Group used their completed role sheets to discuss the book *Charlotte's Web* (White, 1952) in a structured manner. Although this book was below the instructional level of all of the group members, Ms. Shaw chose it because the students in the group requested it. In addition, *Charlotte's Web* is a complex text that offers ample opportunity for deep discussions about characters, theme, setting, and plot. Recall that the instructional focus for this group is discussing theme and exploring how characters respond to challenges.

One of the assigned roles for discussion in an early lesson with the literature circle format was that of connector: a person assigned to explain the connections she or he made to the text during the reading. The following is an excerpt from one lesson that highlights this role:

Anna: I like animals. Fern likes animals. Fern was so sad when she had to give her pig away. I was sad when I had to give my kitten away.

Jacob: I can see that connection. But Ms. Shaw says you have to explain how that helped you understand the text. Why did you understand the chapter better when you felt sad?

Anna: Well, because I could see how attached Fern was to Wilbur, how much she loved him. I know that feeling. So then it made sense when she got so angry at her dad for saying that Wilbur had to go. She just loved Wilbur so much and it didn't seem fair.

Mari: So you could really understand how Fern felt, and that helped you understand her actions in the story, didn't it?

Anna: Yes, and it reminds me of how mad I get when my dad tells me to do something that doesn't make sense.

Derek: I get that… When my dad…

Ms. Shaw: Did anyone else have a connection to the text they can share, or are you ready to move on to another role?

Each student read an assigned portion of the text independently prior to the small-group meeting. The students in the group used the role sheets to scaffold their discussion, and Ms. Shaw was present to monitor the discussion and elaborate or clarify points if needed. Proficient readers learn to think more deeply about books when they have opportunities for authentic conversations such as these.

CONCLUSION

There are many factors for a teacher to consider when determining the focus (i.e., lesson content) and structure (i.e., lesson process) of a differentiated reading lesson. Most important are the strengths and needs of the learners in the group. However, students' interests, state or core standards, and curriculum are also important factors. Ms. Shaw used all of these criteria to help her plan effective small-group lessons to complement her whole-class lessons, while tailoring instruction to individual learners.

Practical Application

Mr. Moffett has completed his baseline assessments and entered the assessment data in the table below. Complete the following using the information in the table and in this chapter to guide you.

1. How many groups would you suggest Mr. Moffett form for his small-group instruction? Explain your answer.

2. Name the different groups, and list the members of each group.

3. Explain why you formed the groups as you did.

4. What lesson structure do you feel would be most important for each group? Why?

STUDENT NAME	QSI	INSTRUCTIONAL READING LEVEL (DRA2+)	WRI (AREA OF NEED)	COMPREHENSION RUBRIC (OVERALL)	NAEP ORAL READING FLUENCY SCALE	INTEREST INVENTORY
Gabriella	Within-Word Pattern	24	Decoding multi-syllabic words	Instructional	Nonfluent Level 2	Historical fiction Animals
Rebecca	Syllables & Affixes	40	Proficient	Independent	Fluent Level 4	Sports Realistic fiction
Hope	Within-Word Pattern	30	Decoding multi-syllabic words	Advanced	Fluent Level 3	Animals Realistic fiction
Connor	Syllables & Affixes	50	Proficient	Instructional	Fluent Level 3	Fantasy Animals
Alyssa	Within-Word Pattern	28	Proficient	Advanced	Fluent Level 4	Realistic fiction Historical fiction

Taylor	Within-Word Pattern	28	Decoding multi-syllabic words	Independent	Fluent Level 3	None
Noah	Within-Word Pattern	30	Decoding multi-syllabic words	Instructional	Fluent Level 3	Sports fiction Sports biography
Lauren	Syllables & Affixes	50	Proficient	Instructional	Fluent Level 4	Realistic fiction
Owen	Within-Word Pattern	34	Proficient	Instructional	Fluent Level 4	Fantasy Biography
Juliet	Within-Word Pattern	40	Proficient	Independent	Fluent Level 3	Nonfiction Biography
Sari	Syllables & Affixes	50	Proficient	Instructional	Fluent Level 3	Realistic fiction Fantasy
Emma	Within-Word Pattern	38	Proficient	Instructional	Fluent Level 4	Fantasy Historical fiction
Joseph	Syllables & Affixes	44	Proficient	Advanced	Fluent Level 4	Realistic fiction Sports
Ellie	Within-Word Pattern	50	Proficient	Independent	Fluent Level 3	Realistic fiction Animals
Devin	Within-Word Pattern	34	Proficient	Independent	Fluent Level 4	Prehistoric life Historical fiction
James	Syllables & Affixes	44	Proficient	Instructional	Fluent Level 3	None
Kate	Within-Word Pattern	38	Proficient	Advanced	Fluent Level 4	Sports Historical fiction
Daniel	Within-Word Pattern	28	Proficient	Instructional	Fluent Level 4	Biography Historical fiction

Recommended Resources

The following resources offer additional information on various structures for small-group reading lessons:

Guided Reading

Lesley University. Guided reading: Working with small groups of students at similar reading levels, www.lesley.edu/guided-reading/

Orange County Public Schools. What is guided reading? www.ocps.net/cs/services/cs/currareas/read/IR/bestpractices/GL/What%20is%20guided%20reading.pdf

ReadWriteThink. Using guided reading to develop student reading independence. www.readwritethink.org/professional-development/strategy-guides/using-guided-reading-develop-30816.html

Richardson, J. (2009). *The next step in guided reading: Focused assessments and targeted lessons for helping every student become a better reader.* New York: Scholastic.

Book Clubs

Brock, C. H., Boyd, F. B., & Caldwell, D. (2015). Book Club: A view from Mrs. Nguyen's grade four classroom. *Practical Literacy, 3* (20), 5–8.

O'Donnell-Allen, C. (2006). *The book club companion: Fostering strategic readers in the secondary classroom.* Portsmouth, NH: Heinemann.

Raphael, T. T., Florio-Ruane, S., & George, M. (2001). Book Club *Plus*: A conceptual framework to organize literacy instruction. *Language Arts, 79* (2), 159–168.

Small Planet Communications. About the book club program. www.smplanet.com/planetbookclub/about

Literature Circles

Daniels, H., & Steineke, N. (2004). *Mini-lessons for literature circles.* Portsmouth, NH: Heinemann.

Laura Candler. Literature circles. www.lauracandler.com/strategies/litcircles.php

Literature Circles Resource Center. Overview of literature circles. www.litcircles.org/Overview/overview.html

ReadWriteThink. Literature circles: Getting started. www.readwritethink.org/classroom-resources/lesson-plans/literature-circles-getting-started-19.html

REFERENCES

Daniels, H. (2001). *Literature circles: Voice and choice in book clubs and reading groups.* Portland, ME: Stenhouse.

Fountas, I. C., & Pinnell, G. S. (1996). *Guided reading: Good first teaching for all children.* Portsmouth, NH: Heinemann.

Gardiner, J. R. (1980). *Stone Fox.* New York: Harper & Row.

McMahon, S., & Raphael, T. E. (1997). *The book club connection: Literacy learning and classroom talk.* New York: Teachers College Press.

Tomlinson, C. A. (2000, August). Differentiation of instruction in the elementary grades. *ERIC Digest.* Champaign, IL: ERIC Clearinghouse on Elementary and Early Childhood Education. (ERIC Document No. ED443572). Retrieved from http://www.education.com/reference/article/Ref_Teacher_s_Guide/.

White, E. B. (1952). *Charlotte's web.* New York: Harper & Brothers.

Selecting Texts

Text matters in learning to read" (Hiebert, 1999, p. 552). This statement is simple and definitive, and it indicates that text selection is an important instructional decision, particularly when a teacher is tailoring reading lessons to meet the needs of every child in the classroom. Nearly any text may be used for small-group reading instruction, as long as it is carefully matched to the strengths and needs (and interests, when possible) of the learners in the group. A well-chosen text can serve as an instructional scaffold to help developing readers (Fountas & Pinnell, 2012a; Hiebert, 2013; Mesmer, 2010) and can provide the teacher with opportunities to differentiate the content and process of a small-group lesson (Tomlinson, 2000).

Proponents of differentiated reading instruction recommend that teachers use instructional-level texts for small-group lessons (Clay, 2006; Fountas & Pinnell, 2011). The notion of matching readers to instructional-level text for differentiated instruction originated decades ago. Emmett Betts (1946) first published a framework for reading levels in 1946, based on his colleague's study of fourth-grade readers (Halladay, 2012). The framework (see Exhibit 5.5) has changed only slightly since its original publication and has become firmly rooted in classrooms today. Classroom teachers typically reference a table such as the one in the exhibit. When learners read text at their instructional level, the text provides ample opportunities for successful processing, such as fluent and accurate reading with good comprehension. Still, instructional-level text contains some challenges, as well. Challenges might include a word that is difficult to decode, a novel word with an unknown meaning, or complex presentation of content that requires the reader to infer meaning. These issues present opportunities for the reader to problem-solve and, if necessary, for the teacher to lend some support. This is the point where the teacher, as the "more knowledgeable other," prompts the student in accord with Vygotsky's (1978) zone of proximal development theory (see Chapter 1).

Leading scholars have recently called into question the assumption that books used for small-group reading instruction should be limited entirely to instructional-level texts (Fisher & Frey, 2014; Halladay, 2012; Shanahan, 2015). Because the teacher can provide as much support as necessary to individual readers during small-group lessons, many experts feel that more complex texts, often at a higher reading level, may be used in this instructional context. Research also indicates that when learners are interested in a topic, they can read texts beyond their instructional level (Pardo, 2004). It is assumed that higher-level texts can expose readers to more sophisticated vocabulary and opportunities for deeper comprehension. This argument has gained attention since the adoption of the Common Core State Standards.

The CCSS address the issue of text selection by stating that "all students must be able to comprehend texts of steadily increasing complexity as they progress through school" (National Governors Association Center for Best Practices & Council of Chief State School Officers, 2010, Appendix A, p. 1). Some educators perceive this call for increasing complexity in text as a mandate to use difficult (i.e., frustration level) texts, rather than instructional-level texts, across instructional contexts (Stahl, 2012). Because the teacher is present to scaffold students' reading during small-group lessons, it stands to reason that with additional support, students—especially those in the transitional and self-extending stages of literacy development (see Chapter 1)—may be able to read and comprehend text beyond the instructional level successfully during these lessons. However, it is essential for the teacher to monitor students' progress during reading, so that each student receives necessary levels of support to navigate the text. Equally important is to provide students with opportunities to read texts at their independent rather than their instructional or frustration reading level during instructional contexts such as independent reading sessions. This allows developing readers to practice behaviors of proficient readers.

WHAT MAKES A TEXT EASY, HARD, OR COMPLEX?

Teachers can determine students' instructional reading level through assessment, as explained in Chapter 5. However, the fact that *Charlotte's Web* (White, 1952) is considered a frustration-level text for some students doesn't mean that it is a "hard book." The average first-grader may stumble through Wilbur's story, but most fifth-graders would breeze through the book. Text difficulty is relative; that is, it depends on who is processing the text. The students in any given classroom represent a range of development, which means they possess varying competencies; therefore, instructional reading levels vary within and across classrooms. Still, texts do vary in complexity; more complex texts require readers to apply higher-level competencies to the task of reading. For example, *Brown Bear, Brown Bear, What Do You See?* (Martin & Carle, 1967), with its short, predictable, rhyming text and explicit picture cues, does not require readers to apply the same level of competencies as the longer, less predictable book *Green Eggs and Ham* (Seuss, 1960).

Effective teachers match texts and students based on several factors. It is important to consider a text's readability level, its complexity, and the features that make it conducive to teaching a specific skill or strategy to help each student progress along the continuum of literacy development. This means that the teacher carefully selects texts to support teaching in such a way that each student can move from one literacy phase (e.g., emergent, early, transitional, self-extending) to the next. Refer to Exhibit 1.2 for a description of literacy phases of development.

Text Readability

Educators have attempted to describe the readability (i.e., how easy or hard) of text for nearly 100 years (Hiebert & Mesmer, 2013). For the most part, the formulas for determining text readability have been simple, based on word variation (versus

Grade level to Lexile equivalence.

GRADE BAND	CURRENT LEXILE BAND
K–1	N/A
2–3	450L–730L
4–5	640L–850L
6–8	860L–1010L
9–10	960L–1120L
11+	1070L–1220L

Source: https://lexile.com/using-lexile/lexile-measures-and-the-ccssi/text-complexity-grade-bands-and-lexile-ranges/

frequently repeated words) and sentence length. In essence, texts with simple sentences, many high-frequency words, rhyming patterns, and/or words that repeat (e.g., *Brown Bear, Brown Bear, What Do You See?*) were considered beginning-level texts, according to these formulas. That is, they were considered "readable" for emerging and early-level readers (see Chapter 1). In contrast, texts that contain many different and sophisticated words, along with complex sentences (e.g., *Charlotte's Web*), have been assigned a higher readability level, because the reader must be more strategic while reading the text. One popular current readability formula based on word- and sentence-level criteria is the Lexile Framework for Reading (https://lexile.com). What is lacking in these traditional formulas is a consideration for the reader's background knowledge. For example, *Winnie the Pooh*, by A.A. Milne (1926), has the same Lexile readability level as *To Kill a Mockingbird*, by Harper Lee (1960). Clearly, the content in Lee's book requires deeper reader knowledge than Milne's book. Exhibit 8.1 provides the grade-level equivalents of Lexile levels.

Text Complexity

The CCSS have reframed readability as text complexity in order to address the variance of books beyond just the word and sentence levels. Text complexity is defined in the CCSS by three measures: quantitative, qualitative, and "reader and task" measures. The quantitative measures are similar to traditional readability formulas; they include word length, frequency (versus variation), sentence length, and the cohesion of the text. The quantitative measures are easily calculated with computer software for a quick measure of a text's complexity. Qualitative measures of complexity include the following:

- levels of meaning within the text
- the text structure
- conventionality of the language
- background knowledge required to read the text

These factors are not easily measured by software programs, so they must be considered by human readers (e.g., the teacher).

Reader and task variables are factors specific to each reader (e.g., background knowledge, experiences, motivation) and the task set before the reader (e.g., reading for pleasure, reading to learn new information). Considering these three factors provides a more comprehensive view of text complexity and more accurate matches of texts to readers. For example, students living in a rural town in Iowa are likely to lack the prior knowledge necessary to read a text about life on a beach, whereas children living in Hilton Head, South Carolina, will probably have ample background for the information in the book. Therefore, the text will likely be "easier" for the students in South Carolina to read than for those from Iowa, although its reading level (e.g., *DRA2+* or Fountas and Pinnell level) is the same for both groups of students.

English learners may find a given text more challenging than it is for native English speakers for several reasons. One reason may be background knowledge and experiences; therefore, it is important to select culturally relevant texts for these students to read. When books are culturally relevant, students understand the content more completely, and this increases their engagement with the text. In addition to ensuring that English learners have the background knowledge for the text, teachers must consider the vocabulary in the text. Words with multiple meanings, similes, metaphors, and idioms may be confusing for some of these students. Finally, it is important to consider the text's syntax. Since it is likely that English syntax (i.e., sentence structure) is different from the student's native language, books with relatively simple sentence structures will present fewer challenges to English learners. For example, the first, two-sentence, statement below is likely to be easier to comprehend than the second, one-sentence statement.

> He took my shoes. He took my hat.
>
> He took my hat after he took my shoes.

TYPES OF MATERIALS FOR SMALL-GROUP INSTRUCTION

Usually when teachers engage their students in whole-class lessons, learners are exposed to text of varying complexity, often above their instructional reading level. In addition, most teachers provide time for independent reading of self-selected text, so learners have time to practice reading skills and strategies with texts they enjoy. The purpose of this section is to describe texts matched to learners for the purpose of small-group instruction.

Leveled Readers

Leveled readers are sometimes called "little books." These little books are meaningful whole texts written with careful consideration of text structure, appropriate picture support, and naturalness of language (Fountas & Pinnell, 2012b). Exhibit 8.2 shows examples of leveled texts. In general, leveled texts are organized by gradient of text difficulty, which means that lower-level

Leveled texts.   **EXHIBIT 8.2**

EXHIBIT 8.3   Leveled reader libraries.

texts are very supportive for the reader and higher-level texts provide readers less support. One example of the gradient of difficulty is the numerical *DRA2+* levels that Mr. Waverly (described in Chapter 5) used when he assessed his students. Another popular leveling system is the Guided Reading system, which uses letters (A through Z) to signify increasingly challenging texts (Fountas & Pinnell, 1996).

Many publishers produce leveled texts, which vary in quality. Some publishers use simple quantitative measures of readability and complexity; some use multiple measures, including qualitative, quantitative, and reader/task measures. When more measures are used in the leveling, the books tend to be more authentic for the reader, because the language is not controlled by the readability formula. Because of the diversity of students in schools, teachers need access to a large number and variety of books, including leveled texts, for reading instruction. Portions of two elementary schools' leveled reader libraries are pictured in Exhibit 8.3.

Decodable Texts

Also known as phonics readers, **decodable books** are those written with an emphasis on limited spelling or phonics patterns. Decodable text provides the reader with a high proportion of phonetically regular words, which makes decoding easier throughout the book (Mesmer, 2008). The sentences below are examples similar to those that appear in decodable texts. These sentences feature the short /e/ sound.

> Ted went to the shed.
>
> Ted went to get his sled.
>
> Bev went to get Ted's sled too.

The assumption behind the use of decodable texts is that if developing readers can decode the words easily, they will successfully read the book. However, because the text's words are limited to specific patterns, the language in these books is usually contrived, and opportunities to practice comprehension can be lacking. In addition, the syntax in these books is different from the oral language that young readers usually use and can seem inauthentic or unnatural. These factors can make decodable texts difficult for developing readers to navigate. This is especially true of English learners, who are in the beginning stages of learning English syntax rules.

Some publishers of decodable texts use Guided Reading levels or *DRA2+* levels to categorize their books so that teachers can incorporate these books into their resources for differentiated reading instruction. This allows teachers to supplement reading of more comprehensive reading materials with decodable texts, when necessary, for students who struggle with decoding. However, as with all students, it is best to use authentic texts (i.e., those with natural language and engaging content) for instructional purposes, so that readers can focus on comprehension and integrating strategies (i.e., decoding with comprehension), as proficient readers do. Several examples of decodable text are shown in Exhibit 8.4.

Core Reading Programs

Many school districts in the United States use a **core reading program (CRP)** for reading instruction (Education Market Research, 2010). CRPs, also known as basal readers, are programs offered by publishers, primarily designed for whole-class teaching of grade-level materials. They typically consist of one or several large hardcover anthologies of reading selections,

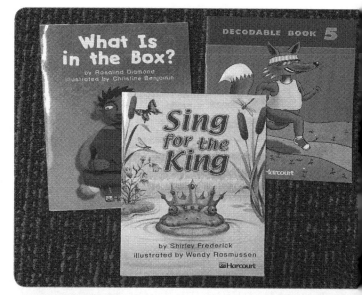

Decodable texts.   **EXHIBIT   8.4**

student workbooks for skill practice, and student tests and suggested assessments, as well as a teacher's manual describing proper use of the program materials. Many publishers offer a limited number of "leveled readers" with their programs, as well. Each CRP provides a scope and sequence for teachers to follow, based on national grade-level norms for literacy development. Because of the various components of CRPs, these are sometimes the only materials teachers have available for reading instruction, so they are used during small-group differentiated lessons and for whole-group instruction in these classrooms. However, content analyses of these programs have demonstrated that they do not provide enough support or sufficiently varied materials for teachers to provide effective differentiated instruction for all learners (Dewitz

EXHIBIT 8.5

Example core reading program.

EXHIBIT 8.6

Trade texts.

& Jones, 2012). Exhibit 8.5 shows the contents of one publisher's CRP.

Trade Texts

Trade texts (e.g., picture books, novels, magazines) are not published for the purpose of teaching reading; they are published for readers to enjoy and gain information. Of course, reading instruction can and should be enjoyable and authentic, so trade texts can serve as good tools for instruction. As long as the teacher can determine that a text is an appropriate match for the learners (considering, for example, text level, students' interests, and appropriateness for the teaching point), trade texts are suitable for small-group differentiated reading lessons. The Recommended Resources section at the end of the chapter provides various resources for determining the reading level of popular trade texts. Several examples of trade texts are pictured in Exhibit 8.6.

CONCLUSION

Instructional reading materials should support the literacy curriculum and teaching. However, it is also essential that the materials be interesting to the learners, so that they become fully engaged in the task of reading. It is important for teachers to use their knowledge about their students, based on assessments, to choose texts that are appropriate for each lesson. Differentiated reading lessons require specific texts, thoughtfully and purposely selected to aid in the development of targeted skills and strategies. Carefully selected texts can serve as scaffolds for reading development if teachers intentionally choose books that provide opportunities to practice teaching points presented in lessons. Instructional-level texts may be the best fit for small-group lessons, although (with additional scaffolding) teachers may match readers to slightly higher-level texts, particularly when the books are matched to students' interests, as well as to necessary teaching points.

Practical Application

1. Use the Book Wizard at www.scholastic.com/bookwizard/ to compare the Lexile reading level, DRA reading level, and approximate grade-level equivalent for each book listed below:

    a. *The Very Hungry Caterpillar*, by Eric Carle

    b. *The Hunger Games*, by Suzanne Collins

    c. *Martin Luther King Jr.*, by Pamela Walker

    d. *Ocean Life*, by Brenda Z. Guiberson

    e. *Sarah Plain and Tall*, by Patricia MacLachlan

2. Consider the chart below. Are you surprised by the level assigned to any of the books in question 1? Explain your thinking.

GRADE LEVEL	TEXT LEVEL (DRA)	LEXILE BAND
K	A–2	N/A
1	3–16	230L–420L
2	18–28	450L–570L
3	30–38	600L–730L
4	40	640L–780L
5	50	730L–850L
6	60	860L–920L
7	70	880L–960L
8	80	900–1010L

3. Compare all of the books in question 1 to grade-level expectations, using the Lexile level first and then the DRA level. Why do you think these leveling systems sometimes don't indicate the same grade level?

Recommended Resources

The following resources provide information on how to level trade texts:

Fountas, I. C., & Pinnell, G. S. (2005). *Leveled books K–8: Matching texts to readers for effective teaching.* Portsmouth, NH: Heinemann. Also: www.fountasandpinnellleveledbooks.com/aboutleveledtexts.aspx.

Mesmer, H. A. E. (2008). *Tools for matching readers to texts.* New York: Guilford.

The following resources will match a text to a specific level (e.g., *DRA2+* or Fountas and Pinnell levels):

A to Z TeacherStuff, http://books.atozteacherstuff.com/leveled-books/

Level It Books, http://levelitbooks.com/ (describes an app for Apple and Android devices)

Scholastic, www.scholastic.com/bookwizard/

REFERENCES

Betts, E. (1946). *Foundations of reading instruction: With emphasis on differentiated guidance.* New York: American Book.

Clay, M. M. (2006). *An observation survey of early literacy achievement.* Portsmouth, NH: Heinemann.

Dewitz, P., & Jones, J. (2012). Using basal readers: From dutiful fidelity to intelligent decision making. *The Reading Teacher, 66* (5), 391–400. doi:10.1002/TRTR.01134.

Education Market Research (2010). *Elementary reading market: Teaching methods, textbooks/materials used and needed, and market size.* Rockaway Park, NY: Author.

Fisher, D., & Frey, N. (2014). Scaffolded reading instruction of content-area texts. *The Reading Teacher, 67* (5), 347–351.

Fountas, I. C., & Pinnell, G. S. (1996). *Guided reading: Good first teaching for all children.* Portsmouth, NH: Heinemann.

Fountas, I. C., & Pinnell, G. S. (2011). *Assessment guide: A guide to Benchmark Assessment System 1* (2nd ed.). Portsmouth, NH: Heinemann.

Fountas, I. C., & Pinnell, G. S. (2012a). Guided reading: The romance and the reality. *The Reading Teacher, 66* (4), 268–284. doi:10.1002/TRTR.01123.

Fountas, I. C., & Pinnell, G. S. (2012b). *The Fountas and Pinnell text level gradient: Revision to recommended grade-level goals.* Portsmouth, NH: Heinemann.

Halladay, J. L. (2012). Revisiting key assumptions of the reading level framework. *The Reading Teacher, 66* (1), 53–62. doi:10.1002/TRTR.01093.

Hiebert, E. H. (1999). Text matters in learning to read. *The Reading Teacher, 52,* 552–566.

Hiebert, E. H. (2013). Supporting students' movement up the staircase of text complexity. *The Reading Teacher, 66* (6), 459–468. doi:10.1002/TRTR1149.

Hiebert, E. H., & Mesmer, H.A.E. (2013). Upping the ante of text complexity in the Common Core State Standards: Examining its potential impact on young readers. *Educational Researcher, 42* (1), 44–51.

Lee, H. (1960). *To kill a mockingbird.* New York: Lippincott.

Martin, B., & Carle, E. (1967). *Brown bear, brown bear, what do you see?* New York: Henry Holt.

Mesmer, H. A. E. (2008). *Tools for matching readers to texts.* New York: Guilford.

Mesmer, H. A. E. (2010). Textual scaffolds for developing fluency in beginning readers: Accuracy and reading rate in qualitatively leveled and decodable text. *Literacy Research and Instruction, 49,* 20–39. doi: 10.1080/19388070802613450.

Milne, A. A. (1926). *Winnie the Pooh.* New York: Dutton.

National Governors Association Center for Best Practices & Council of Chief State School Officers (2010). *Common Core State Standards for English language arts and literacy in history/social studies, science, and technical subjects, Appendix A.* Washington, DC: Authors.

Pardo, L. S. (2004). What every teacher needs to know about comprehension. *The Reading Teacher, 58* (3), 272–280.

Seuss, T. (1960). *Green eggs and ham.* New York: Random House.

Shanahan, T. (2015, March 2). Teaching with books at the students' reading levels. [Reading Rockets Blogs about Reading]. Retrieved from http://www.readingrockets.org/blog/teaching-books-students-reading-levels.

Stahl, K. A. D. (2012). Complex text or frustration level text: Using shared reading to bridge the difference. *The Reading Teacher, 66* (1), 47–51. doi:10.1002/TRTR.01102

Tomlinson, C. A. (2000, August). Differentiation of instruction in the elementary grades. *ERIC Digest.* Champaign, IL: ERIC Clearinghouse on Elementary and Early Childhood Education. (ERIC Document No. ED443572). Retrieved from http://www.education.com/reference/article/Ref_Teacher_s_Guide/.

Vygotsky, L. S. (1978). *Mind in society: The development of higher psychological processes.* Cambridge, MA: Harvard University Press.

White, E. B. (1952). *Charlotte's web.* New York: Harper & Brothers.

Providing Differentiated Support for Students

When teachers differentiate instruction, they plan and conduct thoughtfully varied lessons to account for the strengths and needs of individual learners. Morrow (2011) stated that the most effective teachers "teach skills within a meaningful context and in an explicit manner" and "view all students as capable learners who progress at their own developmental level" (p. 89). This kind of teaching requires deep knowledge of literacy development, pedagogical methods, techniques for assessing learners, and characteristics of appropriate instructional materials. This knowledge allows the teacher to reflect on possible ways to match students to text and then prompt them as needed while reading. In other words, effective teachers know and use methods for scaffolding learners through their reading. Therefore, it is essential for teachers to understand the developmental levels of literacy (presented in Exhibit 1.2) and know how to determine where each student fits in the progression of development. After planning lessons based on students' strengths and needs, the teacher must remain responsive to individual students during the lesson and provide differentiated types of support. That is, the teacher must have the ability to adapt during instruction, in order to meet the students' evolving needs (Parsons, 2010).

THE GRADUAL RELEASE OF RESPONSIBILITY MODEL OF INSTRUCTION

According to Vygotsky (1978), "Every function in the child's cultural development appears twice: first, on the social level, and later, on the individual level; first, between people (interpsychological) and then inside the child (intrapsychological). This applies equally to voluntary attention, to logical memory, and to the formation of concepts. All the higher functions originate as actual relationships between individuals" (p. 57). This statement is related to Vygotsky's (1978) theory of the zone of proximal development (ZPD), discussed in Chapter 1.

Pearson and Gallagher (1983) described a model of effective teaching that explains the transfer of new tasks to developing learners. The gradual release of responsibility model, briefly introduced in Chapter 4, is graphically represented in Exhibit 4.2 (p. 48). According to Pearson and Gallagher, "Any academic task can be conceptualized as requiring differing proportions of teacher and student responsibility for successful completion" (1983, p. 337). In reading instruction, the bar on the left side of the graph represents modeled reading, such as an interactive read-aloud (described in Chapter 2) or the demonstration of a new skill or strategy through a mini-lesson (described in Chapter 3). As the teacher releases responsibility for the task of reading, the students begin to participate in the text reading, as through shared reading (described in Chapter 2); this is illustrated in the second bar of the graph. The third bar of the graph represents guided instruction, where the student assumes most of the responsibility for the task of reading, and the teacher prompts the student only when necessary to aid in problem-solving through difficult portions of the text. This commonly takes place in small-group, differentiated reading lessons. Finally, learners assume all of the responsibility for reading, with very limited teacher support through independent reading; this is illustrated in the fourth bar of the graph. Examples of teacher support during independent reading may include guidance with text selection or redirection of focus when the student engages in off-task behavior.

Margaret Mooney (1990) describes this instructional model as "reading to, with, and by" children, which provides a simple indication of the different instructional techniques teachers use to shift the responsibility for reading from teacher to learner. Regardless of what the model is called, the overarching purpose of effective reading instruction is to provide the appropriate amount of support (i.e., scaffolding) to accelerate learners' development. For students to become proficient readers—or succeed in any academic task—the teacher must foster independence and self-regulation by decreasing the amount of support she or he provides. In other words, the teacher must release responsibility to the learners.

SCAFFOLDING LEARNERS: THE ESSENCE OF DIFFERENTIATION

Instructional support of learners is sometimes referred to as *scaffolding*. The term, introduced in the late 1970s, describes the "process that enables a child or a novice to solve a problem, carry out a task or achieve a goal which would be beyond his unassisted efforts" (Wood, Bruner, & Ross, 1976, p. 90). During small-group instruction, the teacher's careful guidance enables each child to complete tasks that may otherwise be too difficult. As stated previously, the ultimate goal of scaffolded instruction is to foster students' independence and self-regulation in a task. Therefore, during small-group instruction scaffolds must be removed over time to allow the learners to assume full responsibility for reading.

Because scaffolding is a learner-centered construct, it can take various forms, depending on the strengths and needs of the learners within a reading group (Dennen, 2004). Effective teachers make thoughtful decisions about how to differentiate the level of support, as well as the type of support, they provide. One example is a visual aid designed to remind readers to apply certain skills and strategies to their independent reading, such as those listed in the poster displayed in Exhibit 9.1. In this case, a teacher would first demonstrate the use of the various strategies to define unknown words. Then, the teacher can ask students to refer to the poster while reading and use the codes to record the strategies they apply to figure out word meanings. The

EXHIBIT 9.1

Scaffolding visual aid.

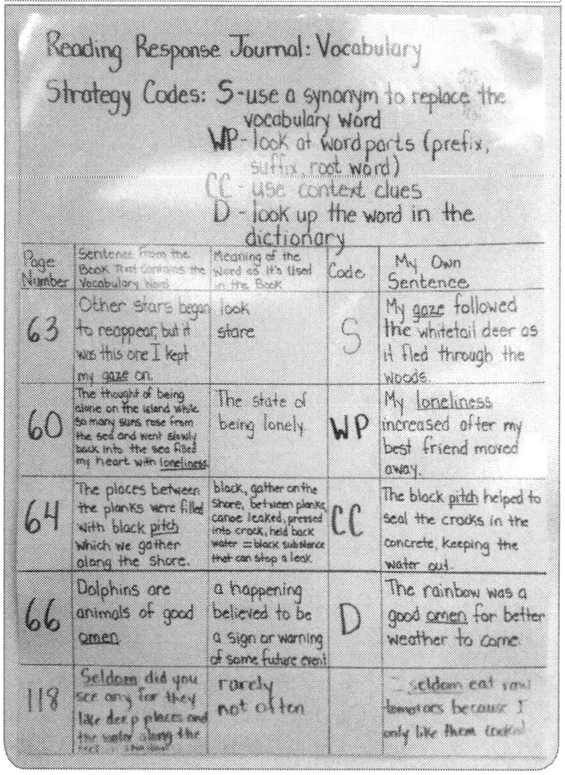

EXHIBIT   9.2

Scaffolding handout for informational text.

Pay Attention!

NON-FICTION TEXT FEATURES

Name: _____   Date: _____

Book Title: _____

Which of the following text features are present in your book?
Record the information in the table below. If you don't find one of the text features,
write N/A in the Page # column.

Text Feature	Page #	Purpose HOW DOES THIS FEATURE HELP YOU UNDERSTAND THE INFORMATION?
Table of Contents		
Chapter Title		
Heading		
Subheading		
Font Change (bold, italic)		
Caption		
Photo/Illustration		
Diagram		
Map		
Graph/Chart		
Glossary		

poster serves as a scaffold to remind the students how to document their use of vocabulary strategies in their journals while reading and eventually apply the strategies without coding them.

Teachers may also create scaffolding handouts to help readers attend to specific features in a text. Exhibit 9.2 contains a handout that a teacher designed to help transitional and self-extending readers focus on key text features in informational text. After Mr. Metzgar (featured in Chapter 3) introduces various text features to his students, he demonstrates how to use the features in a series of mini-lessons. Then he requires his students to complete the handout (Exhibit 9.2 and Appendix A.8) while they read several different informational texts; this ensures that the students will consciously focus on different text features while they read independently. Similarly, a fourth-grade teacher may provide a scaffolding handout for her students to help them record key information from narrative texts, such as a comparison of characters (Exhibit 9.3 and Appendix A.9). Like the handout featured in Exhibit 9.3, this handout can be used with many different texts; it is not limited to only one book. For example, after students read an assigned text for guided reading, the teacher may ask the students to complete the handout to record details about two characters, in preparation for a discussion comparing these characters. Alternatively, a teacher could use such a handout as a scaffold to help students focus on character description and development during self-selected independent reading.

The reading material itself can be considered a scaffold that a teacher provides to help students develop their literacy skills. The teacher carefully selects each text (see Chapter 8) to ensure that the contents provide just enough support and challenge for the readers. Verbal prompts, such as questioning, providing suggestions, and affirming approximations, also serve as scaffolds. These verbal scaffolds (explained in more detail in the next section) are essential to effective small-group lessons.

Regardless of the type of scaffolds used during a lesson, the teacher should constantly adjust the level of support to meet the needs of the learners. Emergent-level readers generally require more teacher support than other readers because they are just beginning to develop their literacy understandings. Remember, however, that students' ability constantly changes as a result of instruction and practice; therefore, the level of support will change over time, as well. In addition, even self-extending readers (Exhibit 1.2) require teacher support, particularly when they are learning a new skill or strategy or reading a particularly complex text, such as a novel with a nonlinear structure or an informational book on an unfamiliar topic.

Scaffolding handout for narrative text.   **EXHIBIT 9.3**

Fantasy Novels
Reading Response
Key Ideas and Details: Comparing/Contrasting Characters and Events

Character A	Character B
Winnie	**Jesse**
Differences in dialogue & thoughts:	*Differences in dialogue & thoughts:*
Winnie thinks a lot about different things, in the beginning she thinks about running away a lot. But she's also considerate because she thinks killing animals or anything is wrong, she even cried when she killed a wasp. She also thinks about Jesse and wether or not the Tucks secret is true. She talks about the spring and asks questions, shes very curious about things and	Jesse thinks alot about Winnie, he thinks about her knowing the secret and wether she'll marry him or drink the water. He seems to plan ahead with things too because he seems to have it all planned out "would it be if you wait til your 17 same age as me—back that's only six years off and then if you could drink the spring water and go away with me." Jesse is also consider and not afraid to ask questions.
Differences in actions & events:	*Differences in actions & events:*
When the man in the yellow suit told the Tucks his plan to sell the water, all the Tucks jump up and yell at him but Winnie so stunned, she doesn't know what to do, shes too shocked to react to things. When they are getting Mae out of the jail cell, Winnie tries to stay calm and quiet not to give Mae away. She does think before she makes decisions	Jesse is clumsy and careless, he seems to not think before he does something, He ate poison toadstools, he climbed to the middle of a tree a fell, and imediatly jumped into the lake, clothes and all. If he didn't drink the water hed probably be dead by now. When they were rescuing Mae and Miles Jesse was pushing her but was it really her jump for and
Explain their similarities:	

Jesse and Winnie both are pretty lonly because Jesse really doesn't have any friends since he moves around so much, and he can't get a wife because shed get suspicious about how he seems to not be getting older and Winnie doesn't really have any friends because people thought she was too "clean" to be a real friend, the only friend she had before the Tucks was her "pet" toad. They also both are not really afraid to ask questions. They both feel for eachother too, they both love eachother. They like to explore new places too, Winnie, coming into the forest loved seeing and discovering new things and Jesse, he's always going to new places and getting new jobs and stuff "So, Jesse, he does whatever strikes him at the moment, working in fields or in saloons, stuff like that."

VERBAL SCAFFOLDING

In differentiated reading instruction, the goal is to move students from their current level of literacy development (e.g., emergent, early, transitional) to the next level, through the collaborative use of strategies that are on the verge of development. Collaboration occurs through scaffolded instruction, where an expert (i.e., more knowledgeable person) provides support to a novice in order to accomplish a goal. Simply put, when teachers scaffold student learning, they are applying Vygotsky's (1978) theory of ZPD, as well as Pearson and Gallagher's (1983) GRRM. In small-group reading instruction, knowledge is mediated through the teacher, who gradually releases control of specific tasks (e.g., application of reading strategies) to the students (Wozniak, 1980).

One tool that teachers use to mediate knowledge is language (Wertsch, 1985). The teacher can use spoken interactions that take place in meaningful conversations with a student to guide and extend the student's learning (Mercer, 1995). Therefore, when these interactions occur during small-group reading lessons, they may be thought of as verbal scaffolding, because they can lead the student to engage in effective reading strategies and critical thinking (Duke & Pearson, 2002).

Each teacher–student interaction is unique. There are times when a developing reader needs an explicit explanation about how to read a word or understand a key detail in text. At other times the same reader may need less support, such as a simple reminder (i.e., prompt) to apply a previously taught strategy to decode a word or locate specific information in a text. Therefore, teachers provide differentiated verbal scaffolds, depending on the level of support that the student needs. Exhibit 9.4 provides a list of common types of verbal scaffolding, along with examples taken from a small-group lesson in a kindergarten classroom. Because this type of support occurs in response to a student's reading approximations and questions, the conversation cannot be scripted or pre-planned; these decisions must be made in the moment. Peter Johnston (2004) said it best when he wrote, "Thinking through what we are going to say next as we interact with children would mean that we were not giving them our full attention and not being genuine" (p. 7).

Each example in Exhibit 9.4 serves as an illustration of this point. The teacher provided a direct explanation of the text feature (caption) only after asking the students in the reading group to describe the purpose of a caption. When none of the students could provide an adequate explanation, the teacher provided the explanation. That would not be an efficient use of instructional time if the students already knew the purpose of a caption. As stated before, teachers must possess deep knowledge of content and must use assessments in order to know students' strengths and needs and participate in interactions responsively and authentically.

According to Rodgers, "Studies suggest that teachers scaffold children's reading behaviors by using language effectively; they respond to a student's reading behaviors with talk that is designed to bring the student a little further along" (2004, p. 505). It is important for teachers to consider the different levels of support offered by various verbal scaffolds and provide only the needed amount. If a teacher provides more support than a student needs, there is the risk of taking too much of the responsibility for reading away from the student, which may stifle

		Types of verbal scaffolding.	**EXHIBIT 9.4**
VERBAL SCAFFOLDING TYPE	**DEFINITION**	**STUDENT'S READING BEHAVIOR**	**EXAMPLE OF TEACHER'S VERBAL SCAFFOLDING**
Verification	Confirmation of valid or correct student response	Student points to a crying boy in the text illustration. "Oh, no! He got hurt!"	"Your inference makes sense! The boy in the picture is crying. The book tells us he fell down. We cry when we fall down because it hurts; I bet you are right. The boy got hurt."
Invitation to participate	Statements that the teacher uses to encourage student participation by eliciting students to provide explanations, elaborations, or direct evidence from text	After the teacher reminds the students of the purpose of a caption, one student notes that the photograph on the book's cover does not have a caption.	"What do you want to tell me about this photograph on the front page? Does anybody have something that they would want to write?"
Clarification	Guided discussion or questioning that the teacher uses to help correct a student's misunderstanding	The text states, "The girl put on her jacket." The student reads, "The girl put on her coat."	"That looks like a coat, but look how the word starts. Could that be *coat*? What else could it be if it starts with a *j*?"
Explicit modeling	Verbal demonstrations of strategy application, including think-alouds and talk-alouds	The students in a small group consistently ignore the captions when they read informational texts.	"Let me think … when I take a look at this photograph, I think, what does the author want me to notice here? What additional information can I learn from this photograph? So then I read the caption so I can find out the important information. This caption tells me that 'rocks can come in many shapes, colors, and sizes.'"
Direct explanation	Explicit statements that the teacher makes to assist students in understanding a concept or strategy	When the teacher asks, "Do you know what a caption is, or why it might be in a book?" the students answer that they do not know what a caption is.	"A caption is when the author adds words near the picture to describe the photograph. Look on this page. The sentence under the picture tells us all about this dolphin's teeth."
Telling	The teacher provides an answer for the student in order to continue the discussion or the reading. Telling is typically reserved for occasions when problem-solving prompts may not work; for example, if a word is not easily decodable for the student, or if a picture or other type of clue is unavailable or inappropriate.	The text states, "Mom is in the house," and the student reads, "Mom is in tuh-huh-eh?"	"That word is *the*."

Source: From Ankrum, Genest, & Belcastro (2014). Used with permission. Adapted originally from Roehler & Cantlon (1997).

the student's development in using strategies independently. This is supported by Taylor, Pearson, Peterson, and Rodriguez (2003), finding that student achievement increased when teachers used verbal coaching (e.g., explicit modeling, clarifying) more often than providing students with answers (i.e., telling) during lessons.

LESSON FREQUENCY

long with considering the different levels of scaffolding that may be provided to students, it is also important to consider how often differentiated lessons will be provided. Generally speaking, emergent readers (see Exhibit 1.2) require more support than children in later stages of development. This is because, for children at the beginning stages of literacy development, all skills and strategies are new. For example, this is when readers begin to understand what a letter is and how a letter is different from a word. There is much to understand about how print works! In addition, because emergent readers are typically very young, their attention span is often quite limited; therefore, concise lessons conducted daily are beneficial to these readers. It is most effective for the teacher to meet for a short period of time each day with emergent readers.

Children in the early and transitional stages of literacy development (Exhibit 1.2) have progressed in their understandings about reading. Teachers often schedule small-group lessons two to four times per week with these readers. If the members of a group of transitional readers are considered to be reading at or above grade level, for example, the teacher may meet with them twice per week. However, if the majority of the class is composed of self-extending readers (Exhibit 1.2), then the group of transitional readers is considered to be reading below average for the class. In this case, the teacher would meet with the group three or four times per week.

Late transitional and self-extending readers can generally read longer texts, such as chapter books or lengthy informational texts, over many sittings. It is important that teachers allow time for these students to engage in independent reading of assigned texts between small-group lessons. Students at these stages have developed the competencies necessary for reading complex texts, but they need to practice in order to build stamina and strengthen the independent use of strategies. Therefore, teachers typically meet with groups at these stages once or twice per week, mainly to discuss key elements of texts and the strategies the students use when reading.

CONCLUSION

ffective teachers carefully select appropriate texts, based on students' interests and reading level, for the students in each reading group. In addition, teachers consider using supplemental materials, such as handouts, to help students navigate texts during lessons. Verbal scaffolding and lesson frequency are other methods for differentiating support for developing readers. All of these supports allow students to read successfully within their zone of proximal development, where accelerated learning can take place. This careful planning, along with in-the-moment teacher responses, ensures that students experience success, as well as learning opportunities, throughout each lesson.

Practical Application

1. Create a visual aid or scaffolding handout to help students understand the following elements of a story: characters, plot, and setting.

2. Use the information in Exhibit 9.4 to identify the type of scaffolding that is provided in each example below.

TEACHER'S VERBAL SCAFFOLDING	VERBAL SCAFFOLDING TYPE
"You were chunking! That is great. You put the sounds together to figure out the word."	
"If it doesn't make sense, you have to stop reading. That little voice in your head should say, 'Whoa, whoa, whoa, I have to stop here,' right?"	
"Why do you think Opal loved Winn-Dixie? Go back into the book and find some evidence to share with the group."	
"That word is *stifle*. It means to stop something from happening. Like if you stifle your laughter, you stop yourself from laughing."	
"You said, 'They runned to the store.' Does that sound right? We don't say runned. Check the word again. Say it with me. R-an. Ran. They ran to the store. That's better!"	

3. Complete the table below by writing a verbal scaffold for each reading behavior, and then identify the type of scaffold. There are many possible answers; try to write a different type of verbal scaffold for each response.

READING BEHAVIOR	TEACHER'S VERBAL SCAFFOLDING	VERBAL SCAFFOLDING TYPE
The text states, "The boy shrieked when he heard the news." The student reads, "The boy sh-shry-shryked?"		
The text states, "The family lived in a chalet in the woods." The student pronounces the *ch* like *change*, and says "ch-al-it."		
After reading, the student says, "I think that Fern was sad about Wilbur."		
The text states, "The girl ran to her house as fast as she could." A picture shows a girl running up to a house. The student reads, "The girl ran to her horse as fast as she could."		

REFERENCES

Ankrum, J. W., Genest, M. T., & Belcastro, E. G. (2014). The power of verbal scaffolding: "Showing" beginning readers how to use reading strategies. *Early Childhood Education Journal, 42* (1), 39–47. DOI 10.1007/s10643-013-0586-5.

Dennen, V. P. (2004). Cognitive apprenticeship in educational practice: Research on scaffolding, mentoring, and coaching as instructional strategies. In D.H. Jonassen (Ed.), *Handbook of research on educational communications and technology* (2nd ed.), pp. 813–828. Mahwah, NJ: Lawrence Erlbaum.

Duke, N. K., & Pearson, P. D. (2002). Effective practices for developing reading comprehension. In A.E. Farstup & S.J. Samuels (Eds.), *What research has to say about reading instruction*, pp. 205–242. Newark, DE: International Reading Association.

Johnston, P. H. (2004). *Choice words: How our language affects children's learning.* Portland, ME: Stenhouse.

Mercer, N. (1995). *The guided construction of knowledge.* Bristol, PA: Multilingual Matters.

Mooney, M. E. (1990). *Reading to, with, and by children.* Katonah, NY: Richard C. Owens.

Morrow, L. M. (2011). Developing effective reading curricula for beginning readers and the primary grades. In T. V. Rasinski (Ed.), *Rebuilding the foundation: Effective reading instruction for 21st century literacy*, pp. 89–112. Bloomington, IN: Solution Tree Press.

Parsons, S. (2010). Adaptive teaching: A case study of one third-grade teacher's literacy instruction. In S. Szabo, T. Morrison, L. Martin, M. Boggs, & L. Raine (Eds.), *Building literacy communities: The 32nd yearbook of the Association of Literacy Educators and Researchers*, pp. 135–147. Commerce, TX: ALER.

Pearson, P. D., & Gallagher, M. (1983). The instruction of reading comprehension. *Contemporary Educational Psychology, 8*, 317–344.

Rodgers, E. M. (2004). Interactions that scaffold reading performance. *Journal of Literacy Research, 36* (4), 501–532.

Roehler, L. R., & Cantlon, D. J. (1997). Scaffolding: A powerful tool in social constructivist classrooms. In K. Hogan & M. Pressley (Eds.), *Scaffolding student learning: Instructional approaches and issues*, pp. 6–42. Cambridge, MA: Brookline.

Taylor, B. M., Pearson, P. D., Peterson, D., & Rodriguez, M. C. (2003). Reading growth in high-poverty classrooms: The influence of teacher practices that encourage cognitive engagement in literacy learning. *Elementary School Journal, 104* (1), 3–28.

Vygotsky, L. S. (1978). *Mind in society: The development of higher psychological processes.* Cambridge, MA: Harvard University Press.

Wertsch, J. V. (1985). *Vygotsky and the social formation of mind.* Cambridge, MA: Harvard University Press.

Wood, D., Bruner, J. S., & Ross, G. (1976). The role of tutoring in problem solving. *The Journal of Child Psychology and Psychiatry, 17* (2), 89–100.

Wozniak, R. H. (1980). Theory, practice, and the "zone of proximal development" in Soviet psychoeducational research. *Contemporary Educational Psychology, 5*, 175–183.

Parting Thoughts

ur classrooms today are filled with diverse students. It is essential for us as teachers to understand how to meet their individual needs and capitalize on each student's learning strengths. With the goal of meeting individual student needs, lessons should be tailored for each group, each day, each school year. Small-group differentiated reading instruction, often called *guided reading,* is one instructional context where this can happen. However, effective differentiated instruction is challenging. It takes information, practice, and hard work, and no recipe or "how-to" manual can make it a simple process.

Effective teachers are informed professionals. To successfully help our students to develop as readers, we need knowledge. We must understand the developmental phases of literacy acquisition and how to discover each student's phase through meaningful assessment. Once we understand each student's strengths and needs, it is time to apply knowledge of effective instructional techniques to help them move along the developmental continuum. This process also must consider students' interests, allowing us to select appropriate texts that will engage, as well as scaffold, developing readers. Finally, we must know the grade-level standards and curriculum that will guide instruction.

Developing deep knowledge allows teachers to conduct effective differentiated literacy instruction. I hope that the information in this book serves as a starting point and that it will be a valuable reference as you go forward. As you become proficient in one aspect of small group teaching, such as forming groups, I hope you will revisit the text to become proficient in another area. Stay the course! Differentiated instruction is complex, but once you see the results in your students' achievements, you will find it very rewarding. And so will your students.

Appendices

APPENDIX **A.1** Peer Conference Form

Peer Conference

Author: _____

Conference Partner: _____

Title of Piece: _____

Three things I liked about the piece:
(Also explain why you liked each aspect.)

1.

2.

3.

One wish:
(One suggestion for revision; to add clarity, detail, etc.)

Checklist

Name: _____

_____   I wrote the date at the top of my page.

_____   I drew a beautiful picture. I colored it in.

_____   I wrote about a small moment.

_____   I wrote more than 5 sentences.

_____   I wrote no-excuse words correctly.

_____   I have punctuation at the end of each sentence.

_____   I used capital letters at the start of each sentence and
with special words.

APPENDIX A.3 | Literacy Center Routine Reminders

Knowing where to go!	• Provide an explicit explanation of the centers each time students are assigned to new centers.
	• Introduce activities at a morning meeting where all students gather around a chart or display of the week's centers.
	• List student names next to the center activity so they can reference the task board or display to determine where they should begin working.
	• Release responsibility to students, allowing them to determine their starting point each day based on the display.
Center rotation	• Decide how many centers each student will visit each day.
	• Change the display to indicate where students will work if they will visit only one center each day.
	• Explicitly describe the manner of rotation if students will work in more than one center.
Accessing and returning materials	• Introduce students to each center and the materials available within it.
	• Explain where materials belong for easy access as needed and return to the proper place for efficient clean-up.
Working with others	• Provide direction regarding the expectations for working with others.
	• Conduct various lessons explaining to students:
	• How to keep their voices at an acceptable level,
	• How to help others without completing the other person's task, and/or
	• How to offer constructive and positive feedback.
Seeking help	• Establish the common rule of effective classrooms: "Ask three before me."
What do I do when I am finished?	• Refer students to literacy activities (e.g. word games, reading texts, writing activities).
	• Allow students to read silently or browse texts quietly.
	• Set the goal of engaging students in literate activities.
Transitions	• Determine transitions for times when students move between centers.
	• Allow the students to move freely as they finish each task.
	• Provide a signal (e.g. ring a bell or blink the lights) when it is time to clean up an area and move to another task.
	• Choose whether to provide a five minute warning, so that students may wrap up a task before cleaning up.
Where to meet following clean up	• Clarify where students should meet once center activities end.
	• Invite students to gather at the whole-group meeting area for a recap of the day's literacy events.
	• Provide directions for the next event on the agenda.

Reading Ticket

Name: _____   Date: _____

Book Club: _____

Have-To's

	MON	TUE	WED	THUR	FRI

Choices

	MON	TUE	WED	THUR	FRI

Digging In the Dictionary

Name: _____   Date: _____

My word is: _____

I found my word on page _____

The guide words are _____ and _____

My word means

_____

_____

_____

My word is: _____

I found my word on page _____

The guide words are _____ and _____

My word means

_____

_____

_____

Flip Camera Fluency

Name: _____   Date: _____

_____ Practice reading a text that is good for you from the basket. Read the text out loud for the best practice. If you are stuck on a word, ask your partner to help you figure out what the word is.

_____ Then, have your partner use the flip camera to record you reading the text.

_____ Watch the video of yourself.

_____ Talk to your partner about the good things you saw and how you could improve your reading.

_____ Practice reading the text again.

_____ Have your partner use the flip camera to record you reading the text a second time.

_____ Watch the video of yourself.

_____ Talk to your partner about these questions:

Did your reading improve the second time?

_____

What did you like best about how you read?

_____

_____

How did practicing your reading help you to sound better on the video?

_____

_____

APPENDIX **A.7**   Building Compound Words Using Ladybug Wings

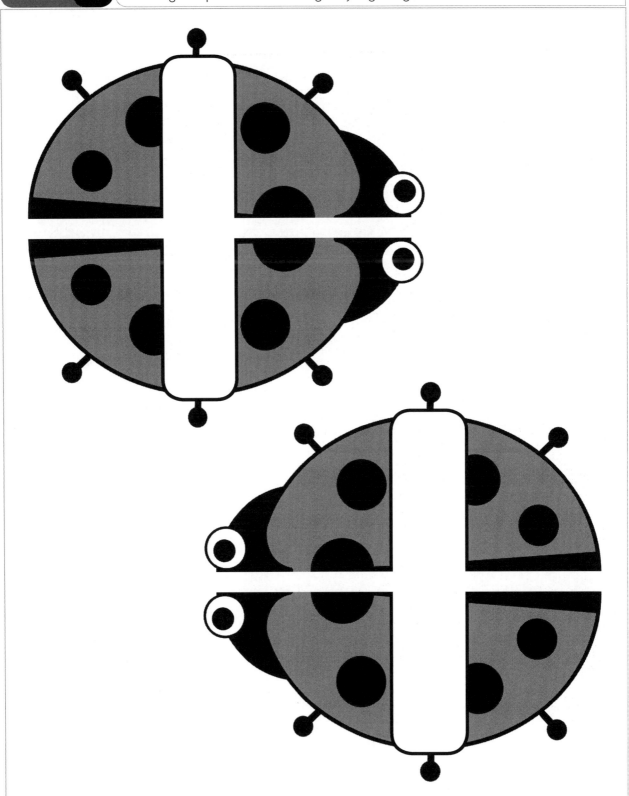

Pay Attention!

INFORMATIONAL TEXT FEATURES

Name: _____   Date: _____

Title: _____

Which of the following text features are present?

Record the information in the table below. If you don't find one of the text features, write N/A in the Page # column.

Text Feature	Page #	Purpose HOW DOES THIS FEATURE HELP YOU UNDERSTAND THE INFORMATION?
Table of Contents		
Chapter Title		
Heading		
Subheading		
Font Change (bold, italic)		
Caption		
Photo/Illustration		
Diagram		
Map		
Graph/Chart		
Glossary		

Reading Response

KEY IDEAS AND DETAILS: COMPARING/CONTRASTING CHARACTERS AND EVENTS

Name: _____   Date: _____

Character A	Character B
Differences in dialogue and thoughts:	Differences in dialogue and thoughts:
Differences in action and events:	Differences in action and events:
Explain their similarities:	

Concepts About Print Assessment   APPENDIX   B.1

Student: _____   Date: _____

		YES	NO
1.	Knows which is the front of the book.	○	○
2.	Holds a book correctly.	○	○
3.	Knows that the words, not the print, are what is read when asked, "Where do I start to read?"	○	○
4.	Knows that one reads from the top of the page to the bottom.	○	○
5.	Knows that one reads the left-hand page and then the right-hand page. Can point to where to go after completing the left-hand page.	○	○
6.	Knows the return sweep concept (where to go when he/she reaches the end of a line).	○	○
7.	Is able to point from word to word.	○	○
8.	Knows the difference between		
	a word	○	○
	a letter	○	○
	a sentence	○	○
9.	Knows letter order is important and different in each word (recognizes the misspelled words).	○	○
10.	Is able to identify the first and last letters in words.	○	○
11.	Knows the purpose of		
	a period	○	○
	question mark	○	○
	exclamation mark	○	○

Source: Los Angeles County Office of Education. (2000). *Kindergarten and Grade One Reading: Basic to Success.* Retrieved from http://teams. lacoe.edu/documentation/classrooms/patti/K-1/teacher/assessment/print/concepts.html.

APPENDIX B.2   Letter/Sound Identification Assessment

Directions: Ask students to identify all upper case and lower case letters, using the following directions:

1. Place the letter identification sheet on the table in front of the student.

2. Ask, "Can you name these letters? Can you say the sounds they make?"

3. Mask the letters with a sheet of paper showing one row of letters at a time. You may want to point to each letter for the child, or let the child point to the letters naming them.

4. Use the upper case sheet for letter and sound identification. If the student does not automatically say the letter name and sound at the same time, let the student name the letters, then ask him/her to return to the beginning of the sheet, saying the sound for each letter.

5. Use the lower case sheet for letter identification. Sound identification on this lower case sheet is optional.

Scoring: Place a check mark in the column if the child identifies the letter or sound correctly. Record any letter or sound the child names incorrectly in the boxes. Count the checks (correct letters or sounds) and total them onto the score sheet.

Score as correct for letter identification:

1. An alphabet name.

2. You could also score as correct a response in which a child identifies the letter and a word that has the letter in it (e.g. "There's a 't' in 'cat.'")

Score as correct for sound ID:

1. A sound that is acceptable for the letter.

2. A response in which the student says, "It begins like . . ." giving a word that has that letter sound as its initial letter.

Record for further teaching:

- The student's preferred mode of identifying letters (i.e. name, sound, or word that contains the letter).

- The letters a child confuses. It is recommended that one confused letter is taught to mastery before introducing the next confused letter. Thus, confused letters are kept apart in the teaching program.

- Unknown letters.

Sources: Used with permission of Teachers College Reading and Writing Project (TCRWP) http://readingandwritingproject.org/resources/assessments. Including information from Neuhaus, G. F. (2003). What does it take to read a letter? The International Dyslexia Association quarterly newsletter—Perspectives, pages 27–31 and Samuels, S. J. (1972). The Effect of Letter-Name Knowledge on Learning to Read. *American Educational Research Journal*, Vol. 9, No. 1. pp. 65–74.

Letter Identification Assessment

Name: _____   Date: _____

	Name of letter	Sound of letter	No reply or not correct		Name of letter	Sound of letter	No reply or not correct
A				a			
W				w			
P				p			
K				k			
F				f			
Z				z			
U				u			
J				j			
O				o			
H				h			
B				b			
				a			
M				m			
Q				q			
L				l			
Y				y			
C				c			
I				i			
X				x			
S				s			
N				n			
D				d			
T				t			
V				v			
R				r			
G				g			
E				e			
				g			

Known letters: Upper case _____ Lower case _____ Known letter sounds _____

List unknown letters: _____

What do you notice? (Does not know names, but recognizes in words; knows names, but no letter/ sound match; reversed letters; straight line known, curved unknown, etc.)

For benchmark scoring rubrics please see the Benchmarks for Primary Assessments document.

©TCRWP

APPENDIX **B.2** (Continued)

LETTER IDENTIFICATION ASSESSMENT—STUDENT COPY

A	W	P	K	F	Z
U	J	O	H	B	
M	Q	L	Y	C	
I	X	S	N	D	
T	V	R	G	E	

a	w	p	k	f	z
u	j	o	h	b	a
m	q	l	y	c	
i	x	s	n	d	
t	v	r	g	e	g

APPENDIX   B.3   Generic Retelling Assessment Template

Name: _____   Date: _____

Retelling

Before administering this assessment, choose a book from the classroom library. On the form you create using this template, record the important story events beneath the appropriate heading (Beginning, Middle, and End). Then, during the retelling, circle the events the student mentions.

Story Summary

Close your book and begin retelling what occurred in the story. Be sure to include events from the beginning, middle, and end of the story.

Beginning

Middle

End

Summary Guiding Prompts:

If the student is unable to relate many of the story's events, use the following prompts, recording the student's response to any you use:

How does the story begin?

Who are the main characters?

What are the important things that happened in the story?

How does the story end?

Reflecting Prompts:

What part of the story did you like best? Why?

What part of the story did you like least? Why

Connecting Prompt:

What connections did you make to your own life or other books you have read when reading this story?

Written Retelling Rubric for Narrative Text   APPENDIX   B.4

Name: _____   Date: _____

Aspects of retelling	1 (very little comprehension)	2 (some comprehension)	3 (acceptable comprehension)	4 (good comprehension)	Score
Story structure	Events are not structured and are retold in disconnected manner.	Events may include a beginning, middle, or end, but are retold in a disconnected manner.	Events are retold mostly in a logical sequence.	Events are retold following a logical sequence that includes a beginning, middle, and end.	
Character description	Does not name or describe characters from the story.	Names or describes main character from the story.	Names or describes main and secondary characters from the story.	Names and describes main and secondary characters from the story.	
Setting	Does not mention setting.	Describes either time or place of setting.	Describes time and place of setting.	Clearly describes, with details, the time and place of the setting.	
Statement of problem and solution	Does not describe the problem or solution.	Describes either the problem or the solution.	Accurately describes the story's problem and solution.	Provides a detailed description of the story's problem and solution.	
Word choice	Does not use language from the selection.	Uses appropriate language similar to that in the selection.	Accurately uses one example of a phrase or special vocabulary from the selection.	Accurately uses several examples of phrases or special vocabulary from the selection.	

Adapted from H. Brown and B. Cambourne (1990). *Read and retell: A strategy for the whole-language/natural learning classroom.* Portsmouth, NH: Heinemann.

APPENDIX B.5 Written Retelling Rubric for Informational Text

Name: _____   Date: _____

Aspects of retelling	1 (very little comprehension)	2 (some comprehension)	3 (acceptable comprehension)	4 (good comprehension)	Score
Main idea or topic	Retelling does not indicate any understanding of topic or main idea.	Retelling indicates a limited understanding of the topic and main idea.	Includes an accurate attempt to describe topic and main idea presented in selection.	Clearly describes and demonstrates understanding of topic and main idea presented in selection.	
Retelling of details	Restatement contains inaccurate details or provides no supporting details.	Restatement contains both accurate and inaccurate details.	Clearly and accurately restates most key details.	Clearly and accurately restates important and supporting key details.	
Word choice	Does not use language from the selection.	Uses appropriate language similar to the vocabulary and/or key phrases from the selection.	Accurately uses one example of a key phrase, language, and/or vocabulary from the selection.	Accurately uses several examples of key phrases, language, and vocabulary from the selection.	
Development of ideas	Retelling indicates little or no development of ideas.	Presents ideas in a random or disconnected order.	Retells most details in a logical order.	Main idea and key details are retold in logical order.	

Adapted from H. Brown and B. Cambourne (1990). *Read and retell: A strategy for the whole-language/natural learning classroom.* Portsmouth, NH: Heinemann.

Interest Inventory

Name: _____   Date: _____

How much do you like each topic?

	🙂	😐	☹️
animals			
sea creatures			
sports			
space			
countries around the world			
plant life			
computers			
weather			
trucks and cars			

What is your favorite sport?

What is your favorite animal?

What is your favorite book?

APPENDIX B.7   Blank Running Record Form

Student: _____   Date: _____

Teacher: _____   Reading Level: _____

Text: _____

Number of Errors: _____   Percentage: _____

Running Words: _____   Level for Student: Easy, Instructional, Frustration

Comments:

TEXT		ANALYSIS		
		Number		**System Used**
	E	SC	E	SC
Page				

Form for Recording and Analyzing Spelling   APPENDIX   B.8

Name: _____   Grade: _____

Word	Emergent	Alphabetic	Within-word Pattern	Syllables + Affixes	Derivational Relations
1.					
2.					
3.					
4.					
5.					
6.					
7.					
8.					
9.					
10.					

Words Spelled Correctly: _____   Spelling Stage: _____

APPENDIX **C.1**   Planning for Assessment

Class: _____   Date: _____

What do I want to know about my students' knowledge?	Why do I need to know it?	How can I best discover what they know (which assessment)?	What kinds of learning tasks can I plan for small groups to support students' learning?
Knowledge of letter sounds			
Ability to recognize words			
Degree of fluency in reading			
Instructional reading level			
Degree of comprehension at instructional level			
Other:			

Template for Assessment Data Compilation Form   APPENDIX **C.2**

LITERACY ELEMENTS BEING ASSESSED → Assessment Used: → STUDENT: ↓	Developmental Spelling Level	Word Recognition	Benchmark Text Reading Instructional Level	Fluency	Interests	Other:

APPENDIX C.3 Literacy Assessment Correlation Chart

Grade Level	Developmental Spelling Level (QSI)	Word Recognition (WRI)	Text Level (*DRA2+*)	Text Level (Fountas & Pinnell)	Literacy Stage
K	Emergent	n/a	A,1	A	Emergent
K.5			2	B	
1.0	Early Letter Name–Alphabetic	Preprimer 1	3	C	
1.1		Preprimer 2	4	D	
1.2	Middle Letter Name–Alphabetic	Preprimer 3	6–8	E	Early
1.4	Late Letter Name–Alphabetic	Primer	10	F	
1.5	Late Letter Name–Alphabetic		12	G	
1.7	Early Within-Word Pattern	Grade 1	14	H	
1.8			16	I	
2.0	Middle Within-Word Pattern	Grade 2	18	J	Transitional
2.3			20	K	
2.6	Late Within-Word Pattern		24	L	
2.9			28	M	
3.0		Grade 3	30	N	
3.3	Early Syllables & Affixes		34	O	
3.6			38	P	
4.0		Grade 4			
4.3			40	Q	
4.6	Middle Syllables & Affixes			R	Self-Extending
				S	
4.8			44	T	
5.0		Grade 5		U	
5.3	Late Syllables & Affixes		50	V	
5.6				W	
6.0		Grade 6	60	X	
6.5				Y	
7.0	Early Derivational Relations	Grade 7	70	Z	
7.3					
7.6					
8+		Grade 8	80		

Author Index

Subject Index

Made in the USA
Middletown, DE
02 December 2021